Women in Egyptian Public Life

WOMEN IN EGYPTIAN PUBLIC LIFE

EARL L. SULLIVAN

SYRACUSE UNIVERSITY PRESS   1986

The paper used in this publication meets the minimum requirements of American National Standard for Information Sciences — Permanence of Paper for Printed Library Materials, ANSI Z39.48-1984. ∞"

Library of Congress Cataloging-in-Publication Data

Sullivan, Earl L.
  Women in Egyptian public life.

  (Contemporary issues in the Middle East)
  Bibliography: p.
  Includes index.
    1. Women in public life — Egypt.   2. Women in
politics — Egypt.   3. Women in business — Egypt.
I. Title.   II. Series.
HQ1391.E3S85   1986   305.4'0962   85-26221
ISBN 0-8156-2354-2 (alk. paper)

Manufactured in the United States of America

To the People of Egypt

EARL L. (TIM) SULLIVAN is Professor of Political Science at the American University in Cairo, where he has taught since 1973. He received a B.A. in Political Science from Seattle University, a Ph.D. in International Relations from the Claremont Graduate School, and taught for six years at the University of Portland before going to Egypt. Dr. Sullivan's other publications include *The Impact of Development Assistance on Egypt* and *Women and Work in the Arab World*.

Contents

Preface

CONVENTIONAL WISDOM invokes an image of the Arab world in which women are neither visible nor important, confined by custom to traditional and subordinate roles, either hapless victims of the status quo or passive recipients of changes not always in their favor. This book is an antidote to that view. While it is clear that women, especially poor women, do not participate in public life to the same degree men do, this book will demonstrate clearly and unambiguously that a growing number of Arab women are important in politics and business and are seen to be so.

I thought about doing this study a long time before beginning the systematic research which led to this volume. Having lived and worked in Egypt since 1973, I was stimulated by a growing awareness of the gap between the Egypt I read about and the Egypt I observed in daily life. The chasm between theory and reality seemed especially serious in the case of women active in Egyptian public life. At first I considered doing a short monograph on the subject, similar to one I had done a few years earlier on the female labor force in Egypt. However, conversations with numerous Egyptian women, some of whom are subjects of this book, convinced me a longer piece would be more appropriate. They also persuaded me that, even as a foreign man, I was in an especially advantageous position to do research on women in the political and economic elite.

Over the course of nearly a decade on the faculty of the American University in Cairo, I had taught hundreds of students from fami-

lies active in politics or business, and had come to know numerous
intellectuals and other people active in public life. I was not a stranger
getting off a plane and asking impertinent questions. Although a foreigner, I had elected to live, work, and raise my family in Egypt and
was not a total outsider. As the book took shape, it included women
in four categories: those who had served in Parliment; the wives of
Egypt's presidents; women in the political opposition; women in business. As it turned out, each group included former students, the parents of former students, or other people I had known for several years
before starting research on this book. Without that head start, and
the concomitant trust it involved, I doubt the research could have been
done.

By quoting and otherwise reflecting the views of indigenous
people, a foreigner can give indirect but legitimate voice to people
whose nationality he does not share, especially if that foreigner cul-
tivates both sympathy and empathy for the people being studied. The
result is bound to be imperfect, but it can help stimulate other research and offer useful insights.

In Egypt as elsewhere, questions pertaining to the roles and status of women are controversial, and the tone and intensity of the debate suggests considerable ambiguity rather than broad consensus about
these issues. In Egypt, women have not only been the subjects of debate, they have been and continue to be contributors to the creative
tension in Egyptian public life on many issues, but especially regarding gender roles. As this book shows, the twentieth century has seen
considerable change in the tone and content of this debate and the
composition of these roles. Egyptian women have not been mere recipients of such changes; they have helped produce them.

This book was not designed outside Egypt in the context of theoretical questions raised in a western university. Rather, it was con-
ceived in Egypt, evolving from the author's direct and long-term observation of the system at work. There is a theoretical dimension to
it, however, with theory used relative to its applicability to the empirical evidence to be presented. The resulting customized theoretical
framework integrates work from women's studies with research on the
Egyptian polity and economy in a way which may be useful to others
engaged in similar ventures. Still, in my opinion, the chief merits of
this book lie in its empirical dimension and its demonstration that,
in Egypt, politics and business are not the exclusive preserve of men.

Women in Egyptian Public Life adds depth and scope to our understanding of the family, polity, and economy of Egypt and shatters the unidimensional image of women in this particular Arab country.

When men view the roles of women in society, they often see little more than the reverse of their own self-image. Women, on the other hand, frequently see a more objective picture of themselves *and* of men. Critics may dispute the implication that a woman's perspectives on society are clearer than those of men, but few would doubt the two are different. In this study of women in Egyptian politics and business, I have attempted to look at the world from both points of view and wish to suggest the resulting gender-sensitive vision produces a set of images of enhanced clarity and dimension. I hope the majority of readers will share my conviction that the result is worth the effort.

Authors have a serious obligation to thank those who influenced the progress of research from the stage of being a mere glint in the author's eye to the finished product. Rather than try to mention all those who have had an influence on my life, I have opted for a brief mention of those who had a direct impact on this book.

Up to and including the penultimate draft, this study was designed and executed in Egypt. I received early encouragement from many people active in Egyptian public life as well as from students and colleagues, whose support and constructive criticism helped me start this project and persevere with it. Limitations on space prevent me from naming all of them, but Heba Handoussa read and critiqued an early draft of chapter 5, and Charles Butterworth and Marina Ottoway did the same for portions of the Introduction and chapter 1. Part of chapter 2 was presented in a paper at the 1983 Middle East Studies Association, and Art Goldschmidt, Ray Hinnebusch, Monte Palmer, B. J. Furnea, Ali Dessouki, and Lou Cantori, among others, made comments on it which proved helpful.

Were it not for John Gerhart and Ann Lesch of the Cairo office of the Ford Foundation, this project would have been stillborn. A grant from the Ford Foundation enabled me to hire research assistants and devote full time to the project during the summers of 1982 and 1983. In addition, three Ford Foundation scholars, Ann Lesch, Cynthia

Myntti and Barbara Ibrahim, read early drafts of portions of the manuscript and made numerous constructive comments on what they read. I cannot exaggerate the importance of these people as far as this book is concerned.

Although I had lived in Egypt for nearly ten years before beginning the research which led to this book, I needed help from Egyptian and other Arab women to make the project work. It was my good fortune to have a number of able and conscientious research assistants, without whom this study could not have been conducted. Amany al-Khattib, Iman Hamdy, Nadia Abdel Nabi, Maha Ghalwash, Taroub Abdel Hadi, Laila Henein, Manal Abdel Meguid, and Shahira Idriss all helped at various stages, with Amany, Nadia, Iman, and Taroub having the longest and most intense involvement. Throughout this study, but especially in its early stages, I consulted many members of Egypt's political and business community. They helped identify women to be included in chapters 4 and 5 and enabled me to check the accuracy of a number of details. As most wished to remain anonymous, I shall refrain from mentioning any names here and thank them myself, privately.

I am also pleased to express special gratitude to my friendly in-house critic and amanuensis, Jeanne Sullivan, who saw this book through all its stages and who was helpful at each.

The final draft of the manuscript was written during the 1984–85 academic year, while I was on sabbatical leave from the American University in Cairo. During that time I had the good fortune to be a visiting scholar at the Claremont Graduate School and at the Von Grunebaum Center for Near Eastern Studies at UCLA. After seventeen years of university-level teaching, the freedom to read and write unfettered by a set schedule was delightful. I am thankful to AUC for granting me the sabbatical and to UCLA and Claremont for a place to hang my hat and for providing access to their excellent research facilities.

George Blair of Claremont and Georges Sabagh and Afaf Marsot of UCLA were especially helpful, the latter two with constructive criticism as well as institutional support. Professor Marsot read and commented on the penultimate draft and made numerous suggestions which I adopted and whose help I acknowledge here. Nancy Gallagher, Clement Moore Henry, Ibrahim Karawan, Maridi al-Nahas, Ahmed Emany, Iman Ghazalla, and Noha al-Mekkawi all provided collegial support at UCLA and gave me a little bit of Egypt during my temporary stay in America.

While research was still in progress, several people afforded me the opportunity to test my ideas on audiences in the United States. Michael Hudson and Ibrahim Oweiss of Georgetown, Hamied Ansari and Bill Zartman of Johns Hopkins (SAIS), Brice Harris at Occidental College, and Glenn Goodwin at Pitzer College were especially helpful.

Final thanks are reserved for the women about whom this book is written and without whose cooperation and support it could not have been done. They granted interviews, helped facilitate appointments with other people, and, in some cases, argued with me about matters of theory, ideology, and even the structure of the book. I am responsible for whatever errors of fact or judgment remain. The people mentioned in this acknowledgment, especially the women in this book, share responsibility for whatever worth it may have, as it is their lives and fate that form its heart and substance. This book is dedicated to them and to the cause all have served.

Women in Egyptian Public Life

Introduction

THIS IS a study of ambitious and successful women whose membership in Egypt's political and economic elite would have been inconceivable a century ago. It is also a study of the transformation of the institutions, traditions, and structures within which they function. The process of change affecting the roles and status of women is one of the most important developments to have taken place in twentieth-century Egypt, and the debate about that transformation has been a vital feature of the country's intellectual and political life. Islamic reformists, nationalists, and architects of modern development have all, regardless of their own sex, grappled with this issue. Consequently, auditing the debate about the "proper" role of women is one of the best ways to learn about Egypt, to understand her past and present, and gain insights into her future.

The subjects of this book are the women within Egypt's current political and economic elite, chosen because their careers illustrate both the rewards and the challenges facing women in public life in Egypt today. As a group they are talented and impressive, yet few observers of modern Egypt know who they are, what they do, how they reached their current positions, or what sacrifices they have had to make along the way. In what follows, these topics will be considered and their significance discussed in light of the political and economic environment within which Egyptian women have struggled to get ahead.

This study also provides an opportunity to ponder a question crucial to Egypt's prospects for development. Is the presence of a rela-

tively large number of Egyptian women in business and politics a temporary situation, or the early phase of a long-term trend? While many
factors are essential to the development process, it is difficult to exaggerate the necessity for investment in human capital. Women represent about half this capital. Moreover, they give birth to and raise the
other half. Future generations will be shaped by the decisions taken
or avoided by today's leaders. Some of Egypt's women are helping to
make these decisions or are contributing in other important ways to
the economic, social, and political development of the country. This
is a recent and encouraging change, but most Egyptian women are
still confined to traditional roles played out in traditional ways and
consequently excluded from this process. One thesis of this book is
that actions taken in the 1980s will substantially affect these roles. Will
Egypt continue to tolerate a high rate of mass illiteracy, especially among
women, or will a major effort be mounted and sustained to educate
the population? More basic, will women continue to be able to experience a public life? The women in Egypt's current political and
business elite will influence the system's response to such questions.
The importance of these women should not be overestimated; neither
should it be ignored.

This book is not intended to be a definitive study of women in
Egyptian public life. Rather, it is an exploratory work, in which the
most obvious features of the terrain are mapped and interesting areas
for future investigation are identified. Ambitious as it may be, its
findings will be tentative and conjectural, but should nevertheless
stimulate thought and further research on Egypt as well as on women.
Because of the nature and importance of the subject, it is intended
to be of interest to both specialists and the educated public. Because
this is a study of women in Egyptian politics and business, it takes
into account a disparate body of theory pertaining to women's studies
and research on the Egyptian polity and economy. Extensive discussion of the literature in each of these areas is not necessary, but a few
comments are in order so that readers, who need not share my biases,
will understand them.

Even a cursory glance at the literature in the field shows that
quite a bit of research has been done on the general topic of women
in the Arab world.[1] Remarkably little, however "has been done on the
political roles of women in the Arab region."[2] Most noteworthy are
works which have dealt with the nationalist and feminist movements

and, in general, the political and economic roles played by some Egyptian women in the first half of the twentieth century.[3] In addition, a few important articles have been written which include a discussion of the political roles of Egyptian women, but they do not have the same focus or scope as this book. One author has concentrated on bedouin women,[4] while another discusses "elite" women in a general way.[5] To the best of my knowledge, there is no systematic research on female entrepreneurs in the contemporary Arab world, although some work has been done on the general topic of "emancipation" which includes entrepreneurial activity as evidence of emancipation.[6]

Western scholars have tended to account for the recent liberation of Arab women by reference to such concepts as modernization, Westernization, or urbanization. Arabs have also used these terms, and have tended to approach the issue in polemical tones, with most of the argument centering on Islam and male control of female sexuality.[7] Both themes find some echoes in this book, but neither modernization theory nor polemics lie at the core of this effort to understand the ongoing drama of the changing status of women in Egypt.

In designing this study I could stand on the shoulders of other authors to some degree and have done so in constructing the hypotheses and research questions identified in the "Theoretical Framework" section of this Introduction. This theoretical framework is custom designed for this research and represents an eclectic synthesis abstracted and modified from work in women's studies, comparative politics, and political economy. First we shall consider some relevant theories of women's studies, then theories of the Egyptian polity and economy which have been used to guide this research. Readers uninterested in theoretical issues may wish to skip ahead to the section of this Introduction called "The Women in This Book" (p. 14) for a brief, nontechnical review of what is to come and why particular groups were selected for study.

THEORIES OF WOMEN'S STUDIES

Most recent discussions of theory and methodology in women's studies have emphasized the need for more theory and criticized previous work as merely descriptive and displaying a male bias which tends, among other things, to regard what women do as being of little importance.[8] This book, by contrast, begins with the premise that what its subjects have done is important. While a serious and concerted effort has been made to avoid inserting a male bias into this book, perfection is an unlikely achievement. Readers may decide for themselves the degree to which this effort succeeded. The book is, however, more descriptive than some feminist writers may wish it to be. That empirical quality is justified, in my opinion, because no similar study has been done. We are exploring relatively uncharted territory, and a good topographical map will help those who follow. While descriptive, this study is not devoid of theory, and should help stimulate more precise empirical work as well as studies devoted to breaking theoretical or methodological ground.

Amal Rassam, a leading Arab social scientist, has noted in a UNESCO-sponsored symposium that most general research on women has been done within an intellectual framework which has accepted either what she calls the "Nature/Culture Duality" or the "Social Evolutionary Approach" to understanding human societies.[9] In the nature/culture duality, the realm of nature is viewed as passive and "female," in the sense that it is the world of nature to which women belong. By contrast, the realm of culture is considered to be creative and dominated by men. Studies of the Middle East often use an analogous set of ideas and posit that society is divided into two separate, complementary, and unequal spheres: the private world of the household, in which women have important but subordinate roles; and the public world of politics, business, and religion, in which men monopolize all significant roles.[10]

Clearly, this book differs from much of the research which has preceeded it in that it seeks to understand how Egyptian women have come to undertake important tasks in the public world supposedly monopolized by men. Like Amal Rassam, I am troubled by the public-male/private-female dichotomy, and am not willing to accept it as a valid depiction of social reality in the Arab world, which is much more complex and dynamic than this essentially static and descriptive theory would have us believe.

Some of that complexity and dynamism is reflected in the work of women researchers who have focused on the dialectical nature of male/female relations in Arab and Islamic culture, particularly those whose work has centered on the patriarchal nature of the Arab family and the ways in which female labor, sexuality, and fertility are controlled. Much of this research is part of a general theory of social change and elaborates on the theme of how patriarchy perpetuates the subordination of women to men. It also focuses attention on the household as a unit of analysis.[11]

My research differs from most of this work in at least two important ways. First, its focus is not the continued subordination of women, which I do not deny, but on ways in which social processes affecting male/female relationships are undergoing transformation. Second, the empirical focus of this book is on a specific group of women who function within the context of Egypt's polity and economy as well as the household. As explained below, the book deals in separate chapters with four groups of women. In each of these chapters, a section will be devoted to the "formative years" of the subjects, concentrating on the childhood household and the members of that household as socializing agents. Also, a section will deal with marriage and family, and the role of the adult household in the lives of these women will be examined. Additionally, each chapter will contain extensive discussion of the public lives of these women. Thus, the household will be one of the foci of analysis but not the only one.

One important feature of research in the field of women's studies is that much of it hopes to bring about improvement in the status of women.[12] This book can perform that function in a number of ways, not the least of which is by highlighting as role models women who have played important parts in Egypt's political and economic life.

I have been conscious throughout this study of the need to be true to the subjects of this research. They are quoted, sometimes at length, and I have tried to highlight their perception of what is important in their lives and in the lives of other women. This follows the logic of Cynthia Nelson's proposition that "our theoretical perspectives about the position of women in Middle Eastern society must be the common sense world of the actors themselves."[13] Also, they have had a real impact on the structure as well as the content of this book. The chapters on presidential wives and opposition women, for example, were not part of the original concept of this study but were added, in part, as a result of repeated suggestions from several women who were subjects of the chapters on women in parliament and business.

The subjects of this book are a carefully selected group of Egyptian women, and I have tried to make it their book to the greatest

degree possible. Theories of women's studies have helped form its theoretical framework, giving parts of it a normative tone, altering its
outline, and determining that the household must be an important
focus of analysis. Futhermore, studying the role of women in Arab
society leads one easily to the conclusion that what appears on the
surface is only part of the story: a web of complex relationships beneath that surface explain and determine the rules for what goes on
above that level. The habit of looking beneath the surface structure
of society is not unique to women's studies, but it is one of its more
salient features and pervades this attempt to examine at least one sub-
surface layer of Egyptian public life. As Rosemary Sayigh points out,
however, patriarchy is not confined to the household or to gender relations, but is also found in the macro-level political and economic structure. No attempt to explain the changing role of women in twentieth-
century Egypt could be done without including the relationship between
the household and those structures in the analysis.[14]

THEORIES OF THE EGYPTIAN POLITY AND ECONOMY

Studies of the Egyptian polity and economy tend to differ method-
ologically according to their relative emphasis on such factors as:
(1) the role of individuals and personal relations, (2) the role of institutions and organizations, (3) the role of class, (4) the role of economic forces in such processes as modernization, (5) the role of the
state, and (6) the role of foreign actors as important agents in shaping
Egyptian public life. Some studies are more explicit than others in
stating which factors they consider important, but many deempha-
size the importance of institutions. Thus, for those who wish to get
ahead, it is more important, in the view of many observers, to be close
to "the leader" (or some other clearly influential figure) than to be
active in, for example, a labor union or professional association. Similarly, for those who wish to understand past decisions or predict future ones, the typical focus is on the single decision maker, down-
playing or even excluding other factors.

   This has not been the approach used here. In designing the theoretical framework for this study, no a priori judgments were made
regarding the relative importance of each of these six factors. Instead,

I decided to assume that all had potential relevance, and one of the purposes of the study would be to come to some conclusions, however tentative, regarding the importance of each on the integration of women into the Egyptian political and economic elite. The conclusions reached are discussed in the final chapter of the book.

At this point, it is enough to explain what I was looking for throughout the course of the research, so that readers may share the sense of exploration and perhaps come to their own conclusions in interpreting the data presented. This explanation will be put forward in the context of discussing several perspectives found in previous research on the Egyptian polity and economy.

The *personalist perspective* characterizes much of what has been written on Egyptian public life.[15] This perspective emphasizes the importance of such leaders as Nasser or Sadat. It also accentuates the role of political *shillal* (closely knit groups of friends), and patron-client relationships. The political scientist Robert Springborg distinguishes between what he calls "organic" and "political" shillal.[16] Organic groups tend to be formed early in life and are characterized by long-term durability and relative equality among group members. Political shillal tend to be groups of unequals, with one dominant patron who helps and is served in turn by clients. These groups are frequently less stable than organic shillal, but more durable over time and continuity of membership than ordinary political coalitions, which can be expected to change as issues and circumstances warrant. Following the logic of this perspective, we shall be on the lookout for specific examples of women who entered the political or economic elite or who prospered in it as the result of being sponsored or supported by a powerful patron. Conversely, we shall try to determine if the fall of a patron led to the fall of a client.

The personalist perspective also suggests that the role of specific leaders, especially those who have held the office of president, should be examined to see what role they have played in supporting roles for women in Egyptian public life. No observer of postrevolutionary Egypt can ignore the dominant role of the president, but it is possible to exaggerate his importance by ignoring other important actors and features of the Egyptian polity and economy.

Political scientists often organize their study of a particular society by focusing on the political elite. My conceptualization of the elite in Egypt is much broader and deeper than that suggested by the personalist perspective, and is best discussed in the context of corporatism and political economy.

The *corporatist perspective* suggests the strong possibility that the role of private voluntary associations or organizations, such as professional groups or labor syndicates, may be instrumental in helping women achieve success in politics or business.[17] Following this logic, we could try to determine what roles corporatist institutions have played in the careers of the women studied in this book. This perspective also suggests the possibility that an adequate conceptualization of the Egyptian decision-making system should include a role for these organizations, and I have included them in the model of the Egyptian elite discussed below.

A concept such as political elite has no intrinsic operational definition. For the purpose of this study, it is used to describe a much larger group of people than are included in the elite by many other scholars. John Waterbury, for example, uses the terms *elite, regime* and *leadership* more or less interchangeably and in a more restrictive sense than I do. For him, the term *elite* "is used as a kind of shorthand for those occupying the most important positions in the state and military apparatus." Membership in this elite "has typically been more a function of personality and proximity to the 'boss' than of institutional position."[18] What he refers to as the "elite," "regime," or "leadership" is what I call the "top elite" or "presidential elite."

Clearly, most power is held in the hands of the president and the few advisors closest to him. This group sits at the pinnacle of power in Egypt, but it does not monopolize all discretionary authority, nor are its members the only people who make decisions about things that matter. Power may be concentrated at the top, but meaningful decisions are also made elsewhere in the system. Therefore, other levels of the political elite must be included in an analysis of Egyptian public life in order to reflect that reality. While the presidential elite is characterized by personalist relationships, the lower levels of the elite are defined by their position in the political structure or, in the case of groups such as intellectuals, which lack a built-in hierarchy, by reputation. The conception of the Egyptian elite used for this book is illustrated by figure 1.

This depiction of Egypt's elite recognizes that, since 1952, the president and a few people chosen by him have dominated Egyptian public life. It also postulates that Egypt's political life has an institu-

FIGURE 1: THE EGYPTIAN ELITE

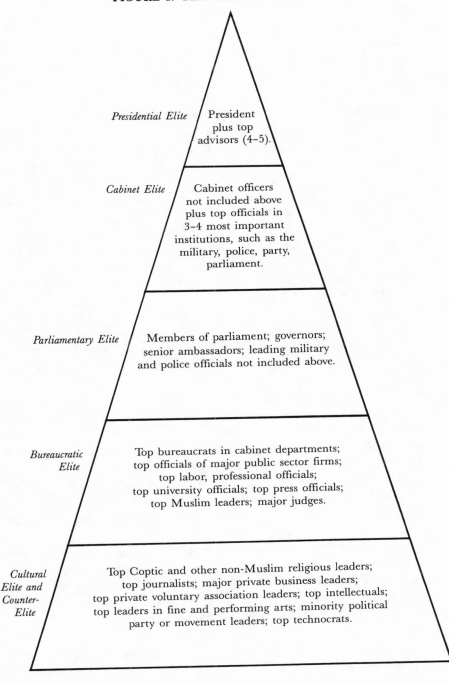

Presidential Elite — President plus top advisors (4–5).

Cabinet Elite — Cabinet officers not included above plus top officials in 3–4 most important institutions, such as the military, police, party, parliament.

Parliamentary Elite — Members of parliament; governors; senior ambassadors; leading military and police officials not included above.

Bureaucratic Elite — Top bureaucrats in cabinet departments; top officials of major public sector firms; top labor, professional officials; top university officials; top press officials; top Muslim leaders; major judges.

Cultural Elite and Counter-Elite — Top Coptic and other non-Muslim religious leaders; top journalists; major private business leaders; top private voluntary association leaders; top intellectuals; top leaders in fine and performing arts; minority political party or movement leaders; top technocrats.

tional and structural dimension to it.[19] Members of the presidential-level elite generally are chosen from those who have achieved prominence at a lower level, and it is quite possible for a person to move in one jump from the lowest to the highest level. In general, I have assumed that relationships between and within the levels of this elite are characterized by varying degrees of personalist and bureaucratic politics. The model should not be interpreted as a static picture of the Egyptian elite but as a way of thinking about its various levels. The examples given are to be taken as illustrative rather than definitive. At times in Egypt's recent history, the institutions mentioned in the figure have had more autonomy and self-direction than at others, but at no time have they ceased to have internally generated dynamism and momentum. Even when regime control has been strong, it has never been total. In short, components of the elite below the presidential level count for something in Egyptian public life, and what happens at those levels is important even if not always vital to the immediate survival of the state.

Egypt can be thought of as having a bureaucratic, welfare-oriented, state capitalist system, in which most power is held by the president, supported, at least tacitly, by the professional military.[20] The state has attempted at various times and to different degrees to co-opt or control most independent institutions or associations. This effort to incorporate organized activity has been only partly successful, the degree of success fluctuating in irregular cycles according to the period and organization in question. Women's associations such as those mentioned in chapter 1, have been among those targeted for special attention, especially by the regime established by the 1952 revolution. Such "democratic" institutions as a free and independent press and independent political parties were circumscribed severely between 1952 and 1979. Since that time restrictions have been loosened though not removed.

The *political economy* perspective is an important aid to understanding contemporary Egypt. Economics and politics may be studied in separate university departments, but in the real world they are linked, and it is doubtful if either can be understood in isolation from the other. The conception of the elite used for this book includes actors from the business sector as well as explicitly political figures. Linkage between economics and politics is especially potent in Egypt, because of policies followed by both the monarchy and the revolutionary regime which succeeded it. For example, Egypt has pursued a policy of import substitution since the time of the Great Depression, attempting to produce products in Egypt and reduce the need for exports. Between 1930 and 1952, a sizable industrial sector was created. After 1952, the policy of import substitution continued to be followed, but most of the major components of the country's leading industries were nationalized. This policy of import substitution dominated by a massive public sector "was in disarray by 1966, and the June War of 1967 delivered the coup de grace to strategies of accumulation of *any* kind."[21] Since the late 1970s, there has been more emphasis on trying to achieve growth via exports, but the economy remains dominated by a huge public sector producing goods for domestic consumption. The private sector, under severe pressure and subject to nationalization and sequestration in the 1950s and early 1960s, has made a gradual but uneven comeback since the late 1960s, doing much of its business with the public sector but also meeting some consumer needs directly.

Egypt is not isolated from world political or economic currents, and in the twentieth century there has been, in succession, a strong British, Soviet, and American presence in the country. This foreign presence has been a mixed blessing and curse, bringing new technology, challenges to traditional values, and constraints on both foreign and domestic policies. Throughout this "struggle for Egypt's soul,"[22] Egypt has remained in the hands of Egyptians and has experienced what can be described as "dependent development," in which the country has become linked to the world economy and foreign states but had used its geopolitical importance to bargain for terms which have helped Egypt experience real growth and economic development.[23]

THEORETICAL FRAMEWORK

To feminists and specialists in women's studies, the topic of this book may seem to have self-evident interest. For nonfeminists and many social scientists, the importance and relevance of studying the political and economic roles of women is not immediately obvious. As can be implied from the brief review of research on the Egyptian polity and economy, and of women's studies in the Arab world, at least three types of arguments could be formulated against doing research of this kind. First, drawing on the notion that politics and business are male monopolies, it could be said that a study of women in national politics and business could not be done because such women do not exist. Variations of this theme were repeated to me several times by several supposedly well-informed foreign and Egyptian observers, mostly male, of contemporary public life in Egypt. As the substantive chapters of this book will make clear, this argument is demonstrably false.

The second argument would discourage work of this kind, deeming it unimportant because, according to one variety of personalist perspective, the only topics of real importance are at the presidential level. This too was a line of reasoning I encountered several times in discussions with people throughout the course of this research. Hopefully, the descriptive portions of this book, especially those pertaining to key changes in law and custom, will suggest to readers that the presidential level is not the only important arena of the Egyptian polity or economy. A third argument against this study, encountered more often than either of the first two, is related to foreign influence, arguing either that progress for women is simply the result of a linear process of modernization, or alternatively, that women in the Egyptian elite are merely Westernized accretions and not authentic to Egypt. According to these views, if you wish to study something important, you must concentrate on the process of modernization, not one of its residual consequences, or on such supposedly more authentic movements as Islamic fundamentalism. I hope the empirical evidence in this book will lead readers to conclude that the women in the current Egyptian elite are not alien icing on an Egyptian cake. The effort to improve the position of women in Egypt is an authentic Egyptian process, the understanding of which is vital to our understanding of Egypt itself. Furthermore, as the research on Islamic feminism by Fadwa al-Guindi suggests, a political victory for fundamentalists does not necessarily imply the end to roles for women in Egyptian public life. As she makes clear, women in Islamic groups on university campuses have their own decision making structure and do not always follow the lead of their male colleagues.[24]

In constructing the theoretical framework for this research I have assumed that no single factor can account for the changes which have taken place in the twentieth century regarding the roles and status of women in Egypt. As this is a phenomenon of complex and multiple etiology, it cannot be conceptualized easily. In order to clarify the situation as much as possible, the subject will be studied at several levels of analysis, more than one type of causal agent will be searched for, and ideas from numerous theoretical perspectives will be employed.[25]

At the *individual level of analysis*, specific examples of leadership will be sought and identified. We shall also seek to determine if patron-client relationships help account for the presence in the Egyptian elite of the women studied in this book.

At the *sub-national level of analysis*, we shall try to find out if certain institutions or organizations help account for the presence of these particular women in the Egyptian elite. Special attention will be paid to the patriarchal household or family as a key social unit. We shall also try to find out if such corporatist organizations as labor unions, private voluntary charitable organizations, professional syndicates, or other such associations were instrumental in helping these women succeed in public life. Furthermore, it is at this level that the question of class as a determinative variable must be considered.

At the *national level of analysis*, we shall try to determine the degree to which law and public policy help account for the ability of women to enter Egypt's national political and economic elite. Participation in this national elite, the components of which have been described above, is the key dependent variable in this study.

At the *international level of analysis*, the issue of foreign influence will be considered. This includes such general phenomena as "world market forces" and "Western culture" and such specific factors as particular examples of direct bilateral relations.

What emerges from this review of relevant research in the fields of women's studies, comparative politics, and political economy are two general research questions and six specific hypotheses. The first research question can be stated as follows:

What has been the role or impact on the careers of women in the current Egyptian elite of: (1) the patriarchal household, (2) patron-client relationships, (3) presidential leadership, (4) private voluntary associations, (5) the state as an agent of change, and (6) foreign influences? As this is but an exploratory work, a precise evaluation of the relative importance of these factors will not be attempted. Rather, it is hoped that general tendencies may be identified as a guide to future research. Second, in an attempt to disconfirm further the stereotype of women evoked by the public-male/private-female model, we shall look for specific evidence that women acting in the public arena have functioned as agents of change, either for Egypt in general or, more specifically, for the cause of Egyptian women.[26]

Supplementing and complementing these broad questions are six specific hypotheses suggested by previous research. These hypotheses state that, when considering women who have succeeded in business or politics in Egypt, it is likely that

1. they will come from a privileged social and economic background;
2. they will be significantly better educated than their male counterparts;
3. they will combine political or professional careers with the roles of wife and mother;
4. they will perform important and necessary roles, often away from the public eye, as mediators and sources of pressure on "their" men regarding changes in public policy and social mores pertaining to women;
5. they will be reasonably well informed about the history of the women's movement in Egypt, identify with "women's issues," and perceive a close, positive, and reciprocal link between national development and progress for women;
6. female entrepreneurs will exhibit the same psychological characteristics attributed in standard studies to entrepreneurs in general.

These hypotheses, the reasons for their selection, and the research upon which they are based, will be discussed more fully in the concluding chapter, where the results of this research will be summarized and discussed in the context of the theoretical framework outlined here.

THE WOMEN IN THIS BOOK

Observers familiar with contemporary Egypt and with the roles played by women in modern Egyptian public life will note that there are many fields in which women are active or prominent. The women whose lives are highlighted here are not the only ones who could have been selected. The first step in settling the substantive focus for research was listing possible categories for inclusion. A book on women in public life could have included chapters on women in

- parliament
- the cabinet
- diplomacy
- the professions — especially medicine, dentistry, law, journalism, and engineering
- business — namely, those who own and manage medium-to-large-scale enterprises
- business — namely, those who own and manage such enterprises as coffee shops, taxi fleets, butcher shops, and other more or less "traditional" businesses which tend to be local rather than national in scope
- agriculture — namely, those who own and manage agricultural land
- politics (due to the positions of their husbands)
- public sector management
- opposition politics at the national level
- education and research
- private voluntary social work
- government bureaucracy — especially those in top positions in the Ministries of Education, Health, or Social Affairs
- the fine and performing arts
- local politics, both pro- and anti-government

In selecting portions of the Egyptian elite for analysis, choices had to be made, some of which may be found infelicitous by some readers. Women who excelled in both politics and business were selected because I wanted to demonstrate that neither politics nor business is a male monopoly although, as explained earlier, many books on Arab culture state that women have no public roles to play in these arenas.

When research began for this book, it concentrated on only two groups of women: entrepreneurs and parliamentarians. These two seemed at the time to be the most conspicuous and obvious of all of the groups of women in the Egyptian elite. Readers should keep in mind that I had lived in Egypt for nearly nine years before research for this book began, and I knew, or knew of, women in all of the groups mentioned above. Based on this familiarity, I suspected that a study of these two groups would contain women from a variety of backgrounds and would thus include representatives from many of the other categories. For example, the parliamentary group contained the only women to serve at the rank of ambassador, all three who served in the cabinet, and several prominent professionals. The entrepreneurs also included women who fell into other categories and represented a portion of the Egyptian elite whose power and importance had grown since the Open Door Policy of the mid-1970s. Between them, these two groups contained examples of women from eleven of the fifteen groups mentioned, including many of the most prominent women in contemporary Egyptian public life.[27]

Encouraged by a grant from the Ford Foundation, I began research on these two groups. As I learned more about the general subject and about Egypt, I became convinced that two additional and markedly different groups should be included: women in the political opposition and the group I call "presidential wives." Among other things, the addition of these two groups meant that representatives of all fifteen segments of the Egyptian elite referred to above would be included in the study group. Nevertheless, each choice requires explanation.

Opposition women were chosen because one of the most conspicuous but heretofore unremarked features of the opposition is the presence in it of a large number of women. Furthermore, the nature of Egyptian politics is such that few of these women had been in parliament. Not surprisingly, most parliamentarians expressed an essentially pro-regime set of opinions and turned out to be remarkably homogeneous in a number of other ways. Including opposition women in the book helped give a more balanced and representative picture of the range of opinion and behavior characteristic of women active in Egyptian public life, especially following the relative liberalization of 1979.[28]

The chapter on presidential wives was included for a number of reasons. First, it did not seem possible to write a book about women in the Egyptian elite without discussing influential women who affected public policy but held no formal or official position in government. Of all the politically relevant activity by Egyptian women in the twentieth century, this is probably the most conspicuous. It could even be called "traditional." In some cases it has also been the most controversial. This general category would include the women who established the feminist movement, women who ran significant pri-

vate voluntary organizations, and women who were married to powerful men and became involved in politics because of their husband's
position. The first two groups are discussed primarily in chapter 1,
which provides the historical overview for the book. The last is represented by three women who typify three distinct models of behavior
for women in analogous positions. As will be seen, these women are
interesting in and of themselves, but they are also important because
of the role models which they represent, models which are related to
the theoretical framework which shaped this research, particularly to
the patriarcial and personalalist perspectives discussed above.

Strictly speaking, this is not an historical study. Even though it
features details drawn from the life histories of over seventy people,
emphasis is on the present and future more than the past. Nevertheless, the hypotheses which informed and shaped the research assume
a high degree of historical continuity. For that reason, chapter 1 is
devoted to a brief consideration of the main aspects of the feminist
movement in Egypt as well as to changes which have taken place during this century regarding the education and employment of women.
Subsequent chapters deal specifically with women in the political and
economic elite in the early 1980s.

The first to be discussed are those who have held high public
office at the national level. This includes women who have been elected
or appointed to either house of parliament, held cabinet office, or served
as Egyptian ambassador to a foreign country. As all of the approximately fifty women who fit into this category have served in parliament, chapter 2 is called "Parliamentary Women" and concentrates
on this aspect of their careers. These people deserve attention if for
no other reason than their number. Paradoxically, although Western
women usually are assumed to be more "liberated" than those in the
east, there are more women in Egypt's parliament than in America's
Congress or Britain's House of Commons. Egypt's parliamentary
women are also characterized by diversity. For example, in addition
to features already mentioned, they differ in style of dress and type
of education. Many wear traditional Islamic garb, while others are
draped in modest but finely tailored clothes from Paris, Milan, or New
York; some have Western Ph.D.s while others received their entire formal education in tiny rural villages. Diverse as they are, however, they
stand together when circumstances warrant it and use their formal
power to advance and protect the common cause.

The visible and public exercise of power by women is controversial in many societies, but especially in Arab and other Muslim
countries. We shall see how Egypt's parliamentary women deal with
this issue, but, ironically, they have probably been less controversial
than a second group of women who can be considered to form part
of the political elite. These are the wives of high public officials, in
particular the spouses of Egypt's presidents. Although presented with
unique opportunities, they often have been faced with what to them
have been vexing limitations. Because of their positions in the country's political system, and the role models they represent, the wives
of Presidents Nasser, Sadat, and Mubarak will be the subjects of
chapter 3, entitled "Presidential Wives."

Still part of the political elite but far from the center of power
are women in the third group: those who have held high office in an
opposition political party or a leadership role in an opposition movement, or who have the reputation for being important components
of the opposition. The fourth chapter, on "Opposition Women," features those who have experienced the risks and rewards of occupying
such positions, thereby standing against Egypt's bureaucratic and authoritarian regimes.

As for the economic elite, a small number of women have recently become successful entrepreneurs and will be the subjects of
chapter 5, "Women in Business." Because of the absence of reliable
public data on economic affairs, these women, unlike most of the politicians, were identified more by reputation than by position. Several
leading financial and business figures were consulted and asked to
identify women whom they considered to be part of Egypt's business elite. All those nominated were investigated, but only those who
owned and operated their own business, and who also either started
it or "made it what it is today" in some clear and major way, were
selected. While the selection of those who constitute Egypt's economic
elite was, necessarily, more subjective than that of the political group,
I am confident that I located virtually all of Egypt's major contemporary female entrepreneurs.

Most of the information for this study is derived from a series
of intensive interviews with women in the four groups mentioned above.
A total of 74 different women, a few of whom fit into more than one
category, are profiled. Futhermore, a number of individuals were consulted who had special knowledge which they agreed to share, often

on a confidential basis, as were a variety of primary and secondary sources in both Arabic and English. Interviews were conducted in Arabic or English—sometimes a mixture of the two—either by myself or a female research assistant. Some people were interviewed several times, and, with the permission of the interviewee, a few conversations were taped. All in all, over 170 hours were spent interviewing between June 1982, when the study began, and June 1984, by which time most interviews were completed. Except for biographical data, a formal questionnaire was not used. Rather, an interview sheet containing a number of open-ended questions gave a common structure to conversations. Every effort was made to reduce the formal nature of these encounters and to provide each subject with the opportunity to speak at length on issues of personal concern to her, as well as to give the interviewer a chance to probe items of particular interest.

Although this is a study of elite women, its implications are important for women of all classes. It should, for example, help identify the issues of the future for all Egyptian women, not just those in the current elite. Furthermore, elite women are important role models. They provide men and women, in and outside Egypt, with examples of the contributions women can make to political, economic and social development. Focus on the elite does not imply that what nonelites do is of no consequence. Women of all classes and occupational categories are important in their own right as human beings and as resources which may be mobilized in more productive ways than they have been in the past. If the history of Egypt is any guide, the example of the women discussed in this book will stimulate the younger generation and show both sexes how much is to be gained by enabling women to participate more fully in economic and political life.

The Public Role of Women in Modern Egypt

FEMINISTS, seeking equal rights for women, attempt to transform the political balance, moving women from the margins of power to positions where they can participate in society's important decision making. In Egypt it has been argued that the participation of women in public life will be good for both sexes, that it will strengthen the family, and also help society at large by increasing the number of citizens upon whose resources and talents the country may draw. In pursuit of an enlarged public forum, feminists everywhere have faced opposition from women as well as men, and have had to make numerous choices regarding ideology, specific goals, and tactics. Not all have felt that women should seek absolute equality with men, believing that protection and enhancement of a separate sphere for women in the public life of the country is preferable to a totally egalitarian world. Some have accepted the idea of a separate and protected sphere as an interim tactic but profess equal opportunity as the ultimate goal. Others reject separatism even as a tactic, fearing that unless women succeed in competition with men, the effect of protection will be to undermine the legitimacy of their claim to equal rights. Regardless of goals, however, feminists have made a niche for women in the public life of Egypt, one that did not exist until recently, but whose roots can be seen in the not too distant past.

The periodization of history is always arbitrary, but it may be helpful to think about the twentieth-century changes affecting the roles and status of women in Egypt as having gone through four fairly distinct phases and as having entered a new period in 1979. The chronology in the back of the book (pages 171–75) may help orient readers, as it summarizes major events relevant to the public role of women in Egypt.

From about 1900 to 1923, issues were clarified, positions taken, and debate joined. Men as well as women appeared as prominent participants in events during this stage. Some influential women, including a princess, organized fashionable intellectual salons.[1] Both proponents and opponents of an expanded role for women defended their views, most frequently in Islamic terms and in reference to the need to modernize Egypt. In this regard, little has changed since then, and the debate is still couched in these terms, thus supporting the suggestion of a prominent Egyptian sociologist that in Egypt nothing is ever really discarded. Rather, Egyptian history is a process of recycling and accumulation.[2]

The second stage in the women's movement began in 1923 with the establishment of the Egyptian Feminist Union. It ended in 1935, when the process of women's setting the agenda for the movement was basically completed. Upper-class women organized, marched, gave speeches, established private voluntary charitable organizations, defined issues, and staked claims. Women went abroad for higher education, schools for girls were founded, and, in 1928, women were admitted to the Egyptian National University. Feminist leaders such as Hoda Sha'rawi and Ceza Nabarawi made a point during this period of linking feminism with nationalism, but also emphasized that, in their view, women had a right to personal development and fulfillment.[3]

In 1935, the mainstream of the women's movement in Egypt began to be more assertive regarding women's rights. For the first time, the Feminist Union endorsed the principle of full political equality for both sexes. As they were graduated from the university, more women entered the professions. Some worked as active feminists. Others concentrated on professional development, eschewing politics for the time but, consciously or unconsciously, laying a foundation for a future political career. The question of Palestine and the need for Arab unity were new themes taken up by women activists after 1935, but traditional programs also continued, such as the effort to abolish legalized prostitution. This last effort finally succeeded, but not until 1949. In general, women became more active in public life and helped set the tone for the period. Following World War II, political work was accelerated, and more strictly political groups of women were formed, especially after the death of Hoda Sha'rawi in 1947.

Throughout the first half of the twentieth century social feminists, who specialized in attempts to improve social and economic conditions, vied for leadership with political feminists, who advocated direct political participation by women and reform of the Personal Status Laws — laws regulating marriage, divorce, and child custody. The feminist movement adopted, albeit piecemeal, the goals of the political feminists. However, most day-to-day activity fell within the scope of social feminism, by which women established and ran a variety of private voluntary social service organizations.[4] Politically, the most important of these were in the health field, such as Tahsin al-Saha, the Red Crescent, and the Mabarra Muhammad Ali group of hospitals.

One example of their importance can be seen in the response to problems Egypt faced in the aftermath of World War II, in which these agencies were active in efforts to deal with major epidemics of cholera and malaria. The women's associations, particularly the Mabarra, were probably more effective than the government in handling these crises and they, along with the government and some foreign health agencies, were responsible for ending the epidemic.[5] In this and other ways, women demonstrated their value to society and supported the nationalist cause. In the process, in a conscious exercise of linkage politics, they worked to gain support for items on their political agenda.[6] This tactic bore fruit, but not in a major way until after the Free Officers came to power. The 1952 revolution started a new phase of life in Egypt, but for women, the period which began in 1935 did not end until 1956, when the new constitution gave women the right to vote.

Between 1956 and 1979, pathbreaking women participated in Egyptian public life in new ways. Egyptian women started their own businesses, entered parliament, were appointed to cabinet posts, and became increasingly conspicuous and visible. More women became more active in more fields, particularly the professions.[7] On perhaps a more negative note, in the 1960s women's groups were absorbed into the only legal political organization of the time, the Arab Socialist Union, and many of the welfare activities of women were taken over by the state. For a while, the political nature of feminist activity was limited to serving the party and the state. However, even though feminist organizations were somewhat co-opted by the regime, the pace and scope of female involvement in public life was accelerated by the accumulated momentum from past achievements, notably in education. After 1970, when Anwar Sadat became president of Egypt, this trend was given further impetus and encouragement by the regime. The president's wife, Jihan, an ardent feminist, became the focus for both blame and praise as she developed into a public personality and a force in her own right. The period which began in 1956 with women gaining the right to vote, ended in 1979. In that year, with strong presidential support, the Personal Status Laws were reformed, and women were given guaranteed seats in all of Egypt's elected assemblies.

After 1979, Egypt's leading women continued to do the kinds of things they had been doing throughout the century. Now, however, a new role was added: defending and consolidating established rights and protecting the position of women from erosion or wholesale attack. What was a radical and, to many, outrageous program in 1923 is now partly legal, traditional, and even regarded as conservative in some quarters. But for others, all proposals to enhance the role or improve the status of women remain objectionable. The new status quo has been supported by, among others, the Sadat-Mubarak regime and most of the women elected or appointed to high public office. Some feminists, including many in the political opposition, however, want more substantial change in the direction of full equality. Other opposition figures, including some Islamic fundamentalists, advocate enacting legislation which would severely restrict the role of women in public life. Thus, what has been accomplished remains controversial and should not be regarded as permanent.

In many ways Egyptian women are better off today than they were in 1900. Much of this progress is due to Egypt's development, but a substantial portion is the result of the successful struggles of women such as those who are the subjects of this book. However, the fruits of development have not been shared equally between classes and, more particularly, between men and women. Poverty, malnutrition, poor health, illiteracy, and dependence are still experienced more by women than by men. What progress has been made has not been easy and is resented and opposed by many people, even though what has been achieved is little more than a beginning. Readers should keep this ugly reality in mind as they proceed through this book. It is a problem to which we shall return.

FEMINIST ROOTS: ORGANIZING AND SETTING THE AGENDA

The public role of women in Egypt's political and economic life has changed dramatically, even fundamentally, during the twentieth century.[8] This is in contrast to the previous one hundred years, during which pressure accumulated and the stage was set, but little change for the better occurred. (In fact, conditions for women are more likely to have declined rather than improved during the nineteenth century.[9]) At the turn of the century, peasant women worked in the fields as part of the extended family, but other public activities were severely limited. Bedouin women could move unveiled within the tribe, serve behind the scenes as mediators and go-betweens, and even participate in public events and ceremonies, but they were not permitted to express opinions on public issues.[10]

Urban women were even more secluded from public life than their rural counterparts. While under Islamic law they were entitled to own property, in practice they were seldom permitted (presumably by the male members of their families) to administer it.[11] This is in contrast to the eighteenth century, in which the wives of Mamluks often administered their own property as well as that of their husbands.[12] Even though veiled, and therefore hidden, urban women at the turn of the century could not work with men. In fact, to work outside the home in any capacity was considered dishonorable. Virtually all women were illiterate, the exceptions being a handful of privileged, urban women who were more likely to read French or English than Arabic.

Upper-class urban women generally were confined by the rules governing the household. This did not mean, however, that they were necessarily powerless or ignorant of life outside their veiled world. Some, for example, were involved in business and followed political events, but they did not appear publicly to be active in these spheres. Severe social strictures limited all women and prohibited most of them from participating in public life.[13]

However, the most constrained situation was probably in provincial towns, where women were veiled, secluded, unable to work outside the home, and even less likely than urbanites to learn about anything other than the traditional world of women. As Amina Said, one of Egypt's leading feminists and journalists and a member of its current political elite has stated: "The traditions and ideology [in these towns] bear the stamp of the petite bourgeoisie in its worst form and they have affected the women . . . in a very repressive way."[14] For this reason, in the early part of the century, if a rural family wished to educate its daughters, either the girls were sent to Cairo or, as was the case with Amina Said, the whole family moved.

The first government primary school for girls was established in 1873, but it was not until 1921 that the first government secondary school for girls was opened.[15] Virtually all schools for girls were located in an urban area, and most were in Cairo. Later, both primary and secondary schools were available in rural areas, and some members of the current political elite attended them. Change, although slow, did take place.

A man, Qasim Amin (1863–1908), is credited with being the first in the twentieth century to call for basic alterations with regard to the position and rights of women in society.[16] As the historian and Islamicist Thomas Philipp has pointed out:

> The debate over the emancipation of women originated among Muslim reformists. It was their contention that an Islam correctly interpreted and set free of traditional ballast was able to provide a viable system of beliefs and values even under the changed circumstances of modern times. Thus, they felt that the position of women had suffered, not through the commands of the original Islam, but by a misinterpretation of the Quran and later un-Islamic additions.[17]

Qasim Amin was a follower of Mohamed Abduh (1849–1905), the leader of the reformist movement who himself had been inspired by Rifaat al-Tahtawi (1801–73), an even earlier reformist.[18] Early in the nineteenth century, al-Tahtawi "emphasized the necessity and legitimacy of adapting Islamic law to new social circumstances."[19] Among those circumstances were capitalism and imperialism, but the dispute over the role of women in the context of these new forces had to be conducted within the framework of Islamic jurisprudence.

In Sunni Islam, which prevails in Egypt, there are four recognized schools of law: Hanafi, Shafii, Maliki, and Hanbali. The Hanafi school, by far the strictest regarding women and issues affecting personal status, has been followed officially in Egypt since Ottoman times, but many Egyptians still use Shafii or Maliki precepts in their own life. Reformers followed Tahtawi's advice and invoked the principle of *takhyayyur*, "an accepted method of jurisprudence according to which a Muslim in a specific situation was permitted to go outside his own school of law and follow the interpretation of one of the other Sunni schools."[20] It was within the context of this movement that Amin called for the emancipation of women. On the positive side, his chief argument was that women must be educated in order for them to carry out their roles as wives and mothers properly, and to contribute to the development of society. In the same vein, he opposed polygamy, easy divorce by the male, veiling of women, and arranged marriages.

While Qasim Amin, as a Muslim reformer, advocated the rights of women, at least two of Egypt's most prominent nationalists, Talat Harb (1867–1941) and Mustafa Kamel (1874–1908), opposed these ideas on the grounds they were foreign to Egypt. One historian's interpretation is that Talat Harb, the founder of Bank Misr (the Bank of Egypt) and an advocate of the industrialization of Egypt by Egyptians, not foreigners, went so far as to contend that "the emancipation of women was just another plot to weaken the Egyptian nation and disseminate immorality and decadence in its society."[21] Talat Harb's rejection of Amin's ideas on women may have been because Qasim Amin framed his case for reform in terms which made clear his admiration for and wish to adopt many of the customs of the British. In an astute article on Amin, Juan Cole points out that Amin "saw the emancipation of women as an essential step in catching up with European progress. . . . For Harb, the abolition of the veil and seclusion would be a further step toward the total disintegration of the indigenous values of Egyptian Islam."[22]

In this instance, Amin can be seen as a spokesman for the established upper-middle class. He wanted Egypt to strengthen itself for competition with the West by learning from the West, thus drawing on its power. Harb, on the other side, can be seen as a representative of an upwardly mobile new middle class, possibly fearing competition for scarce jobs from women and seeking protection in the comfort of custom and the traditional sense of honor.

As the century began, the issue of greater freedom for women was controversial. No consensus existed, but it was clear to all that questions regarding the role, status, and rights of women were central to both the nationalist movement and the debate regarding the reform of Islam. In succeeding decades much has changed, but the issue continues to inspire divisiveness rather than consensus.

The public debate regarding the emancipation of women may have been started by men, but women soon joined the fray. Often for pragmatic, but sometimes for ideological reasons, some of them took a more conservative stand than that of Qasim Amin. These women tended to be educated and come from the upper class. Malak Hifni Nasif (1886–1918), for example, was the daughter of a follower of Mohamed Abduh and one of the first Egyptian women to be educated. Awarded a teacher's certificate, she worked as an educator but also wrote articles for newspapers and magazines under the pen name of Bahithat al-Badiya.

In 1911, in a speech to the Egyptian Legislative Assembly, she presented a petition which contained ten demands for women. Her petition, all points of which were rejected by the Assembly, centered on giving women more and better education and such rights as free access to the mosque. In addition to her wish to have more women enter the fields of medicine and education, what she wanted was a system which would enable women to do their traditional jobs better.[23] She did not demand full and equal participation by women in public life but, although she did not oppose polygamy or arranged marriages, did request legal protection for women regarding marriage and divorce.[24]

The question of laws and customs pertaining to marriage and divorce was crucial to early feminists and remains so today. At the time of Qasim Amin and Malak Hifni Nasif, a Muslim girl was often married before puberty, could be divorced for any, or even no reason, could be beaten by her husband and, if she left him without his consent, be brought back by force and subjected to *bayt al-taah* (house of obedience), that is, forced to live under his jurisdiction and subject to his authority. In general, matters pertaining to marriage and divorce were, and continue to be, governed by custom rather than civil law, and efforts to achieve change have proven to be exceptionally difficult and controversial, even though liberal reformers have argued consistently that the changes called for by feminists are not contrary to Islam.[25]

The feminist movement in Egypt is usually said to have had its birth in 1919, when a number of veiled upper-class women, led by Mrs. Hoda Sha'rawi (1879–1947) and others, marched in protest against the British decision to forbid the nationalist leader, Saad Zaghloul (1860–1928), from going to Britain to present the demands of the Egyptian *wafd* (delegation).[26] Strictly speaking, the women involved in the demonstrations and marches of 1919 did not march on behalf of the rights of women, but rather advocated the same nationalist points as those presented by the men.[27] The public activity of women was intended to convey their dedication to the main issue of the day, nationalism, and to show that women stood with men and could help the national cause. From its ideological inception, therefore, Egyptian feminism was linked with nationalism and supported the desire to develop Egypt as well as free the country from foreign control.

From an institutional point of view, feminism took a step forward in Egypt on March 16, 1923, when Mrs. Hoda Sha'rawi convened a group of women at her home to organize what soon became the Egyptian Feminist Union. Mrs. Sha'rawi, Ceza Nabarawi, and the other Egyptian delegates to the International Alliance for Women, meeting in Rome in 1923, had returned to Egypt unveiled. This plus the establishment of the Feminist Union, inaugurated a more forceful and visible stage in the women's liberation movement. It was not until 1935, however, that the Feminist Union first began to demand full and equal political rights for women. Before that demand could be made, the leaders of the movement felt that women had to be prepared for it. The primary objective of the new organization was, therefore, "to raise the intellectual and moral level of the Egyptian woman so as to enable her to realize her political and social equality with man from the legal as well as from the moral point of view."[28]

Organized feminism retained its link with nationalism and also tried to align itself with the voices for social reform in Egypt. Thus, it stated its program in terms that made it clear that women wanted changes in the laws affecting marriage, divorce, and the custody of children but also wished "to make propaganda in favor of public hygiene and sanitation," "encourage virtue and fight immorality," and oppose irrational "superstitions, cults and customs."[29] This it did, as the history of the Feminist Union makes clear. What is also clear is the pattern of political activity and the ideological tone established by Egypt's early feminists. The precedent they set has influenced the course of events until the present time.

In order to understand contemporary events, it is necessary to pause and consider what the early feminists were up against. Nominally ruled by a hereditary monarchy, Egypt was effectively controlled by the British. Members of the ruling family were the descendants of Mohamed Ali, an Albanian who took over Egypt in 1805, shortly after the departure of Napoleon. The nationalists, men like Talat Harb, Mustafa Kamel, and Saad Zaghloul, were more concerned about the British domination of the polity and the economy than about the monarchy, but they wished to "Egyptianize" the system in every way possible. As noted above, these men were either unenthusiastic about or frankly opposed to the feminist movement, suspecting it of having a foreign influence and of being "un-Egyptian." Other nationalists, however, men such as Ahmad Lutfi al-Sayyid (1872–1963) and Taha Hussein (1889–1973), belonged to the liberal reformist tradition embracing especially the ideas of Mohamed Abduh and Qasim Amin. Influenced partly by the theories of Herbert Spencer, these Egyptian "progressives" were advocates of evolutionary rather than revolutionary change.[30]

Most feminists were associated with this group of nationalist reformers, progressives, and modernists who believed that society had to be freed of unhealthy (and, in their view, un-Islamic) accretions before it could experience true liberation. Dr. Taha Hussein, whose French-born wife was listed as a member of the Board of Directors of the Egyptian Feminist Union in the late 1920s,[31] devoted his life to scholarship and educational reform. He was interested particularly in the application of modern research techniques to the study of Arabic, and had a major impact, first as Dean of Arts at the National University and later in a number of other posts, on the extension and reform of education in Egypt. Among the principal beneficiaries of his efforts and those of the other modernists were the increasing number of female students who entered the formal educational system.

An inevitable consequence of the divisions within the nationalist movement was disagreement regarding both strategy and tactics. There was also a certain amount of personal competition and tension among the nationalists, but perhaps most important for our purposes is that a pattern of specialization developed. Talat Harb founded Bank Misr and concentrated his efforts on the indigenous industrialization of Egypt. Saad Zaghloul, while not uninterested in economic affairs, pursued party politics as his chosen venue, principally via the Wafd Party, which he established. Ahmad Lutfi al-Sayyid helped establish the three major political parties of that period but was probably best known for his important service as rector of the Egyptian University.[32] All three men were involved in journalistic ventures, and they and their followers were all nationalists; yet there was little consensus among them, except that all agreed that Egyptian institutions should be reformed and developed, and Egypt should be self-governing.

In 1923, the likelihood of women being granted the franchise was nil, so party politics was not a likely field for successful activity by women, even those of the upper class. Similarly, as few women had any expertise to offer, they could do little to contribute to the industrialization of Egypt at that time, especially given Talat Harb's hostility to feminism and to women's playing public roles. By default, if nothing else, the early feminists were thus left in a loose alliance with the nationalist reformers whose strongholds were in education and journalism, and who functioned primarily as a pressure group favoring general nationalist causes, legal reforms, and social action. Not surprisingly, then, most of the early gains achieved by feminists were in the areas of social reform and education.

Feminism was essentially an upper-class movement, and it was probably only the upper-class status of its leaders that permitted them to develop and then advocate their ideas in public. However, while class provided a certain freedom, it may also have reinforced conservative restraints and caused them to restrict their agenda, at least initially, to a relatively small number of issues. What they did not advocate is probably as important as what they supported. For example, women were not encouraged to avoid marriage, nor was support for birth control on the list of early Feminist Union proposals.[33] In general, women were not urged to become independent from men. They were taught to respect themselves and their sex, and to demand and earn respect from their husbands as well as from others with whom they would come in contact.[34] It was assumed that virtually all women would marry and have children. Thus it was to the institutions of marriage and the family that early feminists turned their attention. Their reasoning went something like this: the family had to be strong; educated men needed educated wives to run the household and raise children; if women were married too early or could be divorced without valid cause, this weakened the family and ultimately weakened Egypt. Thus, the cause of women and the family was part of the national cause.

Even though feminists achieved little in the way of reform at first, they kept a number of issues on the nationalist agenda for several decades. Most important, perhaps, they established certain functional areas as legitimate arenas in which women could work. For example, by concentrating activity on the fields of education and social reform, upper-class feminists of prerevolutionary Egypt made it possible later for women of all classes to seek education and for women to claim special insights into social reform. It is not an accident that all three women who have served as cabinet officers have headed the same ministry, Social Affairs, which is, in effect, Egypt's welfare ministry. It is now widely accepted that this is a legitimate and "traditional" field for women, but it is a legitimacy established since the foundation of the Feminist Union and made traditional as a result of the extensive activity of the early feminists in "social" activities, that is, charitable good works of a private, voluntary nature.

THE FEMINIST LEGACY

What happened to the legal and social reforms pertaining to marriage, education, employment, and political freedom for women that Hoda Sha'rawi and her colleagues pursued? Some changes were made. In 1924 the legal age of marriage was established as 16 for girls and 18 for boys, and both sexes were given a legal right to education.[35] However, these laws were not always enforced and even today not all children, especially not all young girls, go to school, even though primary school education is legally mandatory for both sexes. Issues of enforcement, as well as the remainder of the feminist agenda, continued as primary elements of feminist and, because of linkage politics, nationalist concern.

There were also several attempts to change the Personal Status Laws. For example, in 1920 and again in 1929, legislators undertook to change the divorce laws. Using the principles from the Maliki school of Muslim law, the new rules identified four kinds of problems which could enable a woman to sue for divorce. Thus, if the husband failed to provide *nafagah* (maintenance), the wife could, after 1929, go to court and petition for a divorce. She could also do so if her husband had a serious contagious disease, if she had been deserted by her husband, or if she had been seriously maltreated by him.[36] Additional attempts to improve the rights and status of women were made in 1943 and 1945. Aimed mainly at restrictions on polygamy, they failed.

When the Free Officers came to power in 1952, they began to implement some of this program and, in the Constitution of 1956, granted women the right to vote, indicating a real, if delayed, pay-off for tying feminism with nationalism.[37] This was done in spite of the opposition of the Sheikh of al-Azhar, who issued a *fatwa* (religious ruling) stating that women were too unstable to vote. The Nasser regime finessed the situation in characteristic fashion. The Sheikh was made Egyptian ambassador to Yemen, and soon after he left Egypt the new law was passed.[38]

This reform may, however, have been due in part to increased pressure from political feminists more militant than those associated with the Egyptian Feminist Union. For example, in 1948, Mrs. Doria Shafik Regai and others founded an organization called Bint al-Nil (Daughter of the Nile). Bint al-Nil had two principal purposes: to establish full political equality between men and women and to abolish illiteracy. The period between 1948 and 1952 witnessed extensive and frequent expressions of dissatisfaction with the way Egypt was governed, and some women from Bint al-Nil contributed to the revolutionary atmosphere in 1951 by briefly occupying parliament and demanding representation for women in that body.[39] They failed in their immediate objective but succeeded in making clear that part of the process of overthrowing the old order involved changes in the status of women.

Mrs. Shafik and her followers continued to work for women's suffrage even after their party was abolished by the new regime in 1953. In 1954, she and a few others threatened to fast unto death unless the government, in the new constitution then being planned, gave women the right to vote. Her ten-day hunger strike ended when President Neguib, Egypt's first president following the 1952 revolution, promised that her petition would be given serious consideration.[40] Two years later, the right of women to vote was made part of the law of the land in the new constitution promulgated by Neguib's successor, Gamal Abdel Nasser.

Egyptian women now have many of the legal rights for which they and their male supporters have long struggled. Rather than recount the history of how those rights were gained, I will discuss what appear to be the principal issues of the law as it is today, as well as present a brief survey of the main dimensions of female education and employment in Egypt. These three fields—law, education, and employment—are so linked that their significance for women can only be understood if they are considered together.

Female illiteracy, especially in rural areas, is still high, even though primary education has been legally mandatory for both sexes since 1924. In 1976, official government figures indicated that 71% of Egyptian females and 43% of the males were illiterate.[41] Housewives and peasant laborers are the most numerous and perhaps most important female workers in Egypt, but because their work is not remunerated they are excluded from reporting in official statistics.[42] By law, men —fathers, brothers, husbands, sons—are obliged to support "their" women, and this law is reinforced by social custom and the code of honor by which many people in Egypt live.[43] However, not all women and families are adequately supported by their men, and many families are headed by women, notably widows and divorcees.[44] Thus, many women, particularly in urban areas, find it necessary to seek employment outside the home.

Women entering the labor force are protected by Law 91 of 1959 against discrimination on the basis of sex. Once employed, they also enjoy certain benefits, which can make it more expensive to hire women, such as paid maternity leave, guaranteed job security, time off with pay to nurse an infant, and the right to retire earlier than men. In fact:

> The Egyptian government has been active and successful in enacting legislation to insure the protection and welfare of female workers. As is the case in other areas, not all laws are enforced at all times. However, Egyptian women do have a line of legal defense against discrimination or ill-treatment and, compared to many developing countries, labor laws in Egypt related to female employment are relatively progressive and enlightened.[45]

Most women employed outside the home in today's Egypt are at least literate, and about 15% (as of 1976) had a university degree. Change in this area is both recent and striking. In 1961, almost 83% of the female labor force, excluding unpaid peasant and housewife labor as well as most "cottage industry," was illiterate. By 1976, only 31.2% of the female labor force was illiterate.[46] Virtually all growth in female employment is accounted for by education, with most employed women working as teachers, clerks, health workers, and government civil servants. It is difficult to find a good job in Egypt, but as university graduates enjoy guaranteed government employment, it can be expected that growing numbers of women will seek the degrees that lead to jobs. As of the early 1980s, female enrollment in university programs has stabilized at about 32% of the total, having remained at that level since 1979.[47] Although women still constitute less than 15% of the formal labor force, the number of working women is increasing as is their percentage contribution to the total labor force.[48] It is difficult to exaggerate the significance of this development. Although by Western terms the progress achieved to date may be considered modest,

> these are not western women, and it is a mistake to assume that . . . social or sexual liberation will take the same form as it has in the west. In the Egyptian context, the mere fact that education and employment take women outside the home, unsupervised by "their" men for a good part of the day, is significant as a *de facto* challenge to the social limits placed on the public behavior of women. For at least part of the day, these women have a private life in the public world, separate from the role of daughter, wife or household manager. Men may continue to hold the same ideas regarding the "proper" limits on female behavior, but women who work and go to school are challenging those limits [daily] in effective ways.[49]

In 1928, a handful of pioneers entered Cairo University as the first women students at that level. By the early 1980s, over 150,000 women had earned university degrees and entered professions that were once male preserves.[50] As they worked their way up in a seniority-conscious society, some of the most able and lucky ones acquired prestige, wealth, and power and probably made it easier for those who followed. Many male preserves still exist, however, and today's generation of leaders has a great deal to consider. It was not until 1979 that a woman, Dr. Aisha Rateb, reached the rank of ambassador, and in 1985 there were still no female judges in Egypt and relatively few women active in the legal profession.[51] Tradition in Egypt holds that women may not serve as judges because they are too emotional. A taste of what women must contend with regarding this issue may be ascertained from the response of the Sheikh of al-Azhar to a question from a reporter regarding the propriety of women working as judges. He said, "There is no objection in the cases which do not affect women emotionally like civil cases, personal status and delinquency. Beyond this, they are not allowed to interfere due to their emotions which cannot bear the excitement of criminal cases."[52]

Confronting these problems perhaps will be harder, perhaps easier, but certainly different from what it would have been in the past. This is so because Egypt now has a relatively large number of women occupying significant national and local public offices, due primarily to changes in the law made in 1979.

In the recent history of Egypt, 1979 was a tumultuous year. Not only did it see the Treaty of Peace between Egypt and Israel, but it also witnessed considerable alteration of the domestic political structure. After the treaty with Israel was signed in March, parliament was dissolved and new elections were held. Political parties, including some relatively tame opposition groups, contested elections for the first time since the 1952 revolution. Emergency degrees were rescinded and rules for a new house of parliament, *Majlis al-Shura* (Consultative Assembly), were included in a new "peace" constitution. In the midst of this atmosphere, certain important legal changes were made affecting women. First, by Law 21 of 1979, *Majlis al-Shaab* (the People's Assembly) was enlarged to include 30 seats reserved for women. Furthermore, the law of local government was changed to guarantee that 10% to 20%, depending on the circumstances, of the seats on local councils, from the governorate to the village level, had to be reserved for women. The principle is that there must be at least one seat reserved on each council for a woman. Finally, when the new, enlarged parliament was assembled, one of its first acts (Law 44 of 1979) was to ratify an emergency decree promulgated by President Sadat amending the Personal Status Laws to include many, but not all, of the demands first made by Egyptian feminists over fifty years before. Six years later, the 1979 amendments to the Personal Status Laws were declared unconstitutional on procedural grounds: the emergency decree was not valid. The main elements of the amendments are worth a brief review because of the substantive issues at stake and because most of the provisions of the 1979 laws were reintroduced in a new law in 1985.

The major terms of these reforms included the right of the wife to a divorce if her husband took an additional wife without her consent; the necessity that the wife be informed in the event of divorce;

the right of the mother to retain custody of children until boys are ten and girls are twelve years of age; the right of the wife to alimony; and the right of the woman to remain in the matrimonial home until she remarries or until her period of custody of the children has expired. In this area, women were still not equal to men, but they had more rights and security than before the 1979 changes, and by 1980 the divorce rate apparently had gone down.[53]

In 1979, it looked as if much of the original feminist program had been achieved. A hard and long battle had been fought and won but, as later events indicated, complaisance was not in order. The legal changes affecting women were controversial, both for their content and because of the methods used by the Sadat regime in getting them approved. This was true especially in the case of the Personal Status Laws. It was common to hear them called "Jihan's Laws," referring to the wife of the president, who, even though she had no legal power, was credited with, or blamed for, their passage. Critics also pointed out that parliament had little choice but to ratify the presidential decree which preceded their enactment into law. Three years later, the constitutionality of the 1979 changes in the Personal Status Laws was challenged and, on December 12, 1982, the issue was referred from a circuit court to the Higher Constitutional Court. After December 1982, the 1979 laws were not enforced with any consistency by Egyptian courts.[54]

After a long delay, the case was resolved in May 1985 when the Higher Constitutional Court declared the 1979 amendments to the Personal Status Laws unconstitutional on the grounds that the initial emergency decree which promulgated the laws was issued in the absence of a genuine emergency and hence was not valid. This posthumous slap at President Sadat's authority, which conceivably could be used to invalidate other laws he issued by decree as well as limit his successors, did not rule on the substance of the issue at hand. Nevertheless, it was a major blow to reformers.

Two months after the 1979 Personal Status Laws were declared unconstitutional, the saga of the reform effort took another turn. Against the objections of leading Islamic fundamentalists, the Mubarak regime supported new legislation similar to that issued by decree in 1979. In a compromise between fundamentalists and feminists, the 1985 laws provided that a wife no longer had the automatic right to divorce if her husband took a second wife. Granting the fundamentalists one of their key demands, the highly patriarchal judiciary system was given a measure of discretionary authority. A first wife who wanted a divorce would have to prove to the court that she sustained material or moral damage as a result of her husband taking a second wife. Furthermore, the husband would have to provide his former wife with adequate housing as long as she retained custody of their children. From a feminist perspective, this is not a perfect solution to the problems stemming from polygamy, but the political adage that, in politics, the perfect is often the enemy of the good, may be applicable in this case. As a result of the 1985 reforms, feminists can claim both a present victory and a cause to struggle for in the future.[55]

By 1985, parts of the original feminist agenda had been realized, but the issues remained controversial and subject to attack from many quarters. Parliament had become a central forum for debate and, potentially, for making decisions regarding these questions. During the early 1980s, this debate began and the stage was set for the next phase of activity and thought regarding the role of women in Egyptian public life. Over forty women had the opportunity to participate in that process and they, along with other women who have served in parliament in the past, are the subjects of the next chapter.

Parliamentary Women

PARLIAMENT AND POLITICS

THE FIRST WOMEN to become members of Egypt's National Assembly in the late 1950s joined an unusual institution. Party politics and parliament had been suspended following the 1952 revolution.
When the new constitution was promulgated in 1956 it envisaged a
National Assembly, universal adult franchise, and an organization called the National Union to supervise and guide politics. There were
to be no political parties, as they were perceived by the leadership of
the country to be divisive. The Assembly was to make laws and approve the budget, and as in Britain, cabinet ministers were to be subject to questioning by members of the Assembly. The Suez crisis of
1956 and related events delayed implementation of the new constitution until July, 1957, when the new 360-member National Assembly
convened its first meeting. The constitution permitted the president
to appoint ten members, while the other 350 were elected, two from
each of 175 districts. Two of the successful candidates were women,
one from Cairo, the other from Alexandria. Defeating men in open
elections, they successfully overcame the bias among their constituents against women in politics. As Rawya Attia, elected from Cairo,
said at the time, "I was met with resentment for being a woman. Yet
I talked to them and reminded them of the prophet's wives and families until they changed their opinions."[1] She and her colleague, Mrs.
Amina Shoukry of Alexandria, employed such arguments to win sup-

port but also used their job experience as political assets. Mrs. Shoukry, who had worked with Hoda Sha'rawi in the Feminist Union, was well known as a volunteer welfare worker. Rawya Attia, only thirty-four years old at the time, drew attention to the fact that she was a captain in a women's commando unit. Both won in the second round of elections and thus became the first women to serve in an Arab parliament.

All candidates for the 1957 election had been approved by the Executive Committee of the National Union, an organization created by President Nasser to specialize in policy and serve as the functional substitute for political parties. Parliamentary politics restarted in Egypt as a pale vestige of the frequently lively and sometimes raucous National Assembly of pre-revolutionary times, which was precisely what the new regime wanted. Since that time Egypt has had seven parliamentary elections (excluding the 1960 selection of members for the Assembly of the United Arab Republic), some of which (1964, 1976) have been quite animated. Only two (1979 and 1984) have seen legal activity by political parties. Women fared differently in each election. For example, eight were successful in 1964 but only two, both incumbents, were elected in 1969.[2]

The National Union, created in 1957, with Anwar Sadat as its first secretary-general, was succeeded in 1962 by the Arab Socialist Union (ASU), which lasted until 1978. When it was abolished, an experiment with a controlled, multiparty political system began. Both the National Union and the Arab Socialist Union were intended to be the center for policy guidance, while the unicameral National Assembly was to concentrate on implementation of policy through legislation. Neither the National Union nor the ASU ever became creative guides for policy, perhaps because the Free Officers "seemed never to be clear in their minds" about the role of such organizations.[3]

By the mid-1960s, the Assembly and the ASU had become rivals, largely because the members of the Assembly were not always willing to accept the limitation which the National Union tried to impose, namely that they were not to deal with policy. The greater flexibility of the regime following the 1967 war plus the election of numerous government and ASU figures to the Assembly in 1969, helped reduce some of the rivalry. The reality of power, however, was that Egypt was ruled by the president, the military, and the bureaucracy. Raymond Baker, in his book on Egypt under Presidents Nasser and Sadat, exaggerates somewhat when he says, "the Parliament has no role in major policy decisions."4 Baker's is typical of the conventional view of most observers. He notes that the Assembly may debate and discuss a policy, but seldom, if ever, does it make any major changes in important government proposals. This does not mean, however, that membership in the Assembly is meaningless or necessarily marginal, as we shall see later in this chapter. Institutions, including parliament, have more importance than is commonly recognized.

Until 1980, Egypt had a unicameral parliament of 350 elected members and 10 members appointed by the President. The country was divided into 175 supposedly equal electoral districts, each of which sent two delegates to the Majlis al-Shaab, or People's Assembly. Since 1964, it has been stipulated in the Constitution that at least half of the members must be peasants or workers. This is achieved by "reserving" one seat in each district for peasant and worker candidates. In some instances, "worker" or "peasant" status is more formal than real, and may reflect more about what the individuals were than what they are.

The ten appointed members include some individuals of distinction from the nonpolitical world. This device also permits the President to appoint distinguished (but loyal) members of the Coptic minority to parliament, as very few Copts have ever won office in elections.

By law, voting is mandatory, but not all adults are registered to vote. This was illustrated in 1979 when Ismail Fahmy, the former foreign minister who resigned in 1977 in protest against Sadat's trip to Jerusalem, was disqualified from running for parliament as a punitive action for breaking rank with the President. The excuse used to support this was that he had not registered to vote. Furthermore, while the law stipulates that men must register and vote, women are free to do so but are not similarly obliged. Some elections (1976) have been interesting and engaged the public's attention, while others (1979) have been relatively dull.

Once elected, parliament sits for a period of five years unless dissolved by the president. The budget must be approved by Majlis al-Shaab, but the greatest power the Assembly has is probably the ability of delegates to the Assembly to question members of the cabinet on matters of policy and implementation of policy. This practice, modeled after the custom in the British Parliament, often produces spirited exchanges and acerbic comments.5 The Majlis al-Shaab works through eighteen standing committees which hold hearings on all proposed legislation, most of which originates with the government with only a few private bills emanating from members of the Assembly. All new laws or amendments to existing legislation must ultimately be approved by the full Assembly. The People's Assembly is also involved in the selection of the president of the republic. It is the business of the Assembly to select a single candidate, who is then submitted for approval by the people of Egypt in a plebiscite.

In 1979, the constitution was amended to create a new parliamentary body, Majlis al-Shura (Consultative Assembly). This institution of 210 members is one of the most curious creations of Egypt's late President Sadat, who apparently envisaged establishing something of a cross between Britain's House of Lords and America's Senate. It is also reminiscent of Majlis al-Nuwab, the lower house in Egypt's prerevolutionary parliament. In one important respect, however, it is unique. Majlis al-Shura has only one major power: it owns, and hence nominally supervises, the fourth estate in Egypt, the press.[6] It assumed this role from the Arab Socialist Union, which ceased to exist in 1979. Other than that, this body of distinguished Egyptians is available to give advice on matters of policy, when asked by the government to do so. Like Majlis al-Shaab, it works through committees but, because it has no law-making capacity, it has only five, each covering a broad field of subjects. Since its inception, many of its members have been seeking ways to expand its scope while others question its importance, even thinking it should be abolished.[7] But until it is either terminated or made more significant, its members receive the same pay as do those in Majlis al-Shaab. In 1983, this was 120 £E per month plus 30 £E per day for each session attended. Thus, a diligent member of parliament could earn over 3,000 £E a year, a not insubstantial sum in a country whose per-capita national income was about 500 £E a year. The parliamentary season runs from mid- to late October until July. Each house meets on alternate weeks in sessions which start on Saturday and last for three to five days, depending on the nature of the business at hand.

Even though the 1979 elections were calmer than those of 1976, they were interesting and important for two reasons relevant to this chapter. For the first time, a relatively large number of women were elected to the Majlis al-Shaab, due to the creation in that body of thirty seats specifically reserved for women, including at least one from each governorate. These new seats were additions to the total number of members in the Majlis, so that men could not complain that they had "lost" anything. Thus, the new Majlis al-Shaab had a total of 390 members, almost 9% of whom were women. Only women were permitted to contest elections for the reserved seats, but both men and women were allowed to vote. These elections involved over 200 female candidates for thirty places. In addition, two women were appointed, one in 1979, the other in 1981. Three ran against men and defeated them. Thus, by 1982–83, when the field work for this portion of the study was done, thirty-five women were members of Egypt's Majlis al-Shaab. In Majlis al-Shura, 140 of the seats were filled by elections held in 1980. The elections were on the party list system and no seats were reserved for women. Two women were on the list for the government party, however, and were elected. The remaining seventy seats, five of which went to women, were filled by presidential appointment, bringing the number of women in Majlis al-Shura to seven out of 210 and the number of women in both houses of parliament to forty-two, which is 7% of the membership. This group included almost all of the women who served in elective or appointive capacity in previous parliaments and they, plus former parliamentarians about whom sufficient information could be gathered, constitute the "Parliamentary Women" discussed in this book.[8]

The second important feature of the 1979 and 1980 parliamentary elections was the presence of three political parties. In 1979, the Arab Socialist Union was formally abolished as was the center platform or group which had represented the government in parliament. The left and right platforms within the ASU were also ended, and three political parties were permitted to organize, publicize their activities, and contest elections. The largest of these, holding 90% of the seats in Majlis al-Shaab in 1979, was the government party, the Hezb al-Watani al-Democrati, the National Democratic Party (NDP). President Sadat was its first president and Hosny Mubarak its second. All but one of the women in parliament between 1979 and 1983 were listed as members of the NDP. The other two parties represented in parliament in the early 1980s were two of the three legal opposition parties in Egypt. The Muslim Brothers were not permitted to form a party because religious parties are proscribed. The Wafd al-Gideed (New Wafd), the inheritor of the mantle of pre-revolutionary nationalism and legitimacy, "dissolved" itself in 1978, rather than deal with continual government harassment.[9] Thus, neither of the two po-

tentially largest opposition groups contested elections in 1979. This
left the role of opposition to three minor parties. The smallest in parliament was the Liberal Socialist Party, usually referred to as al-Ahrar,
which, despite its name was not socialist, advocating an expanded role
for private enterprise. On the left was a new party which had roots
stretching back to the prerevolutionary Misr al-Fatat (Young Egypt),
founded by Ahmad Hussein. This organization, the Socialist Labor
Party (SLP), was mildly leftist, and, like al-Ahrar, was a loyal, perhaps even tame opposition. The third legal party, clearly leftist, was
the Hezb al-Taqamua al-Watani al-Taqadumi al-Wahdawi, the National
Unionist Progressive Party (NUPP). This party failed, due to strenu-
ous government opposition, to win any seats in parliament in the 1979
elections.[10] Opposition was legal, but the government retained control. It was thus in an atmosphere of a controlled multiparty system
that parliamentary women in Egypt functioned since 1979.

Remarkably little is known about the average Egyptian parliamentarian. Virtually all have been males. In many ways the pattern
has not changed much since 1957 when, as Robert Stephens has noted,
"Most of the candidates and those elected, apart from government
ministers, were middle class, professional men, lawyers, journalists,
doctors, senior civil servants, ex-army officers, some businessmen, land
owners and farmers, village headmen and local mayors."[11] Since 1964,
the number of those parliamentarians listed as "farmers" or "workers"
has been at least 50% of the total. While in some cases this is an accurate designation, in many instances it is only a formal title which
somewhat masks other work activity. For example, some "workers" are
actually managers, while some "peasants" are rural landlords or village headmen. Parliament is dominated to a large degree by essentially urban people, but linkages between the urban elite and the rural
"second strata" constitute an important mechanism in Egyptian politics, and help enable the rural elite to continue to control the countryside while the urban elite controls the country.[12] Membership in parliament is one of the major ways by which ties between urban and
rural elites are developed and sustained.

One of the most salient characteristics of Egyptian parliamentarians is loyalty. This can be expressed as loyalty to the political system, the regime, the National Union or the ASU, or, since 1979, the
NDP. Loyalty can also be thought of in more personal terms, as many
parliamentarians are regarded as the clients of one or more individu-

als at the top of the Egyptian political system. Thus, those members of Majlis al-Shaab or Majlis al-Shura who are truly independent are a small minority and stand out from the rest. A few of those true independents are women. Before discussing them, however, it is necessary to have a profile of the whole group in order to have an overall perspective regarding typical Egyptian female parliamentarians.

WOMEN IN PARLIAMENT

The typical woman in Egypt's parliament in 1983 was forty-eight years old, married, and mother of two children.[13] She married in her twenties, usually after finishing her education, which, in most cases ended with a university degree. Today, she is manager of a successful career in addition to running a household. As a child, our typical parliamentarian is most likely to have attended a school in which instruction was in Arabic but she is also likely to speak at least one foreign language, usually English or French. Most came from economically privileged families and, as adults, developed an active record of service in one or more private voluntary charitable organizations. The average female parliamentarian has had a busy, multifaceted, rewarding life and, as near as I could tell, looked forward to more of the same.

Throughout this discussion of parliamentary women, reference will be made to two general categories, urban and rural, in recognition of one of the most obvious differences among them. Out of forty-six women, twenty-five are categorized as urban and twenty-one as rural. Within the latter group there was also one obvious difference: twelve wore so-called Islamic garb while the remaining nine dressed the way their urban colleagues do, in modern Western-style clothing. Thus, the rural group is divided for discussion and statistical purposes into two sections, according to their style of dress, enabling readers to see the degree to which female politicians in Islamic dress do or do not differ from their Western-dressed colleagues. This division also has the effect of highlighting diversity within the group itself. Occasionally, these women will be referred to as "veiled," but readers should be aware that none of them actually cover their faces. They do, however, wear a version of Islamic dress approved by contemporary fundamentalists: the hair and neck are covered and they wear a high-necked, long-sleeved, ankle-length dress. Rather than ask why they dress this way, and stop there, we shall concentrate on examining the degree to which their background or behavior differs from that of the other women.

One of the most interesting and important characteristics of women in parliament is their diversity. Their differences, as well as significant similarities, will be illustrated in the discussion that follows. Divided into four sections, the first deals with the early childhood and formal education of Egyptian women who later became success-ful politicians. Then we will consider the circumstances associated with marriage and family for such women and next, with the various paths to power they have taken. Finally, we shall discuss their behav-ior in parliament.

FORMATIVE YEARS

All of the forty-six women in the parliamentary group were born dur-ing the first half of the twentieth century, a time when Egypt was a staging ground and battlefield for other people's wars, when it was effectively occupied and controlled by the British, against whom Egypt's nationalist leaders rallied. Only a few of the youngest were brought up in the fifties and are, therefore, children of the 1952 Free Officer Revolution. The rest are products of the same period that produced Nasser and Sadat. For many of their male counterparts, the key year was 1936, when the military academy was opened to "ordinary" Egyp-tians. For the women, the year which changed the future the most was probably 1928, when the first women were admitted to Cairo Uni-versity. Among the women admitted that year was Soheir al-Qalamawi, one of the more successful members of parliament and, since the Na-tional Democratic Party was formed, the leader of its Women's Sec-tion. As early protégé of Dr. Taha Hussein, much of her life has been directed toward teaching Arabic literature, but she has been involved in politics since 1952.[14]

The families into which these women were born tended to live in one of Egypt's urban areas (Cairo, Giza, Alexandria, Port Said, or Ismailia) or in a provincial capital. This is shown in table 2.1.*

---

*In order to avoid cluttering the text, all tables pertaining to this chapter are

Only eight were born and raised in one of Egypt's villages, where at that time the vast majority of Egypt's population lived. Egypt's cities may well have been more livable and manageable then than they are now, and virtually all respondents reported pleasant memories of their youth.

All but four parliamentary women are Muslim and most, whether Christian or Muslim, were raised in religious households, many learning the Koran or the Bible at home as well as in school. For almost every member of the group religion was seen as a positive force in their lives, even though many indicated that the attitude of some religious authorities often impeded progress for women. For roughly one-third of the group, religious or other solace was needed for the major childhood trauma reported: the death of a parent. Ten future parliamentarians reported the death of a father while four lost their mothers. None was orphaned but a large minority were raised by a single parent or, in a few cases, by a natural parent plus a stepparent. This pattern is indicated by table 2.2.

The death of such a large number of fathers would seem to suggest that many would report that mothers had been the dominant influence in their young lives. However, as table 2.3 illustrates, fathers are more than twice as likely as mothers to have supported the notion that their daughters would be educated and prepared for roles in addition to those of wife and mother. Almost all those interviewed reported that their fathers enjoyed their work or profession and conveyed a positive attitude toward work to their children, including, and in many cases especially, to their daughters. Many women whose husbands died supported active roles for their daughters, but an equal number did not. In a few cases (four) the most supportive role was taken by a stepparent or, most frequently, grandparent, but the leading role of the father in the Egyptian family is illustrated clearly by the fact that even though 25% of the fathers of this group died before they could motivate their daughters, fathers were the dominant influence in their daughters' lives in over one-third of the cases.

Women in parliament who today wear Islamic dress are more likely to have experienced the death of a parent than are the women

---

located in an appendix at the end of the book. This also enables readers to peruse all of them at a glance rather than separated by text. The contents of each table are discussed in the chapter text.

in any other category. Six of the twelve members of this group lost a parent while young, accounting for 42% of the total parental deaths. They are also more likely than others not to have received parental support in their desire to have a career in addition to that of wife and mother. Both situations, however, are due more to rural origins than anything else. Six of the veiled women grew up in small villages and five in provincial capitals, where old men often married young girls, health conditions were grim, and traditional role values were seldom challenged. Clearly, this small group of women have persevered against considerable odds to achieve their current status. Each has, in this regard, been strengthened in her resolve by religion.

While we did not specifically inquire about the siblings each of our respondents had, it seems clear from those who did provide this information that most came from families of three or more children. Virtually none grew up as the only child. Over half were especially bright and apparently were given more parental attention because of this. Only seven members of the group reported that neither parent encouraged or helped them to become what they are today.

Given the supportive role taken by all but ten of the fathers of the future parliamentarians, it is important to reflect on what work they did and on their educational background. As far as profession is concerned, no pattern is discernible: there are almost as many job categories as there are fathers, ranging from plumber to sheikh to cabinet member. Most were educated in some way, however, as is illustrated in table 2.4. The urban group was especially well-educated, with the fathers of fourteen of its twenty-two members having earned a university degree. The least well-educated fathers are those whose daughters now wear "Islamic dress," but this was not unusual for people in rural villages at that time. The clear majority of men in all categories can be considered to have been at least adequately educated for their time and location and considerably better educated than the vast majority of their male Egyptian colleagues. In this respect, most could be considered privileged.

Education for women is still not the norm in much of Egypt, and it is against this background that the schooling of the mothers of the study group must be considered. As shown in table 2.5, none of the mothers had received a university degree. Six of the rural women and one urban mother were illiterate. In more than one instance, however, having an illiterate mother, or one who was educated at home rather than in school, had a positive impact on the life of a future parliamentarian. As one of them put it, "My mother was illiterate and, therefore, insisted that I go to school because she did not want the same things to happen to me that had happened to her." This kind of parental support was demonstrated in a number of ways. One widowed father moved his family from the countryside to Cairo in order to send his daughters to school, but most parental activity focused on "character building" and education. For example, one veiled respondent said about her father: "He gave me trust. He was quite proud of me and had a great influence on my character." About her mother the same woman said, "She gave me patience and power."

The fact that any of the mothers was educated at all, and that twelve had completed secondary school, means that the families of Egypt's future female parliamentarians were unusual and privileged, even though some were clearly not upper-class or even upper-middle-class. The attitudes of the parents toward education was more crucial than the assets of the family. Whether rural or urban, aristocrat or lower-middle-class, education for all children, including girls, was considered a necessity and not a luxury in all of the families of the women in this group. It was this, perhaps more than anything else, that was to lay the groundwork for what was to come.

Education for this group of future politicians did not, in most cases, end with primary or secondary school. As illustrated in table 2.6, nearly 75% of the group have received a university degree (all but one in Egypt), and one-quarter of them have gone on to earn graduate degrees, several from major universities in the West. The urban group is markedly better educated than those from rural Egypt, and those with Western dress are more likely to have a university degree than are those with Islamic dress, half of whom were born and raised in small villages and have remained close to home. However, a clear majority of women in all three categories have at least a university degree. Precise figures are not available for their male colleagues, but it is doubtful that their overall level of formal education is anywhere near as high as that of the women.

In the period since 1962, Egypt has had three female cabinet members, all three of whom have earned Ph.D.s. They are included in table 2.6 as part of the urban group with postgraduate degrees. All three have held the same post, Minister of Social Affairs, for periods ranging from three to eight years. This small group will be discussed in more detail later, but one additional characteristic they share has to do with language. As illustrated in table 2.7, roughly 37% of the total group of parliamentary women has "good" Arabic plus a working knowledge of at least one foreign language. The circumstances surrounding this situation require explanation.

Roughly speaking, Egypt has two types of primary and secondary schools that have been attended by women in this study group. The most widely used (67%) may be called an "Arabic" school, i.e., classes are taught in Arabic and a government-prescribed curriculum is followed. The other kind of school is usually referred to as a "foreign language" school, where a government curriculum is followed but instruction is in another language, usually French or English. Many of these are private schools. Most Arabic schools are government-run but some, at least at the time when our group was in school, were private. For the most part, all were good schools. (The poor educational conditions in Egyptian schools today are a relatively recent development due to over-crowding and shortages of funds, teachers, materials, and even school buildings.) One result of doing well in such schools — and nearly every member of the study group claimed to have been a better-than-average student — is that students emerge with "good" Arabic, i.e., they have learned the grammar, vocabulary and pronunciation of an educated Arab. It is difficult to exaggerate the importance of this variable. In general, Egyptians respect and even revere those who have a good command of Arabic, and rhetorical ability is an enormous political asset. Almost regardless of what you say, you are likely to be listened to respectfully if your Arabic is polished. Interviews with leading members of both houses of parliament indicate that, with a few exceptions, those delegates who do not have good Arabic speak seldom, if at all, in sessions of parliament. It is, after all, an assembly for debate and discussion in which words are deeds. Those who are not good speakers have a difficult time competing in parliamentary politics. There is an effective social prohibition against speaking if one does not use proper, formal Arabic, but two-thirds of the women in parliament, whether urban or rural, need not fear this unwritten rule. Furthermore, several of them are well known for their Arabic.

Another hallmark of women in parliament is the knowledge of at least one foreign language, a skill shared by over 60% of them. While this is a clear mark of separation from the Egyptian masses, it also means that those members of parliament who know a foreign language well are more likely to have credibility when debating or discussing foreign policy issues, because if one knows a foreign language it is assumed that one has some knowledge of the world outside Egypt. But those with the greatest potential credibility on a broad range of issues are those who have good Arabic (and thus enhanced domestic legitimacy) plus a foreign language. One of the women, Dr. Laila Takla, who is not in parliament at present, served as the elected chairman of the Foreign Affairs Committee of Majlis al-Shaab during the early and mid-1970s, the most critical and exciting period of President Anwar Sadat's diplomacy. She attended a private school with an Arabic curriculum, which also did an excellent job of teaching foreign languages. Her classmate in school, Dr. Farkhounda Hassan, served as vice-chairman of the Foreign Affairs Committee in the early 1980s. Both have a Ph.D. from a major American university. Neither is likely to have achieved as much as they have in politics without the excellent foundation their parents provided.

Large, supportive, stable families are almost universal characteristics of the formative years of Egypt's future female parliamentarians. In most cases, one or more of the senior members of the family (parents, grandparents, etc.) encouraged the young girls to flout tradition in at least one major respect. As Amina Said, one of Egypt's foremost journalists, put it when speaking of her father, "He was proud of his daughters. He wanted us to be men in frocks." Dr. Farkhounda Hassan elaborated on the same point speaking of her father.

> My father encouraged me to do things that were not the normal things [for a girl]. In a way he put in me the feeling that I can do anything I want as long as I want it. And he wanted me very much to be like a boy . . . in the sense of achievement because, you know, at the time [of my youth] boys were the ones to achieve . . . for the family, to bring the honor to the family.

What happens when, in Amina Said's words, little girls are raised to be "men in frocks"? Virtually all of the women discussed in this chapter were brought up to conform to conventional Egyptian notions of femininity. [15] However, they were encouraged to be like men in one specific way: to bring "honor to the family" by achievement in the world of work, a world which was occupied at that time almost

entirely by men. Thus, they went to school in order to have a different kind of life than their mothers had. However, they shared at
least one thing with their mothers: most of the women in this group
married and had children. Consideration of their marital circumstances
and private lives will help expose a key dimension of the complex issues facing women who have public roles in contemporary Egypt.

MARRIAGE AND FAMILY

In Egypt it is hard to avoid marriage, but few of the country's female
parliamentarians have tried to do so. Marriage and family are central
features of their lives rather than peripheral or troublesome aspects
of complex careers. As table 2.8 indicates, marriage is the norm and
divorce is rare: 95% of the women in the study group are or have
been married, and only a few have been divorced. All divorces involving members of this group have been brought about in whole or in
major part by the husband's inability to coexist with his wife's lifestyle
and public prominence, and the refusal of the wife to compromise.
In some cases the woman was more successful in her career than the
man was in his, leading to strains in the marital relationship. Nevertheless, most husbands have been successful in their work and have
supported their wives' careers and ambitions. However, if an impressionistic observation may be permitted, while most seem to have reasonably happy marriages, the stress of sustaining the complex lives
these people lead is easy to detect and has not escaped the notice of
children and friends.

Given the numerous pressures upon the private lives of women
who have successful political careers in Egypt, what factors account
for the notable durability of their marriages? The results of this study
suggest that relatively late marriage is probably an important element.
Table 2.9 illustrates part of the picture; it shows that of those for whom
reliable information was available, roughly 65% married in their twenties. For the group as a whole, as well as for both the urban and rural
subgroups, the mean age of marriage is 25.42, while both the median
and mode are twenty-five, as is the mean age for those wearing Islamic
dress. For rural women wearing Western dress the average age of marriage is slightly higher, 26.5. The strong central tendency of these fig-

ures indicates that virtually all delayed marriage until formal education was complete or nearly complete. Most Egyptian women in the first half of the twentieth century married at a much younger age, usually while still in their teens. Interviews also indicated that most respondents picked or helped pick their own spouses rather than submitting to a family-arranged marriage. Furthermore, whether the marriage was self-arranged or family arranged, a "compatible" spouse was selected, i.e., a husband who would be likely to support or at least tolerate the fact that his wife intended to have some type of career or work outside the home.

Another factor characterizing the marriages of women in this group is that they seldom had more than three children, and that the children tended to have been born at least two years apart rather than in immediately succeeding years. Table 2.10 shows the pattern for the number of children. Veiled women are much more likely to have large families than are any of the others, but they are also likely to live in a rural village or town where large families remain the norm. While the average family has three children, many of the women, particularly in urban areas, have fewer than that and only six have had more than three. Furthermore, most had servants to help with some of the work or could draw on the extended family system for assistance. Some had servants as well as family help, and a few even reported that their husbands, in a remarkable departure from Egyptian custom, helped with some household chores and with the children. One veiled respondent indicated that, when she went to Cairo for sessions of Majlis al-Shaab, her husband willingly took care of the children, because he supported what she was doing in politics. Nawal Amer, who has represented a poor district in Cairo for nearly two decades, is divorced but has been helped in housework by her mother and has involved her children in her political life, especially during election campaigns. While there are some exceptions, the pattern seems to be that of ambitious and bright young women leaving supportive and encouraging parents and establishing a household with a supportive husband and, later, children who support or at least are not an obstacle to their mother's career.

The professional work of women in parliament is an important aspect of the lives of the women and has an impact on their families. As table 2.11 shows, only eight could be described as housewives. Over 80% of the group had successful professional careers before becoming members of parliament. Furthermore, most continue to practice their profession, treating politics and parliament as a second job, except for those who are retired from their work or the few for whom politics has become their vocation. As the table shows, Egyptian women with successful political careers are likely to have a professional background in education, law, or journalism. Education and journalism are fields in which women have well-established niches, whereas the legal profession is still somewhat restrictive as far as women are concerned. For example, as pointed out in chapter 1, there is not one female judge in Egypt.

Although these three general job classifications account for almost 55% of the total, the most interesting aspect of this dimension of the lives of these women is the diversity of employment and the unconventional nature of some of it. This can be illustrated in a number of ways. For example, Wagiha El Zalabani, a veiled agricultural engineer, represents Beheira governorate in Majlis al-Shaab. There are very few female agricultural engineers in Egypt, but one of them is veiled and in parliament. The group of parliamentary women also includes a well-known singer and actress, the first female professional geologist in Egypt, the first woman to head a major publishing house, the first woman to head Egypt T.V., the first to head Egypt Radio, the woman who established all of the blood banks in Egypt, and the first bedouin from her tribe to earn a university degree. In short, there is a strong tendency among women in this group to have unusual and successful careers prior to getting involved in politics and being elected or appointed to parliament.

Another view of the preparliamentary and extraparliamentary life of the women we are studying can be gained by considering the educational and professional background of the men they have married. This is shown in tables 2.12 and 2.13. The husbands of the study group are even more likely than the women to have a university degree, but slightly less likely to have an advanced degree. Professionally, there are fewer surprises among the husbands, with most having fairly conventional jobs for middle- and upper-middle-class men although they, like the women, tend to have been quite successful in their work. Some have also developed secondary careers in politics; for example, Nabawi Ismail, former minister of the interior, is the husband of Faida Kamel, the entertainer who represents a poor district of Cairo. The fact that the husbands tend to have successful and conventional middle-class careers no doubt contributes to a healthy marital relationship as well as to a stable family: a busy, productive husband is not likely to be jealous of his successful wife. Far from impeding their professional or political lives, many of the women reported that their husbands encouraged them. One stated her husband was happy with her having a career because "It keeps me busy and leaves him free to pursue his own career without having to worry about me being bored with too much time on my hands." This statement accentuates the atmosphere of pragmatic partnership which seems to this observer to characterize many, probably most, of the marital arrangements involving women in the study group. Although stress marks are visible in many marriages, stability, security, and comfort seem to be the major hallmarks of the home life of the women in Egypt's parliament.

PATHS TO PARLIAMENT

What are the principal factors which have enabled women to be elected or appointed to parliament? This is an important but difficult question. In order to try to answer it, the group will be considered as a whole, whether elected in a contest against men, elected to a seat reserved for women, or appointed by the president. In cases where significant differences exist, they will be pointed out. The first issue to be considered is: how much time did it take people to develop whatever the attributes were which enabled them to join Egypt's parliament?

The time between marriage or the start of a career and first entry into parliament is, on average, about twenty-one years. However, the variations around this mean are considerable, ranging from about five years to over fifty, with a few entering parliament in their early thirties, while others did not achieve this distinction until their late sixties or early seventies. As shown in table 2.14, however, rural women have entered parliament an average of four years younger than urban women and, as a group, the youngest of all are those rural women who wear Western-style dress.

The amount of time spent between starting a career and entering parliament may be less important than the quality and type of work done. As indicated above, future female parliamentarians tend to have been successful in their chosen field, regardless of the field, and have spent quite a bit of time establishing themselves and/or managing a household before entering parliament for the first time.

How do women differ in these respects from men? Given the paucity of data it is not possible to answer the question in precise terms, but it is clear that professional backgrounds differ. For example, very few women are engineers, although women have been permitted to specialize in that field since the late 1950s. Only one of the women who have been in parliament comes from the police or military, whereas many male parliamentarians have this kind of background. On the other hand, few men have come to power via a career in primary school teaching. Sex typing in employment has had a notable impact on the recruitment of political elites, but it has not barred women from entry. As far as age is concerned, there seems to be no significant difference between male and female parliamentarians. For example, in 1983, the mean average age for men in Majlis al-Shura was 53.9, while for women it was 53.5 This suggests that, while men and women have somewhat different career patterns, they seem to have spent roughly the same amount of time establishing themselves in their fields, although most women have lost career time due to their roles as wives and mothers. This may not be that much of a political liability, however, because one of the politically valuable work experiences available to women in Egypt, but hardly ever available to men, is volunteer charitable work. How this experience can be politically useful can be seen by digressing briefly to consider the context within which decisions relevant to parliamentary elections or appointments are made.

In Egypt, the regime has created political parties rather than the other way around and has dominated, but not totally controlled, every election since 1957, when the first post-revolutionary electoral contests were permitted. Other than "loyalty," which can neither be adequately defined nor always guaranteed, what have Egypt's top political elite tended to look for in potential parliamentarians? Viewed from the other side, that of the candidate, what qualities are political assets and which are liabilities for the would-be parliamentarian? The procedures involved in the elections of 1979 and 1980 may help to explain at least part of this rather murky aspect of Egyptian politics.

Some candidates filed for election on their own behalf and either ran as independents or sought the official support of a political party. Three of the women eventually elected went to parliament as independents and then switched to the National Democratic Party because, as members of the government party, they felt they could get more done for their constituents. All three independents were from rural areas and wore Islamic dress. One candidate, Olfat Kamel, was an official in the Liberal Party and received its support in her district. The others, whether elected or appointed, were all supported or claimed by the National Democratic Party. In order to be supported by the NDP, candidates for election had to be vetted or approved by a number of people, each of whom can be expected to have viewed the problem from a different perspective. With few exceptions, the process was the same whether candidates were male or female.

As several highly placed and reliable informants explained to me, the appraisal of candidates for the NDP involved four distinct groups. One was the Ministry of the Interior, the department of government concerned with security. Exactly what role Interior played is not clear but it seems that, among its other interests, this agency was on the lookout for reliable political candidates to suggest for consideration at election time. (In this context, reliability refers to the probability that an individual, once elected, generally will support the regime or party.) Another participant in this process was the governor of the province to be represented, who seems to have had concerns similar to those of the Ministry of the Interior. Reliability, electibility, and capability are said to be the most relevant characteristics as far as these officials and the others involved in the selection process are concerned. These "others" include party leaders and, in some cases, the president.

Male and female candidates were treated the same, except that, as far as the NDP was concerned, the opinion of local leaders, usually male, would be supplemented by that of local or national officials from the Women's Section of the party. Thus, in some cases, Soheir al-Qalamawi, or her provincial equivalent, as head of the Women's Section, was very much involved in selecting candidates for official NDP endorsement. In some cases, although probably fewer than either her detractors or admirers suspect, the same role was played by Mrs. Sadat, unofficially "representing" the presidency. It is not clear how many names she actually suggested for inclusion or deletion from the list of those who eventually received the party's support, but she did have significant, if not decisive, impact, particularly on the selection of a few of the candidates for reserved seats in urban areas as well as for those appointed by the president. In her interview with me, Mrs. Sadat acknowledged, but somewhat deemphasized, this role, stating that the women whose names she suggested were such good candidates they did not require her support and had several of the attributes the party was looking for, such as loyalty, previous political experience, a record of professional or other accomplishment, or family reputation.

In Egyptian politics it almost always helps to come from a family which has a "good name" in the area. This is valued particularly in rural areas and helps account for the enduring political (and economic) power of the rural elite, the so-called "second strata" of Egyptian society, which supports the urban top elite in return for the perpetuation of their privileged position in rural life.[16] As shown in table 2.15, 41% of the women in parliament come from families which are prominent in the district they represent. This factor is much more potent in rural areas than in the cities, where only four parliamentarians had this as a major asset. Thirteen (out of twenty-one) of those from rural constituencies come from prominent local families. However, this was not enough to explain success for, as table 2.15 also shows, most women in parliament used more than one major political asset on the road to Majlis al-Shaab or Majlis al-Shura. It also indicates that most women on the route to parliament have had previous political experience and professional connections. Party leaders consulted during the course of this research indicated that these were also the major assets for male politicians. What is unique for the women, therefore, is their work in private voluntary social work and the linkage between this work and political success.

Conventional wisdom in Egypt, reflected for example in ordinary conversation among political cognoscenti in Cairo, suggests that experience in voluntary charity work is the most important factor in the politically relevant background for a female politician. The results of this research suggest that conventional wisdom is wrong. As Table 2.16 demonstrated, in only 15% of the cases was this type of experience the major key to political success, while in 44% of the cases, charity work was unrelated to political prominence. Furthermore, in each of the instances where social service was decisive, the woman in question was a housewife rather than a professional person. However, experience in social service is clearly an important political asset for women, especially in rural areas and particularly when combined with some other attribute. Roughly 46% of the women in the study group reported moderate or extensive experience in one or more of the numerous major private voluntary charitable organizations operating in Egypt, but 68% of these were from rural areas, with non-veiled rural women being slightly more likely to have this background than veiled women. This experience is important politically because it occasions contacts with government and party officials as well as other active women. (In this context, party is used in a broad sense and includes the NDP and, before 1979, the Misr Party, the center platform, the Arab Socialist Union, and the National Union.) Private voluntary social work is one of the socially accepted public roles for women and enables them, when campaigning for public office, to use a record of social service to show public spiritedness, concern about the welfare of the poor, and the ability to get things done. Volunteer social work gives women a distinctive political credibility. Women with this background are at least as likely to stress community service as an issue as are men, who tend to emphasize it more than any other substantive point.[17]

The most important political asset possessed by most successful women in politics is professional experience, with 63% of the members of the study group having this attribute. This factor is present for urban as well as rural women. Veiled women who reside in villages or small towns are no less likely than other rural women to have significant work experience in their background. Clearly, it is the work that women do, whether as paid professionals or unpaid volunteers, that provides the most valuable portion of their political foundation. Many men — unfortunately it is not clear how prevalent this is — have one major asset (such as family prominence) which accounts primarily for their success. Women, however, have at least two, and in rural areas three, suggesting that female politicians must do more than men to prove their worthiness for political office. For urban women, the most likely combination is professional experience plus work with the party prior to election or appointment to parliament. The next most potent combination for urban women is that of social service with party work. But, as shown in table 2.17, 18% of the whole group had little or no party experience prior to entry into parliament. In a sense, it is unusual that anyone could be elected to parliament without prior political experience. This rather peculiar phenomenon may be due mainly to the oddity of the 1979 elections, in which, suddenly, numerous female candidates had to be found and certified. Prior to 1979, few women, especially in rural areas, had any chance to be influential or even active in politics, and hence not many were involved in party activity. In some areas, potential female candidates for office with party experience were unavailable, thus making family background, social work, and a record of professional experience even more important.

In virtually all cases there were five or six candidates for the reserved seats. Three rural women ran as independents and defeated government (NDP) candidates. For them, as well as for a number of other rural women, work experience plus either family or social service were the most common combinations of assets. For veiled women, previous party experience is less likely than for members of either of the other groups but was still a major variable in five out of twelve instances. In rural areas, the most important single quality is family background, with work experience close behind. The combination of these two features occurs in some cases but no real pattern emerges, suggesting that each candidate succeeded for idiosyncratic reasons. It is clear, however, that family is much more important in rural politics than in urban areas, but work experience is crucial in both. Also, a significant number of women use volunteer social service to supplement or make up for the absence of extensive professional or party experience, especially in rural areas, thus serving as something of a "swing" variable increasing the number of politically relevant contacts as well as enhancing a potential parliamentarian's credibility.

Work with the party is important but probably not as significant as the statistics suggest. In fact, in many districts, the candidate contributes more to the party's strength than the other way around. For example, Nawal Amer and Faida Kamel, both of whom represented poor districts of Cairo and who were elected to regular rather than reserved seats, would probably have won regardless of party affiliation. After all, Nawal Amer has been in the Majlis al-Shaab since 1964, defeating men in each election and building up a considerable local and even national reputation fighting for the interests of her constituents. Party experience can hardly be said to have been decisive in her case, and there are other examples of the weakness of party ties.[18] One veiled rural woman, Soheir Gilbana, had been the party representative for women in her governorate, but she ran for parliament as an independent. In her campaign, she viewed party affiliation as more of a liability than an asset. She won and then, after entering parliament, rejoined the NDP in order to get more done for the people of her area. This helps to illustrate that party experience is less important politically than having achieved professional success or having a good reputation in the district. (It also suggests that, in many instances, the NDP as the government party, was more popular with the government than with the electorate.) People who are prominent, whether men or women, are more likely to be recruited into the party than they are to achieve prominence because of party affiliation. As the case of Soheir Gilbana suggests, however, party links are perhaps more important once parliamentary membership is achieved than before. Simply put, it is easier to get things done for your constituents if you are part of the majority party than if you are not. This leads us to consider the roles, achievements, and failures of the women in parliament, particularly with regard to questions pertaining to women, but also touching on a number of non-sex-typed issues.

WOMEN AND PARLIAMENTARY POLITICS

Given the nature of parliamentary politics in Egypt, even a modest achievement by an individual or a group can be thought of as a major accomplishment. Most new laws or policies start with the government and are simply approved, usually with little or no alteration, by Majlis al-Shaab. Majlis al-Shura makes no laws and gives advice only when asked. Although parliament is, by definition, a democratic institution, Egypt is not a full-fledged democracy and, for the most part, extra-parliamentary authorities expect compliance. It is within this atmosphere and hemmed in by these constraints that Egypt's parliamentarians function. Many are more frustrated than exhilarated by playing the role expected of them and do not seek reelection or reappointment, helping to account for the high rate of turnover in membership between parliaments.[19] Some stay for the honor or perhaps even for the money but a small group, including some women, believe they are doing something useful for their constituents, country, or both, and enjoy the work of parliament.

Viewed from one perspective, the women in parliament are indistinguishable from the men. They attend meetings, listen to speeches and debates, occasionally present a report, or participate in debate. They also vote (usually in favor of government proposals) and partake in a variety of public ceremonies designed to present parliament and

Egypt in a positive way. Like the men, they also tend to specialize in one or at most a few issues regarding which they have an enduring interest. One reflection of this concentration can be seen by looking at committee membership.

In both houses of parliament, each delegate may be a full member of only one standing committee. As a general rule, individuals are assigned to the committee of their choice. However, they may also attend other committees if they wish. Thus, while only one woman was a member of the Foreign Affairs Committee in Majlis al-Shura, the majority of the others attended this committee frequently. Table 2.18, reflecting only the principal committee interest of the women in Egypt's present and past parliaments, shows how roughly 18% of those in Majlis al-Shaab have concentrated on one committee, Social and Religious Affairs. It also shows how the others were dispersed in such a way that women were represented on twelve of the eighteen standing committees of Majlis al-Shaab and two of the five standing committees of Majlis al-Shura. In Majlis al-Shaab, women were not represented on the Committee on the Economy, nor were any women full members of the Committees on Proposals and Complaints; Transportation; Labor; Public Security and Mobilization; or Local Government. But it is vital for women's issues that several were members of the Committee on Social and Religious Affairs, as we shall see below, because this committee has dealt with sensitive issues pertaining to religious law and the role of women in society. However, it is equally important that women participate in many other committees and, as near as I could tell, behaved in those forums much like men.

The substantive task performed by women in parliament should be understood in the context of the sense of role definition the women have. Who or what do they believe they represent in parliament? Party identification is strong and almost universal, but there are relatively few party issues per se and party identification does little to resolve the issue of role definition. Essentially free to decide this question for themselves, a large plurality of women in parliament see themselves primarily as representatives of the electoral district which sent them to parliament. Consequently, they specialize in local issues and questions pertaining to their constituents. All of the female members of Majlis al-Shura, plus several members of Majlis al-Shaab, thought of themselves in a wider context and thus specialized in national rather than local issues. Table 2.19 shows how the issue of self-definition was seen by the study group. It also points out some other features of the group as well. For example, all of the female members of the Majlis al-Shura and all of the women who have been appointed to parliament are essentially urban. Not shown in this table, but clear from other data, is that the "national issue" group as a whole tends to be better educated and, with a few exceptions, more likely to come from an upper-class or upper-middle-class background than those who specialize in local issues and constituent service.

Regardless of how they view the issue, all elected members of parliament spend a good portion of their time dealing with problems brought to them by constituents or issues pertaining to their electoral district. Readers should try to understand what this means in the context of Egyptian politics and reflect on the kinds of problems with which parliamentarians must deal. Many of the requests received are attempts to be exempted from a particular rule or law, for example that pertaining to the military draft. Others, probably the majority, are requests for help with a segment of the huge and cumbersome government bureaucracy. Parliamentarians are often approached by constituents who wish them to intervene with the bureaucracy in order to secure something to which the constituent feels he or she is entitled. Often, they are asked to help redress a grievance. Most people, in dealing with any element of Egypt's bureaucracy, feel that a *wasta* (connection) is necessary in order to even have a chance to get anything done.

Many people try to use "their delegate" to parliament as this *wasta*, and delegates are frequently swamped by such requests. Those who have been appointed have an easy out, as they do not represent a district and have no specific constituents. Those who are elected, however, can hardly avoid the issue, and have essentially three choices as to how to deal with these petitions. Some, a relatively small number, can be rejected altogether if the petitioner asks them to do something which is clearly inappropriate. Other pleas must be responded to in a different fashion. One way is that selected by most of those who have decided to concentrate on national rather than local issues. They tend to provide the supplicant with instructions regarding whom to see and, perhaps, what to say or not say. They do not intervene in person. Another method is that chosen by those for whom constituent service is their major reason for being in parliament. In some cases they merely tell people whom to see and what kind of things to say, but they are likely to try whenever possible to intercede directly with the relevant official or officials, attempting to get constituents the service they have requested. Nawal Amer and Olfat Kamel are notable practitioners of this method and have done a great many favors for the residents of the poor districts of Cairo which they represent. Both are also experienced and effective regarding national issues, but tend to specialize in such problems as housing or welfare, which are also major concerns in their districts. In this regard, this group of eighteen women act much like the majority of their male colleagues, for whom efforts to satisfy local demands dominate their parliamentary lives.

Women seem to be more likely than men to try to play the game of national politics, an invigorating but risky business. But in so doing, it is not clear that they think of themselves as representatives of women. Rather, they seek to serve the interests of the nation as a whole.

Were the women in parliament to confine themselves to women's issues, they would have little to say or do, for sex-typed questions do not arise often. Women serve on a variety of committees and tend to participate in sessions where they have some particular professional background or expertise and do not work together as a group very often. While the NDP has a Women's Section, and most of the women in parliament participate in its meetings every other Sunday, there is no organization or regular meeting as such for women in parliament. Nevertheless the majority of the women in parliament in the early 1980s believed that women's needs differ according to class. Thus, urban working women need such things as access to prepared foods and day care centers because, although they work outside, the responsibility of taking care of the home is still theirs. Peasant women need education and better health care. All women, according to the leadership, need to be made more aware of their rights. In responding to these problems, the prevailing pattern is for each individual member of parliament to work alone, especially those who represent urban districts. The most obvious tension among the group is between those who represent rural areas and those who are from one of Egypt's major urban centers. Urban women have received the lion's share of what little public attention has gone to women and many of the rural women, in interviews conducted for this study, stated that they felt somewhat neglected and left out of events. While 44% of those who responded to the question believed that women should work together to present a "women's perspective" on major issues, one-third of the group disagreed sharply with this view, stating that each woman should work alone. About 20% stated pragmatically that they felt it depended on the issue, adding that most problems dealt with were not women's problems as such. While the majority of those elected to reserved seats considered themselves to be "women's representatives," they interpreted this to mean the women in their district, not the women of Egypt.

Women in the group were asked, "Should the women in parliament work together as a group to provide a 'women's perspective' or position on most if not all major public issues?" A large number did not respond to the question, suggesting they did not feel comfortable with it. Several, however, made detailed comments, some examples of which may help us to clarify the variety of perspectives taken by women in this group. One rural woman said simply: "Everyone has her own position and work to achieve." A veiled woman said: "Yes, because in working together they constitute a stronger force." But one of her veiled colleagues felt that: "Everyone works with her own decisions." Sharply defined views were outlined by two urban women. One said: "No. Not at the moment. They should act within their scientific and professional capacities rather than as women." In perhaps the bluntest comment of all, one influential member of the group said her female colleagues should "try to forget about being a woman. After all that has been gained recently by women, now is the time for them to give, not to seek more rights or benefits."

This woman, and those who agree with her, do not wish to consider the issue of female solidarity in the abstract. Rather, she and most of the female parliamentary leadership believe that women must, for practical political reasons, demonstrate clearly that they deserve the rights they now enjoy and can contribute to the welfare of the country as a whole, more now because of their improved status and position. Sadat's presidency was, as many of them put it, "the golden age of women in Egypt," and they feel that now is the time to consolidate gains and demonstrate worthiness rather than risk an antifeminist backlash by pushing for more. This can be seen clearly in the attitude and behavior of parliamentary women regarding two issues: reserved seats for women in public office, especially parliament, and proposed changes in the Personal Status Laws pertaining to marriage, divorce, alimony, and child custody.

With the exception of one woman who did not explain her reasons, there was no expressed opposition among women in the 1979 parliament to the idea of having seats reserved for women in Majlis al-Shaab. However, over one-third of the women in parliament felt it should be a transitional provision "to enable women to prove themselves," after which they would not need such protection. When asked about the length of the period of transition, no one felt it would be brief and many believed that, if women were to be represented at all, separate seats would be necessary for the forseeable future, especially in rural districts. From the fall of 1979 until early 1983, the issues of reserved seats for women could be discussed in the abstract, as an academic or theoretical question pertaining to the early stages of a social experiment. This changed in 1983 when, at the initiative of the government and leaders of the NDP, serious consideration was given to altering the election rules. As part of this "reform" the reserved seats for women were to be dropped, as was the possibility of contesting elections as an independent. Large electoral districts would replace small ones and proportional representation using a Party List electoral system would be introduced. This would mean that political parties, especially the NDP, would become more important and, if women were to be elected they would have to be supported by a strong party and placed high enough on the list to have a reasonable chance for success.

At first, leaders among the women in the NDP apparently supported the proposal to establish the new system but argued that the law must be written in such a way as to protect women from being excluded from the list. Discussion continued within the party and the issue came to a head in July 1983, when Majlis al-Shaab approved legislation to conduct future elections according to a controversial new system. As a brief glance at any of Cairo's major newspapers or magazines published during June or July of 1983 will attest, most of the dispute centered on two aspects of the new rules. First, if a party did not poll at least 8% of the vote nationwide, it would receive no seats in Majlis al-Shaab, even if it received the required number of votes in a particular district. Second, independent candidates would not be permitted to contest elections. Relatively little public attention focused on the issue of reserved seats for women. The story of what happened illustrates how women can become involved in behind-the-scenes bargaining in Egyptian politics and reveals an important aspect of the new power of women: they can use their own formal power as well as the unofficial but real influence they have with "their" men.

By the time it reached Majlis al-Shaab in July 1983, the NDP leadership's proposal was to retain reserved seats for women but reduce their number from thirty to twenty-six. Cairo, having grown since 1979, would be given one new reserved seat, but the five seats in conservative desert fringe governorates would be abolished. Women from these districts organized, protested, and sought support from the other women, and from several men, in parliament. Rural or urban, veiled or not, the women stuck together and used their individual and collective influence to urge that all reserved seats be retained. When the bargaining process ended, the women had won. The reserved seats were restored and the new seat for Cairo added.[20] In short, what started as an attempt to abolish all reserved seats for women, and moved to a compromise position to keep them but reduce their number, ended by adding one new seat to the thirty created in 1979. Reflection on this incident suggests that the base for the participation of women in national politics is not yet secure, even after the gains of the Sadat era and "the golden age for women." But perhaps more important, it also indicates that once in the system, women are able to hold their ground and advance their position.

Even more sensitive than the question of reserved seats for women in parliament is the issue of whether there will be further changes in the Personal Status Laws. As mentioned before, the reform of the laws pertaining to divorce, marriage, alimony, and the custody of children has been a key element in the women's movement in Egypt throughout the twentieth century. Advocacy of change in this area was continued by the women elected to parliament. For example, when Amina Shoukry was elected to Majlis al-Shaab in 1957, she proposed changes in these laws.[21] She did not succeed, nor did those who followed her, until 1979 when some reforms were made enabling, for example, a woman to get a divorce if her husband should take a second wife without her knowledge or permission. Although approved by virtually unanimous vote in parliament, these new laws remained controversial and were opposed by many conservative Islamic leaders.

While there is support by a strong minority of the women in parliament for even more liberal change, as shown in Table 2.20, most efforts by parliamentary women since 1979 have been to protect the new laws from attacks in Majlis al-Shaab. So far, they have been supported by a majority of the most senior officials in Egyptian politics but the presence of many women on the Committee on Social and

Religious Affairs in Majlis al-Shaab is an important added element. Proposals for further changes would, if normal procedure is followed, have to be approved by that committee before they could be taken up by the Majlis itself. The committee in question deals with proposals and problems pertaining to the Ministries of Social Affairs and Insurance, Religious Endowments, and with the University of al-Azhar, the major theological center for Sunni Muslims. The Minister of Social Affairs and Insurance, Dr. Amal Othman, who between 1979 and 1984 held a reserved seat in parliament, meets with this committee.

According to Akila al-Samaa, elected to a reserved seat for Heliopolis, women on this committee were able to kill a proposal made in 1981 by representative Salah Abu Ismail, known to have been a member of the Muslim Brotherhood, to force all working women to wear Islamic dress.[22] They also helped protect the 1979 laws from a conservative backlash in 1980 and 1981, but in 1983 did not believe the issue was settled and expected further efforts to rescind the law, even though it appeared likely that its fate would be settled by the Constitutional Court.

While the law was changed by men — no women spoke in parliament when the issue was discussed in 1979 — women have been quite active as guardians of the new rules, though many of them think that even more liberal changes are needed. Even the one woman who felt the new laws were too liberal did not want to go back to the way it was before 1979. Regardless of religion, place of residence, or style of dress, on this issue the women stood together. Those in parliament who spoke against these laws faced a united front among the women. They also had to be prepared to debate veiled parliamentarians such as Kamla Megahid, who opposed any further changes, arguing that "Anyone who says . . . [the reforms are] against Sharia [Islamic law] does not know anything about religion." The presence of people like this, who feel strongly about the law and who argue its merits in terms of Sharia no doubt improved the chances for its survival and underlined the importance of the continued presence of women in parliament. In July of 1985, after the 1979 laws were declared unconstitutional, the NDP leadership introduced new laws almost identical to those which were struck down in May. They passed with ease, supported by nearly all the male and female members of Majlis al-Shaab. Unlike 1979 the women in Majlis al-Shaab were active participants in the debates which culminated in the passage of the new laws in 1985.

Other than in the summers of 1983 and 1985, on only one occasion since 1979 have the women in Majlis al-Shaab worked together as a unit on behalf of a women's issue rather than leaving the matter in the hands of the members of a specific committee. This involved a proposal in 1981 by the minister of finance, Ali Lutfi, to disperse raises in government salaries in a way which discriminated against women. He wanted to give the raise a married woman would have received to her husband, instead of to her. After several months of trying to get him to change the rule, the women finally went to President Sadat, who backed them. For the most part, however, regardless of personal attitudes toward women's solidarity, the work of the women in parliament is done in their individual capacity rather than as women. In this regard, a few have achieved quite a bit and many have demonstrated they are at least as good as men at parliamentary politics.

Several women have served as heads of standing committees in parliament and, as such, have had an impact on both law and policy. These include Nawal Amer (Housing), Laila Takla (Foreign Affairs), Olfat Kamel (Housing) and Dr. Soheir al-Qalamawi (Culture, Information and Tourism). Drs. Hekmat Abu Zeid, Aisha Rateb, and Amal Othman have all served as cabinet officers and have had a major impact on law and policy in the areas of Social Affairs and Insurance. Their careers are sufficiently impressive, and their accomplishments sufficiently extensive that they deserve separate study, beyond the scope of this book.

An accomplishment of some parliamentary women is that they have retained a degree of independence, even though they are part of the power elite which dominates the country. All but one are or have been members of the government party, but not all have adhered to the party line all the time, even on important issues. All three of the veiled women elected in 1979 as independents have acted this way, as have several others. In the 1975–76 session, Nawal Amer was central to the successful effort to enable working widows to receive the full benefit of a husband's pension as well as their own when they retire. In 1983, Dr. Farkhounda Hassan, with considerable support from both male and female colleagues, succeeded in getting the government to create an environmental authority to deal with growing problems of environmental quality and pollution. This was the culmination of three years of suggestions and well-phrased questions in Majlis al-Shaab to the government.[23]

Dr. Shafika Nasser used her expertise in public health and nutrition to, as she puts it, try to "enlarge the circle of those who believe that the shortest way to Egypt's development is women's development." As the Majlis al-Shura, in which she is an elected member, has no power to make law, she has carried this issue to her colleagues via a 1983 official report on human development, from the Services Committee to the Shura Council. The report noted that whether the problem is curing illness, preventing the spread of infectious diseases, lowering infant mortality or improving education, women are the key. Using education as an example, Dr. Nasser says, "A literate mother would never allow her child to become illiterate." In this sentiment she is joined by many other women in parliament, approximately 40 percent of whom believe that opportunities for formal education are even more important for girls than for boys. As Dr. Zeinab Sobky puts it, "Women constitute half of the society and they educate the other half." Therefore, to educate the women is to educate the nation. Not all of these ideas are unique to these women and many have been expressed elsewhere,[24] but they challenge convention in important ways. It is doubtful that high-level debates on development would take this turn were it not for some of the more independent-minded women in parliament.

Another way to exercise independence is by speaking and voting against the government on major policy issues. However, in the late 1970s one member of the president's party, Dr. Laila Takla, disagreed with the terms of the Camp David accords and said so. She paid the price for such dissent and, in the 1979 elections, withdrew from the election rather than suffer a crushing defeat arranged by the National Democratic Party organization. (After 1979, she became an officer in the Socialist Labor Party. She will be among the people discussed in chapter 4, "Opposition Women.") Another courageous dissenter, still active in parliament in 1984, is Amina Said, a senior feminist and prominent journalist. She has spoken and voted against a number of government proposals, most notably the laws regulating the press. She was one of only three members of Majlis al-Shura to vote against laws which, in effect, regulate and control the press. Such control is not new in Egypt, nor is it unusual in the world today, but it is worth noting that one of the few people in Egypt's parliament to stand up for freedom of the press was a feminist journalist, unwilling to compromise her principles and willing to risk regime disfavor.

Whether they speak for or against government policy, the women in Majlis al-Shaab are more likely to speak than are the men. In the 1984 parliamentary campaign, one of the opposition newspapers published a list of 130 NDP parliamentarians who did not speak in open session in Parliament between 1979 and 1984.[25] Of that group only seven were women. This means that roughly 40% of the male members of parliament did not participate in the debates and discussions which took place between 1979 and 1984, while 20% of the women were silent. Given that one of the main functions of Majlis al-Shaab is debate and discussion, men are twice as likely to shirk their responsibilities to contribute as are women.

The ultimate impact of much that has been mentioned above is still unclear but, for some women in Majlis al-Shaab, their achievements are less doubtful. Nawal Amer, Olfat Kamel, and Faida Kamel all have represented poor districts of Cairo: Sayeda Zeinab, Gamaliya, and Darb al-Ahmar. Their orientation toward constituent service and local issues has paid off in "concrete" terms for their areas. Schools, mosques, housing units, and even a "Faida Kamel Hospital" are proof that these women have been able to make the Egyptian political system deliver benefits to their constituents. While only a few who specialize in national issues can claim to have achieved much, virtually all who concentrate on local problems can point to some fairly specific, if modest, way in which they have affected the operation of the Egyptian system. Thus, while some have made policy or law, many have made the system work for their constituents, most of whom are women who apparently feel more comfortable taking their problems to a female delegate than to a man. Prior to 1979, only women in a few urban districts had this option. Now, it is an exercised right throughout the country, even in the most remote and conservative provinces.

In recent years, political activity by and on behalf of women has increased in both frequency and scope. Dr. Soheir al-Qalamawi, leader of the Women's Section of the NDP between 1979 and 1984, believed more women should become more politicized and, through the party, organized workshops and meetings all over Egypt to encourage women to become more involved in politics. Within the government, thinking about women's problems and what to do about them has become institutionalized through the National Commission for Women, founded in the mid-1970s. Dr. Amal Othman, Minister of Social Affairs, stated in 1983 that as a result of the work of this commission, her ministry started many pilot programs to provide specific services. It is not yet clear how effective either the programs or the commission will be. Skepticism about the ultimate worth of such efforts may be what caused Amina Said to say in a 1983 interview: "The poor government. It is so overwhelmed by problems, such as decaying and collapsing infrastructure, that women have to fight for themselves." Mrs. Said, recruited into feminism at the age of fourteen by Hoda Sha'rawi, has remained faithful to the early principles of solidarity and self-help. For her, this means both collective and individual efforts by women to solve their problems, and, with that, help make additional contributions to improve the quality of life in Egypt. Thus, what seems to be happening in the early 1980s is that government efforts to help women are reinforced by political parties and both are supplemented and encouraged by individual and collective efforts of women throughout the system to help themselves.

CONCLUSION

Before 1979, a relatively small number of women participated in parliamentary politics in Egypt. Women were given the vote in 1956 and a year later two urban women were elected to the People's Assembly, defeating men in open elections. In the following twenty-two years, about a dozen women were elected or appointed to parliament. Three served in the cabinet, all holding the same portfolio, Minister of Social Affairs. In 1979, the number of parliamentary women increased sharply due to a new law which reserved thirty new seats for women in the People's Assembly. Approximately 100 women contested elections for these seats. Those who won were joined by three other women who defeated men in the elections and two who were appointed to the Majlis by President Sadat. In 1980, a new chamber, Majlis al-Shura, was added to Egypt's parliament. Two women were elected to it and five were appointed by the president. Thus, by 1982, when this study began, forty-two women, including some who had been in parliament before, were among the 600 members of Egypt's bicameral legislature. They, plus four women who served in previous parliaments, but are not now in that body, were the subjects of this chapter.

Egyptian women who have served in parliament tend to have

come from relatively privileged families and to have had educated and supportive parents. The role of fathers in encouraging their daughters to get an education and seek a career outside the home is particularly notable. As young girls, these women learned self-confidence, optimism, and an appreciation for the value of work. Of the forty-six studied, twenty-five of the women were urban while twenty-one represented rural districts in parliament. All but four were Muslim. Twelve, all from rural areas, wore Islamic dress while the remainder wore Western-style clothing. Regardless of place of origin or style of dress, the women studied all came from families where education was considered a necessity for all children. Two-thirds went to Arabic schools and, as one consequence, most of Egypt's female parliamentarians developed a good command of the Arabic language. Several also learned at least one foreign language. Both of these linguistic assets proved to be valuable tools for those who possessed them when they entered politics.

On the whole, the women in Egypt's parliament are well-educated. Seventy percent of them have earned university degrees and, of that group, one-third went on to receive at least one advanced degree. Exact figures pertaining to their male colleagues are not available, but it is quite clear that the women are better educated than the men. As one measure of this, women in the Majlis al-Shura accounted for only 3.3% of the membership but 8.1% of the doctorates. Furthermore, virtually all parliamentary women have had successful careers in work outside the home before entering parliament.

When this study was done, almost fifty years separated the youngest from the oldest woman in parliament.[26] Regardless of when and where they were born, however, most married and raised children, with late marriage and relatively small families being the rule. Whether urban or rural, veiled or unveiled, most married between the ages of twenty-five and twenty-six. Average family size was between two and three children, with women from small villages tending to have the largest families. Three women remained single, and one veiled woman did not marry until age fifty-two. Only five had ever been divorced.[27] All divorces were, in one way or another, brought about by the husband's inability to accommodate himself to his wife's role in politics and the wife's unwillingness to give up that life. As a general rule, however, most husbands have supported their wives' careers and ambitions.

It was not until they were in their mid-forties that most of the women in this group became members of parliament. Marriage, family, and professions occupied the time between the completion of formal education and entry into parliament. All but eight had careers outside the home, with education, law, journalism, medicine, and social work being the most common professions. Many, especially the housewives, became involved in volunteer social work. Most of the forty-six women acquired practical experience in party politics during this time and, since then, have been successful at both party and parliamentary politics. This has meant a strong tendency among the group to conform to the norms of the regime on most issues. However, the group also included a number of notable mavericks who use their professional expertise and linguistic skills, especially their command of Arabic, to question or criticize government officials. Some have stood against the majority in parliament on matters of principle. These three attributes — occasionally principled action within a framework of overall conformity, excellent command of Arabic, strong professional background — form the base to the careers of most of Egypt's parliamentary women.

Women in Egypt's parliament have tended to work alone most of the time but have expressed solidarity regarding traditional issues on Egypt's feminist agenda, especially regarding the Personal Status Laws. Not all agree, however, with the idea that women should have a separate sphere, a protected arena, symbolized best by the reserved seats for women in the People's Assembly. Even if they have, in principle, supported these seats only as an interim measure, in practice, they united successfully to defend them when they were placed in jeopardy by attempts to "reform" the electoral laws in 1983.

Clearly, women in Egypt's parliament have a great deal in common. There are also some important differences, however, which serve to highlight diversity within the group. The most obvious of these is the difference between urban and rural women in background, and, in some cases, appearance. Life is harsher and amenities fewer in the countryside than in the cities of Egypt. Thus, rural girls were more likely than urban girls to have a parent die. Later in life, they were less likely to learn a foreign language well or receive a university degree than were the future parliamentarians who grew up in cities. None of them earned a postgraduate degree. On the other hand, five urban women were divorced, while no rural women had this experience. Remaining single was an option exercised by urban women only. What this adds up to is the not surprising conclusion that rural women in parliament come from a more conservative and traditional background and, in general, are less privileged than their urban counterparts. This helps to put into perspective the position and role of the women in parliament who wear Islamic dress.

In contemporary Egypt, wearing Islamic dress is often interpreted as a political as well as religious statement reflecting across-the-board fundamentalist attitudes. Contrarily, some believe that the return to Islamic dress is an effort by women to redefine the code for proper behavior in such a way as to enable them to work outside the home without violating the strict rules of Muslim society.[28] When Hoda Sha'rawi and her fellow feminists stopped wearing a veil across the lower half of the face it was a daring act of assertion and rebellion. They continued, however, to cover the hair and neck and wear ankle-length, long-sleeved dresses. By the 1950s many women, especially in urban areas, were unveiled and, in general, dressed in a more Western style. Change occurred much slower in rural than urban areas. In the 1970s many women and young girls began to "return to the veil." While not actually covering their faces, they wore high-necked, long sleeved outfits and covered their hair. This is considered by most Egyptian Islamic fundamentalists as proper Islamic dress[29] and is an accurate description of how the twelve veiled women in parliament look, that is, the way Hoda Sha'rawi did *after* she took off the veil. Times have changed and, in contemporary Egypt, this style of dress is viewed generally as being traditional and Islamic rather than progressive or modern, as it was in 1923. For the most part, however, the women in parliament who wear Islamic dress are not returning to the veil. Early in life they adopted the style of dress prevalent in rural Egypt. These women conform to the norms of society regarding dress and marriage but also work outside the home and, most unconventionally, pursue active political careers. In the parts of Egypt from which they come, this style of dress is a political asset. Perhaps paradoxically, being veiled strengthens their chances of having a public role rather than preventing it.

It is clear that the veiled women in parliament do not have the same background as the others. What about political behavior and attitudes? All of the women in Majlis al-Shaab in 1983 worked to defend the reserved seats for women from desert fringe areas. Veiled women not only participated in this activity, they helped lead it.[30]

Similarly, as Table 2.20 indicates, there is not much difference between the attitudes of veiled women and the others regarding further
changes in the Personal Status Laws. Some have also been active in
parliament as defenders of the 1979 and 1985 reforms and opposed
efforts to introduce laws which would discriminate against women.
In short, as far as these litmus test issues of feminism are concerned,
there is no appreciable difference between the veiled women, as a group,
and the others. It is true that the most liberal woman in parliament
is urban and actively opposed to veiling, and the most conservative
is veiled, but these individual cases should not mask the overall pattern of similarity between the two groups. When challenged politically, veiled women, even those from small rural villages, are no less
feminist, no less likely to work for the interests of their constituents,
especially the women, than are the most urban and cosmopolitan of
their female colleagues. Western observers, or westernized Arabs, may
find this hard to understand, but the evidence in support of this conclusion is clear.

Diverse, interesting, ambitious, virtually all of Egypt's parliamentary women have learned to work the country's political system
to their own as well as their constituents' advantage. Although there
are dissenters among them, most are conformists who have concluded
that, in order to get ahead in the system you must go along with its
central tendencies and trends. Within that system at least two complementary and coexisting strategic approaches are used by politicians.
One is to attempt to maximize government support for constituents.
The other is to work on self-help projects, some of which are totally
separate from government while others are symbiotic or supplemen-
tary to each other. Most women in parliament follow the first of these
strategies but a few prefer the second. The long-term consequences
of this absence of ideological solidarity are not yet clear.

Most of Egypt's parliamentary women have been able to enter
political life because a separate, protected sphere was created in 1979,
when reserved seats for women in parliament were first established.
Some had political support from Mrs. Sadat at the time, another factor which aided their entrance into the elite. But those who have succeeded in the system have had to do so on their own merits, based
on their individual abilities. Furthermore, success has not been easy.
Each had to struggle against considerable odds in order to succeed
in politics. The attributes which seem, according to the data collected

for this study, to be most crucial in accounting for success are the following.

First, most of the women who have succeeded in politics in Egypt have acquired professional expertise and contacts which have enabled them to make a substantive contribution to debates, discussions, and the making of laws. This background gives them durability and a special place in the system, especially when many of their male colleagues lack this background and have little but their own wits and loyalty to the system, or to a particular leader, to offer as a political asset. These women are clever and loyal, but they also have politically relevant professional experience and are likely to have participated in a number of political coalitions. They are also likely to have long-term value to the system rather than to burn out quickly, outmaneuvered by politicians who have talent for wheeling and dealing as well as professional expertise.

Second, as one consequence of being fairly well educated, women in parliament are likely to have a good command of Arabic. They speak, read, and write the language using the grammar and vocabulary of a well-educated Arab. Given the reverence for the Arabic language in Egypt, it is impossible to exaggerate the political importance of the ability to use it well. Also, parliament is, more than anything else, a debating society. Verbal skill and grace are vital facilities in an arena in which words are deeds, and, as pointed out earlier in this chapter, women are more likely to speak in parliament than are men. In this forum, in which how a thing is said is at least as important as what is said, politicians who have a sophisticated command of Arabic are formidable opponents and valuable allies, able to prosper even in adversity, and thus likely to endure. If nothing else, their proficiency in Arabic guarantees them an audience and the ability to command attention.

Third, most of the women in parliament are known for conventional respectability and adherence to the accepted norms of society. Conservative in such matters as dress and lifestyle, they have married, raised children past infancy, and then entered politics. Although they lead very public lives, they do so with the support of "their" men: fathers, brothers, husbands, and sons. Those who are veiled come from areas where veiling is the norm, and their style of dress, in effect, shields them from excessive criticism regarding their political roles. They, and most of the other women in parliament have done the things society expects of them and convinced voters to send them to parliament. Their position is thus protected by their conventional behavior as well as by public law.

The political success of women in parliament is explained by a combination of factors. The majority have demonstrated professional excellence, speak good Arabic, and conform to traditional values. As individuals and as part of a group, they have been able to circumvent the bias against women in politics. The majority of the women discussed in this chapter are skilled politicians who have earned a place in Egypt's political life. They are not alone in this regard, however, as will be illustrated in the following two chapters in which we shall consider the role played by the wives of Egypt's presidents and then examine the case of women who are leaders in the political opposition.

Presidential Wives

EGYPT'S PRESIDENTS AND THE
ROLE OF WOMEN IN PUBLIC LIFE

I N A POLITICAL SYSTEM in which popular expectations regarding the president are as high as they have been in Egypt, disappointment is inevitable. This problem is compounded if, in the process of development, traditional values are challenged and the domestic power structure is altered. One of the most poignant dilemmas faced by leaders of developing countries is that they are often called upon to symbolize the nation's traditional values and to bring about political, economic, and social transformations which challenge those values. Leaders who attempt to alter the roles and status of women are confronted with this problem. Unless they are to be resisted because they are no longer considered honorable men, they must adhere to convention while attempting to change it. While the presidency is a center of power and discretionary authority and the president is the main recipient of the hopes of the nation, he is also the embodiment of its virtues, and the target for blame when things go wrong. In this regard, the role of the wife of the president can be crucial, for she is the bearer of his honor. She has the potential to help him achieve his overall goals, including those pertaining to women, but she can also make his task more difficult, or even impossible, if her behavior undermines his authority by causing him to lose face.

In this chapter, we are concerned with three women, the wives of presidents Gamal Abdel Nasser, Anwar Sadat and Hosny Mubarak. Whether they have always liked it or not, theirs has been a position of public responsibility. Although bereft of legal authority or national office, each has led, by example if in no other way, or has influenced her husband's behavior or decisions. Each has approached the task differently, and all have had both supporters and critics. Before discussing these women, however, it is necessary to review each of their husband's records as far as the feminist agenda is concerned.

Gamal Abdel Nasser dominated Egypt, and Arab politics in general, for most of the years between the Free Officers' Revolution in 1952 and his death in 1970. He outmaneuvered General Mohammad Naguib, the nominal leader of the revolutionary group, and became prime minister in 1954. Under the Constitution of 1956, he became president of the republic. No feminist-inspired issues were on the revolutionary agenda of the Free Officers when they came to power in 1952, but as nationalist reformers they inherited the obligation at least to consider ideas brought forward by the disparate elements of the nationalist movement, including the feminists. Among those notions were proposals for voting rights for women, reform of the Personal Status Laws, and other social reforms. Nasser moved quickly to acquit some of these claims.

Part of the new constitutional order was the right of women to vote, discussed in chapter 1, a change for which Nasser was partly responsible, as he was the principal architect of the constitution.[1] A year later, the first women were elected to parliament, which passed new labor laws in 1959. Among the provisions of these laws were legal rights and special protection for working women. Law 91 of 1959 prohibited discrimination in employment on the basis of sex, but also proscribed female "employment in activities detrimental to them in physical or moral terms." Men were not so protected. In 1962, President Nasser appointed Dr. Hekmat Abu Zeid as Minister of Social Affairs, thus putting a woman in the cabinet for the first time in modern Egyptian history. The 1950s and especially the 1960s also witnessed increased enrollment of females in schools and universities, and attempts to reduce female illiteracy and raise the general status of women, as part of a policy supported by Abdel Nasser. His appointment of Dr. Abu Zeid as Minister of Social Affairs was of special importance in this regard.

Gamal Abdel Nasser's years in power were, however, a mixed

blessing for women. Women had the vote, could sit in parliament or run a ministry, but women's associations became targets of the regime. Numerous voluntary associations had been created by women in the twentieth century and they had established a clear record of social service in many fields, especially health, education, and welfare.[2] Most of the leaders were women from prominent families and all wished to protect the independence of these organizations. From Nasser's point of view, the social class and the relative independence of these women were objectionable. In the early 1960s, the regime moved to take over most of the functions of the women's associations as state responsibilities and to coopt the organizations themselves into the new political organization, the Arab Socialist Union. Hekmat Abu Zeid implemented these policies, whose intended beneficiaries were female workers and peasants. Some progress was made, but at the official level women's associations lost both momentum and autonomy in the process. Unofficially, according to several women interviewed for this book, the Mabarra Muhammad Ali helped set up rehabilitation centers for the army at this time and various other women's organizations continued to be vital, if secondary, agents of welfare and social reform.

One other feminist issue must be mentioned. Although Nasser gave women the right to vote and enhanced educational and employment opportunities for women, he did little with regard to the effort to reform the Personal Status Laws. Within the ASU in the early 1960s, Nasser kept firm control and rebuffed attempts by women to push for change, leaving some ASU women with the impression that he was not in full sympathy with them on this issue.[3] After Egypt's defeat in 1967, however, the regime moved to accommodate some of its critics, and in 1969 did propose to reform these laws. This effort did not succeed, due to opposition from religious traditionalists, and the problem of how to overcome this obstacle, along with numerous other problems, was left to Nasser's successor, Anwar Sadat.

Sadat moved quickly to establish himself and consolidate his position, and, in May 1971, succeeded in arresting Ali Sabry and other former officials who opposed him. This "Corrective Revolution," as it came to be known, involved more than arresting potential rivals. It also called for a more liberal domestic, economic, and political system, an end to Egypt's close ties with the U.S.S.R., and the return of the land lost to Israel in 1967. We are concerned here with only one part of this program — that portion of the women's agenda that was part of domestic reform. In this area, President Sadat was cautious and tried to protect his regime from attack. On women's issues, the opposition which concerned him most was from the religious right. Trying to please both women and conservative Muslims, the 1971 constitution stated, in section two, article eleven that "the state shall be responsible for making the balance between a woman's duties toward her family and her activity in society, as well as maintaining her equality with men in the fields of education, political, social, economic, and cultural life without detriment to the laws of the Islamic Sharia."

Thus, men and women were equal, but Islamic law would not be compromised. The new constitution should be considered in the context of Egypt's massive domestic and international problems at the time, and in the light of other decisions pertaining to women made in the same year. In 1971, Egypt had a "corrective revolution", a new constitution, a new parliament, and a new cabinet. One conspicuous member of the new cabinet was Dr. Aisha Rateb, who became the second woman to serve in this position. Among her first acts was a proposal to reform the Personal Status Laws. This attempt failed, and, in 1977, another effort was made by Dr. Amal Othman, who had just replaced Dr. Rateb as Minister of Social Affairs. The new laws were still under discussion in 1979 when President Sadat decided to speed up the political process and issued a decree, later passed by the new parliament, making the proposals law. In that same year, 1979, Dr. Aisha Rateb became the first Egyptian woman ambassador, and reserved seats were created for women in the People's Assembly and on all local and provincial councils.

While the new Personal Status Laws did not contain all the demands of the feminists,[4] there is no doubt that President Sadat supported the cause of women in Egypt. He protected the gains made under Nasser and advanced them further, but he also helped make women's issues much more controversial than they had been before. Critics objected to the peremptory nature of Sadat's decree on constitutional grounds, and the specific nature of some of the reforms angered elements of both the secular and religious opposition.[5] For example, one of the provisions of the new law gave a divorced woman the right to evict her former husband from the matrimonial home under certain circumstances. Some people, including some women in parliament, felt that, in a country with such a severe housing shortage, this dealt with one injustice by creating another, and believed that a fair alternative should have been found before the law was passed.

Hosny Mubarak became president of Egypt following the assassination of Anwar Sadat in 1981. When Nasser died, the role of women in public life had advanced considerably from what it had been in 1952, but the issue was not one of Egypt's major controversies. One of the problems inherited by President Mubarak was that the public role of women had become a focus for major controversy. Mubarak's job, as he saw it, was to protect the gains which had been made, but also to reduce or eliminate the controversy. By mid-1985, it seemed he had succeeded on both counts, at least in part. He did so by a variety of tactics, which included permitting the legal system to deal with the Personal Status Laws without presidential intervention. Recognizing that one of his own chief claims to political legitimacy is that he himself obeys the law,[6] President Mubarak, like everyone else in Egypt, decided to wait for the High Constitutional Court to decide the fate of the 1979 changes in the Personal Status Laws. By supporting legality and declining to force change on the population, he put some distance between the presidency and the controversy surrounding women's issues and, in the process, helped reduce the intensity of the controversy itself.

When the court rendered its verdict, it ruled that the 1979 laws were unconstitutional because they were first issued by emergency decree in the absence of any genuine emergency. In July, two months after the decision of the court was announced, President Mubarak's political party, the NDP, introduced proposals for reform similar to those of 1979 with one major exception. The right of a wife to a divorce if her husband took a subsequent wife would no longer be virtually automatic. Rather, she would have to prove either moral or material damage and the case would be decided by a judge. Imperfect as they may be, the 1985 amendments to the Personal Status Laws put women in a more advantageous position than they would be in without the new provisions, and much of the credit for their passage in parliament must go to President Mubarak.

This review of the record on women's issues of Presidents Nasser, Sadat, and Mubarak has been necessary in order that the issues confronting their wives could be understood in an historical and institutional context. Each of these women has added a distinctive element to Egyptian political life and a biographical sketch of each, based on interviews conducted for this book, is warranted. This will set the stage for a general consideration of the main functions of presidential wives in Egypt and a discussion of the principal issues associated with their role in Egypt's political system.

BIOGRAPHICAL SKETCHES

Tahia Kazem was born in Cairo, attended a local school, and was raised in the conventional manner common to middle-class Egyptian families in the years between the two world wars.[7] Her father was a successful tea merchant who had migrated from Iran when he was eighteen years old. Her mother was Egyptian, born in Tanta. Both parents died when Tahia was still in school. This event curtailed her formal education, and for about the next six years she lived with her brother, Abdul Hamied Kazem, owner of a rug factory. Growing up in the 1920s in a comfortable middle-class family, Tahia had learned to play the piano at home and learned French and proper Arabic at St. Joseph's School. Although her family was quite traditional in most ways, she remained unmarried past her teens. Abdul Hamied Kazem was a friend of Khalil Hussein, the uncle of Gamal Abdel Nasser, and in 1943 Nasser and Tahia Kazem were introduced at her brother's home. About a year later they were married. She was an educated, attractive, conservative, urban Muslim woman with a comfortable income of her own, inherited from her father. Gamal Abdel Nasser was the son of a postal clerk in Alexandria, but spent part of his early life in rural Egypt and retained those early rural roots.

By the time of their marriage, he had been graduated from the military academy. He held the rank of captain and his political involvement was as yet minimal compared to what it became a few years later.[8] He was twenty-six, she was twenty-two, and they settled down to a relatively conventional life, with Tahia concentrating on homemaking and Gamal devoting himself to his career and to politics. She became aware of his political activity "right after the marriage." Within less than a decade, he was the master of Egypt and she was the wife of pharaoh. She raised their children, kept house, and stayed out of the public eye most of the time. Affairs of state were discussed at home and she expressed her views freely. For the most part, however, Gamal

Abdel Nasser wanted his home to be a place where he could relax and be a "normal" husband and father. A public person, he also had a carefully protected private life, centered around his wife and children.

When the revolution occurred, Tahia and Gamal Abdel Nasser had been married for eight years. They had four children, Hoda, Mona, Khalid, and Abdul Hamied. Tahia's life revolved around her husband and the children, the oldest of whom was only six years old. Neither parent looked back on a particularly happy childhood. She had had all the material benefits of middle-class life, but found such things alone did not yield happiness. He was shunted about between his father's home, his uncle's, and a boarding school, and "was never close to his father."[9] Perhaps because of this, home life took on special importance for them. As busy as he was, he devoted as much time as possible to his children, playing ping-pong and chess with them and, when they were older, teaching them how to drive a car. Tahia ran the household, helped the children with school work, played the piano. Three years after the revolution a fifth child, Abdel Hakim, was born. With a houseful of infants, it is not surprising that the public saw little of Nasser's wife but, in the 1950s and 1960s, she did play a modest role in Egyptian public life.

Prior to 1952, the women of the nobility and royal family had been involved conspicuously in public life, and occasionally in public scandals. As a deliberate contrast, the wives of the Free Officers who overthrew the monarchy were seldom seen and never heard, especially at first. Even though this was the general rule, when a visiting head of state was accompanied by his wife, Mrs. Nasser was involved noticeably in the attendant ceremonies and receptions. For example, in 1955 when Yugoslav President Tito came to Egypt, he brought his wife and Mrs. Nassar joined in the official welcome.[10] She and the children also traveled with the president on his trips to Yugoslavia. In 1964, when Nikita Khruschev and his wife visited Egypt, Mrs. Nasser was involved in the official receptions and dinners for the Soviet guests. She played the role of official hostess more frequently as the children grew older and "always helped to create a warmer and friendlier atmosphere."[11]

President Nasser died in September 1970. He had been the center of Tahia Kazem's life, and adjustment proved difficult. She has continued to live in the family home. One son still lives with her, and she sees her other children, grandchildren, and old friends frequently.

She travels occasionally, visits friends, goes to the theater, and remembers the past. The record does not show Tahia Kazem ever having played, or wanting to play, a direct role in Egyptian political life, except that she has been a regular voter since women were given the franchise in 1956. As a presidential wife, she was neither forced to adopt a role which she would have found uncomfortable, nor was she constrained by her husband from being more active in public life. She would have liked to travel with him more often and, in general, spend more time with him than proved possible.

Jihan Safwat Raouf was born and raised on Roda Island in Cairo. She and her brothers and sisters attended school near the family home, but before finishing secondary school she met and married Mohammad Anwar al-Sadat. Her father was a low-level Egyptian government employee. Her mother was English.[12] During World War II her mother, Agnes, was proud of the stand the British made in the Battle of Britain. Safwat Raouf, on the other hand, was a staunch Egyptian patriot and pro-German because he wanted the British out of Egypt. Jihan was close to both her parents and her sisters, but even as a preteen child was more interested in politics than either of her parents or any of her siblings. A streak of romanticism was also evident at this early age, and in the mid-1940s she followed what she considered to be the heroic anti-government activities of the Muslim Brotherhood. She also became interested in the story of a young army officer who had been arrested and charged with the murder of Amin Osman, former minister of finance, on January 6, 1946.

His trial did not take place until January, 1948, and lasted until August of the same year when "Sadat was released without conviction after the principal defendant, Hussein Tewfik, escaped."[13] The assassination, trial, and circumstances of his release made Sadat a revolutionary hero in Jihan's eyes. Although he was from a poor, rural background and was neither rich nor handsome, she wanted to meet him. She got her chance shortly after his release from jail when they were introduced in Suez at the home of Jihan's cousin, who was married to Hassan Izzat, an early business colleague of Sadat. While in jail, Anwar Sadat had decided to divorce his first wife and seek another who would be a more suitable companion for a man who felt himself destined to have a major role to play in the political life of Egypt.[14] Apparently, it was love at first sight. He proposed to Jihan on September 19, 1948, and they were married on May 29, 1949, shortly after she turned sixteen. He was thirty.

In the first three years of their marriage, they moved at least three times and Anwar Sadat went into business. He was also reinstated as a captain in the army and posted to Rafah, in the northern Sinai. Following this reinstatement, he resumed his political career, officially becoming a member of the Free Officer Movement in late 1951.[15] He was stationed in Rafah when the coup took place which overthrew the monarchy, and he came to Cairo to participate in the event. Unfortunately on the day of the revolution, he and Jihan were at the movies, sitting through a triple feature. He did, however, get a message from Nasser that he was wanted at military headquarters, and eventually Sadat joined his colleagues and was given the honor of announcing the revolution on the radio.

Tahia Kazem and Jihan Raouf had little in common and, apparently, were never close. Both, however, were wives of Free Officers and conformed to a common pattern of near public invisibility for most of the next eighteen years. The Nassers had children already, but it was not until 1954 that the first child, Lubna, was born to the Sadats. Three more were to follow, with the last, named after her mother, born in 1961.

Until the late 1960s, none of the spouses of the Free Officers pursued any careers other than wife and mother. In a 1957 interview with an Egyptian magazine, Anwar Sadat expressed views regarding women which conformed to the official ideology of the regime. The interview is worth quoting at length.

Question: Do you share secrets of your job with your wife?

Answer: Never. I believe in the values I learned in my village and was brought up with. Working is the duty of the man, and secrets of my work should not be discussed at home.

Question: Do you apply the principle of equality with your wife and female relatives? Do you encourage them to participate in social and political work?

Answer: As for my wife, she has no time except for bringing up our children. This is a great responsibility which is no less important than any social or political work. In fact it is the main responsibility in building a society. Now I believe that educating girls is more [important] than educating boys. We should provide the girl with a weapon with which she could defend her needs and right to live.

Question: Why don't the wives of Revolutionary Council leaders appear in official ceremonies?

Answer: We have revolted against our shameful past, when our women and wives of rulers used to appear in an unrespectful manner under the banner of charity organizations or in official ceremonies. That is why we prevented our wives from attending official ceremonies until we change the old idea. Our women will appear in the manner that suits a country which respects its traditions, customs, and religion.

Question: As a Muslim, what do you think of the female uniform [Islamic dress], on the condition that it would be applicable?

Answer: I don't demand, but wish that the female uniform here would be like the female uniform in Indonesia. This uniform, besides being beautiful, is compatible with religion. I asked my wife to wear it, but did not order her.[16]

When he gave this interview, Anwar Sadat was chairman of the National Union, women had been given the vote only a year before, and two women had just been elected to parliament. Jihan was at home with three children, two girls and a boy, and was only twenty-four years old. Ten years later, however, she was no longer so house-bound, and the strictures against the wives of the country's leaders had begun to be relaxed. In the mid-1960s, Mrs. Sadat organized a weekly study group with some of her women friends, to which they invited experts to give lectures on a variety of subjects. They also collected money for Egyptian and Palestinian charities. However, it was not until the June War of 1967 that she began to be more active in public life, concentrating on voluntary social work, for which she now gained a new respect.

Prior to this time, she had accepted the official line that the women involved in such work were doing it "just for show. . . . something in the newspapers . . . and that's all." When she donated blood, visited the wounded, and worked in other activities of the Red Crescent, she changed her mind. The 1967 War was a military and psychological defeat for the people and leaders of Egypt. Anwar Sadat recorded the effect it had on him in his autobiography: "I was dazed and unable to locate myself in time or space."[17] Mrs. Sadat, by contrast, seems to have been invigorated by the experience of her voluntary social work, and she told him stories of her work to try to raise his morale. Later in the same year, she started her own private voluntary agency at Tala, in Menofia governorate in the delta, concentrating on giving women usable skills and enabling them to earn a cash income. This project can be viewed from many perspectives, but one obvious and important aspect was that it was an effort by privileged urban women to do "something useful" by helping poor rural women learn how to help themselves. As Mrs. Sadat said in retrospect in 1983: "Women who are working have confidence in themselves, they don't rely or depend on their husbands too much, because they have their own salary. They feel secure."

The private voluntary social activities Mrs. Sadat has been involved in since 1967 are too numerous to mention, but the substantive focus was on efforts to help women, children, and the disabled. In the late 1960s and early 1970s, her projects were small and she received no help from the government. This began to change, however, after 1970, when Anwar Sadat became president of Egypt. In the post–1973 War period, Mrs. Sadat, encouraged by her husband, became one of the most active people in Egyptian public life, and her social activities grew in number and scope. Some government assistance was evident, and numerous organizations received funds, volunteers, and publicity that probably would not have come their way had it not been for their links with Mrs. Sadat.

Jihan Raouf was the wife of the president of Egypt from 1970 until 1981. She was an active matchmaker and, during this period, saw each of the four Sadat children married into prominent Egyptian families. The children entered Cairo University, but they were not the only members of the family to do so. Mrs. Sadat had always wanted to complete her formal education and now had both the opportunity and a greater need to realize this ambition. As the wife of the president, Mohammad Heikal says derisively, she sought private tutoring in Egyptology because "she would have to meet and make conversation with distinguished foreign visitors."[18] If all she wanted was to be able to engage in conversation over a range of subjects, a degree was not necessary: home study and reading would have sufficed. She also wanted, however, to prepare herself for a professional career. In the process, she became a highly visible role model for other women. She decided she needed additional formal education, and in 1972 took the British secondary school exam, the G.C.E. (General Certificate of

Education). Having done well on those exams, she entered Cairo University in 1973, the year of the October War with Israel. Her husband urged her to study English because he thought it would be easier for her, but she preferred Arabic literature. In 1978 she received her B.A. in that subject and was admitted to the graduate program. In 1980, she defended her master's thesis, a study of the impact of the English poet, Shelley, on Arabic literature in Egypt.[19] She then became a junior member of the faculty of Cairo University and began work on her doctoral dissertation.

During her husband's presidency, Mrs. Sadat had influence and was not shy about using it, especially on behalf of women. Her public life was an ongoing declaration that women were entitled to become educated, to work outside the home, and to have and express political opinions. If she could do it, others could too. Although there is no record of her having been interested in women's issues in the 1950s or early 1960s, by the mid-1970s she had become the most visible articulator of feminist concerns in Egypt. She joined numerous women's associations and often became their nominal leader. Whenever possible, she used her position to try to advance the cause of women. For example, she lobbied her husband and other leaders for the eventually successful effort to reform the Personal Status Laws. She had the cooperation of most feminist leaders and of the minister of social affairs, but Mrs. Sadat was the most important driving force behind this change. Both opponents and proponents came to refer to these laws as "Jihan's laws." She also worked to get Aisha Rateb appointed as the first woman ambassador, an effort which succeeded in 1979. The idea to have reserved seats for women in parliament was hers, the product of a trip to the Sudan in the late 1970s, where she became aware that Sudanese women already had this right. She discussed it with her husband at the time, but no change was made. Later, when the 1979 elections were held, she raised the issue with him again and persuaded President Sadat to give the idea his personal support. He then assigned the task of getting the necessary legal changes made to Dr. Amal Othman, the Minister of Social Affairs. Mrs. Sadat's involvement did not stop there. When it came time for the National Democratic Party to consider nominations for women to run under the Party's banner, and thus be almost guaranteed victory, Mrs. Sadat participated in the selection process. As she stated in a 1983 interview with me, "I nominated some women whom I felt and still feel . . . are active and can give our country a lot."

Mrs. Sadat was not involved in or consulted regarding all of the most important decisions of the Sadat presidency. For example, she was not involved in plans pertaining to the October War, the Open Door policy, or Sadat's trip to Jerusalem in 1977. Mohammad Heikal, a confidant of both Nasser and Sadat, remembers that on many matters of domestic politics, "Jehan became Sadat's eyes and ears" and helped to provide him with information about what was going on in Egypt.[20] She was also the recipient of numerous complaints and petitions for help, and because she met people the President did not meet, served as an important conduit of information, of both good and bad news, to the president and other officials.

The record of Jihan Raouf as wife of the president of Egypt can be interpreted in a variety of ways. It is not possible, however, to ignore the fact that she became a public figure in her own right and, in the process, the focal point for considerable controversy which helped fuel criticism of her husband's regime.[21] The problem began in the early 1970s and one of the first issues was the title, the First Lady of Egypt, conferred on her by her husband in 1971. This was regarded as an American affectation, an import which had no roots in the Egyptian soil.

The Sadat regime was the political equivalent of a roller-coaster; a series of high and low points, with a slow start, a shuddering conclusion, and plenty of thrills along the way. Throughout the 1970s and early 1980s, Mrs. Sadat contributed to the roller-coaster atmosphere by involving herself heavily in numerous social, charitable, and political activities. Wherever she went and whatever she did, the Egyptian media followed. Occasionally, the foreign media did so as well, not always with happy results. For example, in 1978 she gave an interview to a female free-lance journalist who sold the interview to *Playgirl* magazine.[22] Although pornography was (and is) forbidden to be imported into Egypt, a few copies became available and, among politically conscious Egyptians, the scandal of Mrs. Sadat's interview appearing in the same magazine as nude male photos was the talk of the town for months. In this instance, Mrs. Sadat was the victim of her own naiveté: she did not know the interview would appear in such a publication. This incident, however, illustrates how publicity can have unintended, and often negative, consequences. She was not deterred by this experience but was more cautious with journalists after that event. An even bigger controversy took place in 1979, when Mrs. Sadat sponsored a jet-set gala near the pyramids, complete with

music by Frank Sinatra, and, for the women, special make-up by Rev-
lon and a Pierre Balmain fashion show.[23] In a country as poor as Egypt,
and with extremely conservative mores for public behavior, highly
publicized events such as this were scandalous, and a godsend to the
opposition, who linked fig-leaf bikinis at the 1979 party with Sadat's
Open Door economic policy of 1974 and his Camp David agreements
with Israel and the United States.

Some of the criticism of Jihan Sadat was directed against the
substance of what she did, but in other cases it was because of the
publicity associated with her actions. A good example of this occurred
in 1980, with the nationally televised defense of her master's thesis.
The intention was to demonstrate that she earned the degree and was
not given it because she was the First Lady. Also, it was to show that
women could receive an advanced degree. Those points were lost in
the criticism which followed the event, regarded by most Egyptian
academics as another excess of the Sadat regime, an ostentatious pursuit of publicity for its own sake.[24]

When Jihan Sadat was the first lady of Egypt, she acquired and
exercised political power. She was an important part of her husband's
efforts to "modernize" and update Egypt, and she served as his help-
mate in a variety of ways. She provided him with information and
advice, entertained his foreign and Egyptian guests, and shared the
job with him of representing Egypt to the world. She also served as
an advocate of various causes, especially that of women, and is at least
partly responsible for changes in the laws affecting women and the
family, as well as laws regarding the participation of women in politics. By associating herself with the feminist movement, and using her
position to give it impetus, she helped to make Egypt different from
what it was.

Her power and influence, however, were dependent upon her
husband's position, and when he was assassinated on October 6, 1981,
her base of operations was destroyed. The perquisites of power, the
hangers-on and fair-weather friends, the phalanx of insulating body-
guards disappeared. Within a year Jihan Sadat receded into the background, spending time with her children and grandchildren, teaching
at Cairo University, and working to finish her doctoral dissertation,
a study of the influence of romanticism on Arabic literature in Egypt
between World War I and World War II. She also lectured outside
of Egypt on peace, the problems of women, and aid for the handi-

capped. Interviewed in 1983 and 1984, she stated that she believes the gains made in 1979 must be preserved and, for the future, the problems of working women are at the top of her list of women's issues in Egypt. She hoped the government would continue to provide them with assistance. In addition, she felt it was unlikely that she would ever again play a role in Egypt's politics. In 1985 she was not involved in any major way in the process which led to the passage of new Personal Status Laws. If, however, a new political party with Sadatist principles were to be formed, it would be easy to imagine Jihan Sadat as being one of its main leaders, perhaps even its driving force.

Suzanne Saleh Sabet was born in the upper Egyptian town of Minya, but her father soon moved the family to Cairo, where she and her brothers were raised.[25] Her father was an Egyptian physician who met and married his British wife, a hospital matron, when he was a medical student at Cardiff. Saleh Sabet worked for the Ministry of Health, but after moving to Egypt his wife did not continue with her profession, concentrating on her home and family. Although many physicians' wives donated time to charitable organizations, Mrs. Sabet did not. Suzanne grew up in a comfortable middle-class, urban Muslim home and spent a great amount of time with her parents. She was, however, raised somewhat differently from her cousins on her father's side of the family. In an interview in the spring of 1984, she attributed this difference to

> having a foreign mother. . . . I had more freedom. I was participating in the swimming team; I took ballet lessons; I was always at the club for the swim team or with the dancing school. I was allowed to go on trips to Alexandria with the swimming team. . . . Maybe that might have led to some feeling of independence.

She was trusted by her parents, but "I was not completely free to do what I liked, to be out late, or go to the club dancing parties." Her early experiences helped give her the ability to function independently, an asset which was to become vital in later years.

Suzanne Sabet was educated in local schools, learning English in addition to Arabic. She was still a student at St. Clair's School in Zeitoun, a suburb of Cairo, when she met Hosny Mubarak. He had joined the Egyptian Air Force in 1950 and became an instructor at the Air Academy in 1952, remaining there until 1959. Suzanne's brother joined the academy and, upon graduation, invited his teacher home for dinner. Further visits followed and Suzanne Sabet and Hosny Mubarak were engaged in 1957 and married in 1958. He was thirty, she was seventeen, and for the next several years they lived the typical life of a military family. He was career-oriented and upwardly mobile and held a series of important posts before and after his marriage, until he became vice president of Egypt in 1975. He came from a tradi-tional rural family. His father was a lawyer who worked for the government. He was, however, at least as much a product of his military education as of his early background and was "very different" in his wife's eyes from the rest of his family at the time.

A combat pilot and a teacher, Hosny Mubarak was good at both tasks. As his wife explained in 1984, "Ever since we were married, he was always in an important job." Many of his assignments were dangerous, and most kept him away from home for prolonged periods of time. He flew several bombing missions to Yemen during the Egyptian involvement in the Yemen War, and spent the 1964–65 academic year without his family in the Soviet Union, taking a special course on Soviet jets at the Frunze Military Academy.

During this busy time of the early 1960s, Suzanne gave birth to and raised their two boys and kept the Mubarak home quiet and peaceful. For the next several years her husband was on call or living on a military base rather than at home, and his life was frequently at risk. Social life was limited and sporadic, mainly involving get-togethers with fellow officers and their wives. Like her mother, Suzanne devoted her life to her husband and children. She also remained close to her own parents and learned to cope with the challenges of being a military wife, including the fear. In 1984, she still remembered "the feeling of seeing him packing up in the middle of the night to go on a mission. You have to live with it and just try to push it away from your mind, but it is there. . . . It was a very hard life."

The 1960s and early 1970s were difficult years for the Mubarak family, but not unhappy. Both husband and wife had the satisfaction of a job well done. For Suzanne, the task of raising children was especially gratifying. "I enjoyed it. I loved doing it. I never for a moment thought of doing anything else. I was very happy." In 1969, however, the youngest child started school, and the symmetry of her life was disrupted. On that day she made the decision to continue her own education. Neither her husband, who by this time was Air Force Chief of Staff, nor her parents encouraged her at first, fearing she would not be able to cope with the responsibilities of wife, mother, and student. A year later, she had convinced her husband at least to let her try, and in 1970 she started classes to prepare for the British G.C.E.

She passed the examinations in 1971 and began to think about what to do next. Her youngest child was only eight years old, and Suzanne's duties as wife and mother were still her top priorities. It was then that she heard about the American University in Cairo (A.U.C.) and discovered she could, if necessary, attend as a part-time student. Her English was good and so, in February 1972, she and a woman she met while studying for the G.C.E., enrolled at A.U.C. She was known to her teachers and fellow students as Suzanne Sabet, not Suzanne Mubarak. Occasionally, especially after 1975 when her husband became vice president of Egypt, family responsibilities caused her to take a reduced academic load of three or four courses rather than the usual five. She persevered and, in June 1977, Suzanne Sabet graduated with honors in political science from A.U.C.

Among the things she acquired in her classes was an increased awareness of the devastating impact poverty has on children. She decided to do something about it and, shortly after her husband became vice president, Suzanne and a few women friends, in effect, adopted a public school in Boulaq, one of Cairo's worst slum districts. She had no previous experience in charitable organizations but learned quickly. Her project required work with teachers, administrators, and various government officials to upgrade the school. She and her covolunteers worked in the school, raised money for various projects, and tried to get appropriate government ministries to provide the basic services they were supposed to provide. As she put it: "You don't just go to school and provide a few things. The problems there are buildings, pipes, sewage, cleaning; the whole environment around the school, not just inside the school. We can't do it; we are just an organization. We don't have contractors; we don't have engineers. We can't go digging roads and digging up streets." Within eight years, the Boulaq project had expanded to cover eleven schools, affected thousands of young boys and girls, and had a proven ability to upgrade basic services in and near the adopted schools. Within the same period, Suzanne Sabet's own life changed. In 1981, her husband became President of Egypt. In 1982, she completed a master's degree in sociology/ anthropology at A.U.C., basing her thesis on the Boulaq project.[26]

From the outset of his presidency, it was clear that Hosny Mubarak would approach his office with a different style than that of his predecessor, whose flamboyance contrasted sharply with the stolidity of Mubarak. Although he quickly became the center of attention in Egypt, his wife did not. In fact, for quite some time she had almost no media exposure. Within a week the new president ordered the Egyptian press to leave his family alone. An Egyptian journalist I know telephoned for an appointment to interview the "First Lady" and was told "Egypt has no First Lady."

When Anwar Sadat was assassinated, Hosny Mubarak was with him, and both Jihan Sadat and Suzanne Mubarak were shocked witnesses to the event. It took Suzanne Mubarak a few months to adjust to the circumstances of her new life. Traumatized by the assassination of Sadat and her husband's escape from the same fate, she began rebuilding her world by concentrating on trying to keep a "normal" prepresidential family life intact for herself, her husband, and their two sons. She also worked on the Boulaq project and her master's thesis, which she defended in May, 1982. As was the case when she completed her B.A., she did not attend the graduation ceremony, preferring to receive the degree in absentia. Only a few people knew that the Suzanne Sabet listed in the program was the wife of the president of Egypt.

As has each of her predecessors, Suzanne Mubarak has had to define the role of wife of the president for herself, taking into consideration the circumstances of the time and her own talents and personality. She discussed the problems with many people, including the president, but in the end had to decide for herself. It was not easy because, she said, "You are on your own. You're really on your own." As of the spring of 1984, the role she had selected for herself was multifaceted but did not include frequent photographic appearances in the Egyptian news media. This fits her personality, as she is "a little bit timid, . . . a little bit shy—maybe shy of the cameras. . . . It's not my nature." She also believes her decision not to appear often in the media is wise politically, and will help "calm things down" in the wake of criticism of Mrs. Sadat's frequent appearances on television and in photographs in the daily newspapers. Her avoidance of the news media, however, and the fact that she does not use the title of first lady, may be somewhat misleading, for she is quite active in public life, striving for a "happy medium" between the examples suggested by Mrs. Nasser and Mrs. Sadat. In addition to traveling with her husband when he goes abroad, she greets the wives of foreign dignitaries and acts as hostess at state dinners. Furthermore, she is active in the Boulaq project and the Cancer Society, and has helped organize what might be called a neighborhood improvement society for Heliopolis, the Cairo suburb where the Mubaraks live.

Like Jihan Sadat, Suzanne Mubarak is a self-conscious role model for other women, particularly those married to powerful men. The success of the Boulaq project is now clear enough that she feels she can encourage other women, particularly the wives of provincial governors, to start similar organizations in other areas, using their personal access to decision makers on behalf of the improvement of selected schools in poor areas. Similarly, in 1984, her Heliopolis program opened Egypt's first truly public library. These activities are valid ends in themselves, but they also serve as important demonstration projects for others to emulate and for which they may take credit. She has chosen one field in which to be active — education — and does not believe there are any short-term solutions to Egypt's problems. Before progress can be made, basic services, especially in education, must be improved. Even when asked about the problems of women, she brought the subject back to education:

> I think that many of the problems facing women today are due to the problem of illiteracy. . . . In spite of all that has been done, all the expansion in education we have had since the revolution, still, illiteracy is a persistent phenomenon, of course more in the rural areas and more . . . among the poor. With education, well . . . their self-images are different; their perceptions of life will be different. We will be able to deal with them on matters of family planning, matters of getting women out to work, to better their living, which will solve so many problems of our families.

She is also aware of the class dimensions of the problem and of the need to narrow the gap between the privileged and underprivileged by raising the achievement levels of those on the bottom of the socioeconomic pyramid.

Many people in Egypt, when they are inclined to talk about women, say, "Ah, of course, education. Women are educated, and we are proud to have a minister, we are proud to have an ambassador, we have 30% women faculty members." But is that the Egyptian society? It's quite different . . . with millions of Egyptian women who are still illiterate, who are still living under very, very, hard conditions. . . . The gap is very wide.

With regard to the Personal Status Laws and the participation of women in politics, Mrs. Mubarak supported the 1979 reforms and in 1984 felt that, for the forseeable future, emphasis should be placed on women learning how to exercise their rights more than on seeking additional legal reforms. One thing she did not intend to do, however, was get involved in the political process herself. For example, she played no role in the selection of candidates, whether male or female, for the National Democratic Party's list for parliamentary election in 1984. She stated: "I'm not involved in politics, and I don't think the wife of a president should be. It's not her role. She was not elected."

While she may avoid party politics, Mrs. Mubarak has undertaken at least one important policy-related role. As the president's wife, she is able to be the bearer of bad news. Due to her involvement in voluntary social work, she probably gets out among ordinary people more than he does, and she sees things and hears about problems which she thinks he, or other government officials, should know about. She acknowledges that "my husband likes to come home to a nice quiet atmosphere, no tensions, no complaints, no grumbles." She is also aware that:

I meet a different category of people than he does, so I think it's very important to convey to the president, in a nice way, certain ideas from these people. . . . There's a way of getting the message through, but . . . you don't have to shock him with it. . . . It's also his privilege, in addition to having a quiet home, even if you have bad news, to bring back the news, because these are the ideas that are being generated in society, that are outside his world. I know . . . he has official channels where all this comes to him, but nevertheless, certain things might not reach him as they should.

Suzanne Mubarak is conscious of the complementary nature of her role with that of her husband. He has been concerned with political stability; she has tried to help "calm things down." He has traveled frequently on behalf of Egypt, and has invited many world leaders to visit him; she has accompanied him on most of his trips and has acted as his hostess at home. He has concentrated on improving the economic infrastructure and basic services; she has worked to make slum schools better. He has permitted relatively free and democratic elections to take place; she has not become involved in the political process other than to vote. She has wanted to continue her pre-1981 social work; he has encouraged her to do so, demonstrating that complementarity, for them, works both ways.

CONCLUSION: THE ROLES OF PRESIDENTIAL WIVES IN EGYPT

The post-revolutionary history of Egypt offers three relatively distinct examples of what the role of wife of the president of Egypt is all about. Mrs. Nasser, in the somewhat puritanical early days of the Free Officers, was the wife of a folk hero. It was necessary for her to be perceived as different from the wives of pre-revolutionary leaders such as Mrs. Nahas Pasha. As a consequence, she had little public life. Mrs. Sadat, as part of her husband's effort to be different from Nasser, came to be involved extensively in the public arena. Mrs. Mubarak, seeking a "happy medium" between extremes, is active, but not particulary visible, emphasizing discretion over publicity. These obvious and historically conditioned differences aside, it is important to identify the roles Egypt's presidential wives have and have not played. In the process of identifying and discussing these roles, the idiosyncratic aspects of the postures adopted by Mrs. Nasser, Mrs. Sadat, and Mrs. Mubarak should not be forgotten. Each had to deal with a different set of personal and political circumstances and do so at a particular time in Egypt's history. Given the fact that each of these women has faced unique circumstances, it is interesting that they have so much in common.

All three presidential wives come from an urban, middle-class, Muslim background. They do not come from the same section of the middle class—Jihan Sadat's background was less prosperous than either of the others — but all had at least some of the benefits of middle-class comfort. Furthermore, all three had a non-Egyptian parent and grew up in a family in which Egypt was not the only point of reference.[27] Two of the three were attracted to the arts while young. Tahia Kazem learned to play the piano and Suzanne Sabet studied ballet. Only one, Jihan Raouf, developed an early interest in politics. All three received roughly the same type of education while young, and all stopped going to school at roughly the same age. Even though two of the three were to return to school later in life, none went directly to university from high school.

Compared to the parliamentary women discussed in chapter 2, all three presidential wives married young. None had children within the first year of marriage, but all had children later and enjoyed raising them and managing the household.

All three of the women discussed in this chapter considered it an important part of their job as wife of the president of Egypt to provide the president with the type of home atmosphere he wanted and needed. To these men, home was a refuge from a tense world of conflict, a place where they could recuperate, revive, and live a semblance of a normal life. The task of providing this atmosphere has been one of the most important functions of Egypt's presidential wives. Even on a light day, when things are going well, the president of Egypt must cope with problems of imperialism, poverty, treachery, bureaucracy, sycophancy, and the labyrinthine ways of inter-Arab politics. To enable them to handle the resultant daily stress, their wives have carried a heavy burden and played a necessary, if hidden, role in Egyptian politics.

Associated with this are at least three additional functions. They served as hostess for both domestic political and diplomatic events. Mrs. Nasser studied English, and Mrs. Sadat studied Egyptian history and culture, in order to perform this role better than they might otherwise have done. They also discussed affairs of state with their husbands and offered advice and counsel when appropriate. So far as is known, however, none has been involved in making decisions on such important issues as the nationalization of the Suez Canal or the October War. Of the three, only Mrs. Sadat has been associated directly with the making of legislation, and she confined her activity to laws pertaining to women. All three, on the other hand, served on occasion as a conduit of information to the president from officials and diplomats. Both Mrs. Sadat and Mrs. Mubarak have also done this with other high officials. In this regard, all three presidential wives have contributed to the flow of information among those involved in the high levels of government in Egypt.

Mrs. Sadat and Mrs. Mubarak have engaged in voluntary social work and both also started a voluntary agency and worked in it actively. Mrs. Sadat, however, had a much more prominent record than Mrs. Mubarak and was seen frequently on Egyptian television and in newspapers at various charitable events. Mrs. Mubarak is active, but since President Mubarak came to office, Dr. Amal Othman, Minister of Social Affairs, became more visible, doing many of the ceremonial activities undertaken formerly by Mrs. Sadat. This reflected a policy choice of the Mubarak regime to have this role played by a cabinet officer whose job included formal responsibility for private voluntary agencies.

Mrs. Sadat is the only one of the three women studied in this chapter who became a public personality and political force in her own right. Mrs. Sadat is unique also in that she alone of the three became a center of controversy in mainstream Egyptian politics. Opposition focused on the propriety of what she did and how she did it, but mainly on the fact that she was too public and that her husband did not limit her activities. Thus, criticism of her was criticism of him.

The wife of a president can help her husband and her country a great deal, especially if she concentrates on activity about which there if no controversy. She can help him cope with stress, make sure he receives important information, even if it contains bad news, and help create a warmer and more comfortable atmosphere at diplomatic and political meetings. It is also possible for her to exercise political influence, particularly on behalf of a cause or issue about which she is well informed and known to care a great deal, but this must be done carefully or she will give ammunition to the political opposition, who may attack her for abusing her husband's position and violating social conventions. Although there are no written rules or constitutional guidelines for her, the wife of the president of Egypt has a vital job. In addition to the tasks mentioned above, she is an important role model for Egyptian women and perhaps others as well. In this regard, she faces a paradox. If she is too active, or more to the point, perceived to be too active, she will violate traditional norms and incur allegations of shame. If not active enough, she will be accused by feminists and others of betraying those Egyptian women who have fought so hard and who have so much yet to gain.

Confronted with this dilemma, it is easy to suggest that presidential wives and, by implication, the spouses of other important men, should pursue the golden mean. In the midst of rapid social, economic, and political change, however, the path of moderation may be difficult to define in concrete terms. It may also be too idealistic to expect anyone to stay on such a path for long, even if they find it, given the absence of formal constitutional guidelines.

Opposition Women

THE POLITICAL OPPOSITION IN EGYPT

U NITED ONLY by its stance vis-à-vis the government, the political opposition in Egypt has been rich in talent and eccentricity, characterized by diversity, a penchant for hyperbole and self-righteousness, and restrained as often by the fear of force as by force itself. For most of Egypt's postrevolutionary history, being a member of the opposition has been dangerous but satisfying to the soul. Some opposition politicians may have been charlatans and opportunists, seeking mainly some short-term personal advantage, but most of the leaders have been honest in their opposition. All of the women mentioned in this chapter consider themselves to be sincere patriots, prepared to make considerable sacrifices for their version of political morality. In a country which places a high premium on consensus, some have been jailed and all have suffered in one way or another because of their opposition to or criticism of the government.

Before discussing the women selected to represent the female members of the postrevolutionary political opposition in Egypt, it is necessary to consider briefly two general questions. First, what are the major issues that have tended to arouse the ire of the opposition in Egypt? As a corollary to this question: what specific issues have concerned women? Second, what is the basic institutional structure or framework within which the political opposition has functioned?

What groups, parties, or forums have existed for the expression of rebellion, rejection, or criticism?

These two sets of questions, one dealing with motivation or ideology, the other with institutions and organizations, cannot be understood outside of the context of history. What follows is brief and is not intended to be a comprehensive study of the opposition in Egypt. It is included in order to provide readers with some sense of the ideological and institutional milieu within which the women in Egypt's political opposition have moved since 1952.

Why rebel? More specifically, why rebel in Egypt *after* the Free Officers' Revolution of 1952? Some rejected the legitimacy of the new system, while others denounced only specific policies, people or programs, but many people found a great deal to anger them. Some attempted to bring about change through organized movements, associations, or parties. Others worked as writers or stood as political candidates and challenged the system as independents rather than as members of a party until parties became legal in 1979.

Neither a chronological nor an ideological approach yields a satisfactory understanding of the opposition in Egypt. The post-1952 period could be thought of as divided into the Nasser period (1952–70), the Sadat period (1970–81) and the Mubarak period, which began in 1981. Another form of periodization, using an institutional rather than a personalist framework, would divide the 1952–84 era into two blocks of time. The first, 1952–76, was one in which the regime monopolized political activity and no opposition was brooked. The second, 1976–84, marked the beginning of political liberalization: opposition parties were formed, and opposition newspapers and magazines were published. Ideologically, it would be possible to think of Egyptian political forces in conventional terms of right, left and center, or, in a slightly more complicated version, conservative, liberal, socialist, communist, fascist, or anarchist. The problem is that all ideological and chronological frameworks oversimplify the Egyptian political landscape, even though each casts some light on Egyptian politics.

Presidents do dominate the system and much of political activity has been characterized by support for, or opposition to the president, but many opposition leaders have concentrated their ire on specific policies or laws and have not formulated their ideas as opposition to the president in power. For example, opposing the Personal Status Laws has not necessarily meant opposition to Nasser, Sadat, or Mu-

barak. Another inadequacy of the conventional framework is illustrated
by considering the case of the Ikwan al-Muslimeen (Muslim Brotherhood). It has been part of the opposition to the Egyptian system of
government since its formation by Hassan al-Banna in 1928.[1] To the
Brotherhood, the issue has been more the system itself than the particular leader of the moment. Its members support the establishment
of an Islamic state and government according to the principles of Islamic law. However, there have been significant variations to its tac-
tical stance, according to who is in power. Some of its members or
supporters were jailed or executed under Nasser. Under Sadat, others
were jailed or, contradictorily, permitted to publish a magazine. President Mubarak has allowed them to participate in an electoral coalition with an essentially secular opposition political party, the New Wafd.

Ideological confusion also characterizes the opposition, as illustrated by the Socialist Labor Party, which has been thought of since
1978 as leftist, but whose prerevolutionary predecessor, Young Egypt,
was once thought of as fascist. Its program has changed little since
that time.[2]

A profitable way to think about the opposition in Egypt is to consider its diverse elements in the context of the major historical forces
which have dominated Egyptian political life since 1952.[3] These are:

- The Free Officers' Revolution itself and its self-appointed heirs;
- Individuals and groups who believed they represented that
  revolution better than did the government;
- The Wafd Party, which was the major prerevolutionary, nationalist political party;
- The Muslim Brotherhood, a large religious-political movement
  which has advocated an Islamic state and opposed secularism;
- Other political forces which have existed, such as the Com-
  munists, but have not had as great an impact on the community at large.

The first group can be thought of as the government, regardless of
the period of time in question. The other four, including the relatively
minor groups, are the opposition discussed in this chapter. Some of
these categories of people have been organized, but not all political
figures of importance in Egypt have been members of organized move-

ments or parties. Some have preferred to remain independent, including many of the women.

Over the course of the 1952–84 period, several major issues have been perennial highlights of Egyptian opposition politics. Some people objected to the direction of change, others to the pace, while a great many were upset about the methods the government has used to achieve goals. Thus, under Nasser, people objected to "too much" socialism; under Sadat, "too much" capitalism. With Mubarak, opposition figures complain that he has been too slow to make decisions, and that they are still "Waiting for Mubarak."[4] Before the early 1970s, objections were registered against the American presence in Egypt, and, especially after the Camp David Treaty, the opposition has focused on advocating more support for Palestinian rights and the restoration of Egypt's Arab links. There has been a growing sense, shared by leftists as well as Islamicists, that Egypt has lost its Arab personality and much of Egyptian politics since 1977, when Sadat went to Jerusalem, has been a struggle to reestablish Egypt's Arab identity. One issue which has been the most chronic of all, however, has been the demand for political freedom.[5]

The middle class is probably the most politically relevant stratum in Egypt, as its members are those who staff the military, bureaucracy, and schools, and run both public- and private-sector industries. For this class, freedom of speech, press, assembly, the right to organize groups and parties, has taken on growing significance and unites right, left, and center.[6] In the early days of the Free Officers' Revolution, the regime attempted to unite all political forces under a common umbrella, the most important of which was the Arab Socialist Union (ASU). Even though the ASU was designed in some respects after the Stalinist model, it never dominated Egyptian life to the degree the Communist Party dominated the Soviet Union, partly because it was the creature of the state rather than the other way around.[7] In spite of its formal power, the ASU was not always able to control all of its members, even those in the National Assembly or, after 1971, the People's Assembly. Furthermore, even with a formal monopoly on political legitimacy, the ASU could not prevent significant numbers of independent candidates from winning assembly seats in elections. Its increasing debility was evident especially in 1976 when three *manabir* (platforms) — left, right and center — were created out of the ASU and contested elections. These party-like groupings were to have provided a channel for all legitimate political activity; but over sixty independent candidates succeeded in winning seats in the People's Assembly. To the surprise of no one, the center, that is, the government party, won, while the right gained twelve seats and the left only two.[8]

In 1977, a new law permitted the formation of political parties, and in 1979 the ASU was formally abolished. Under the terms of the 1977 Egyptian law, revised in 1979 and 1983, political parties must be approved by a Committee for Political Party Affairs, a part of the government whose members are appointed by the president. All legal parties must state their support for such principles as national unity and social peace, and parties based on religion or class are proscribed.[9] By 1984, five opposition parties were legalized and four contested elections for parliament. Due to the restriction on the formation of parties, not all potentially important groups participated as organized forces in these elections. Most notable was the absence of a Nasserite party.[10] The Muslim Brothers, although unable to form a party of their own, did create an electoral coalition with the New Wafd, and this strange hybrid was the only opposition party to win seats in the People's Assembly in the 1984 elections.

In addition to the right to contest elections, since the late 1970s legal political parties have been able to publish a party newspaper. In the ensuing years, the opposition press has been lively and filled with controversy. These papers, as well as a few older publications such as *Rose al-Youssef* and *Al-Ahram al-Iqtisadi*, form important outlets for nonconventional opinion. As the pages of the party papers are open to nonparty contributors, they are a more representative forum for political debate than parliament, in which the government party held roughly 82 percent of the seats following the 1976 elections, 90 percent after the 1979 elections, and 87 percent after the 1984 elections.

Part of the reason the National Democratic Party won such an overwhelming majority of seats in the 1984 elections was that the rules were stacked in its favor. Law 114 for the year 1983 created a system of proportional representation. By the terms of this law, unless a party wins at least 8 percent of the national vote, it will not get any seats in parliament, and the votes cast for a party which fails to get the 8 percent minimum will be counted as if they had been cast for the party which won the plurality of votes in that district. Also, the seats reserved for women would go to the party winning the plurality of votes in each district with a reserved seat. All thirty-one reserved seats went to the NDP in the May 1984 elections.

While the apportionment of seats in the People's Assembly does not reflect the real balance of forces in the country, the tally of votes for the 1984 election helps to shed light on the dynamics of opposition politics in Egypt. There was electoral violence, and one female candidate was killed. The NDP won a massive victory. But, lopsided results and violence aside, this may have been the most democratic and honestly reported election in Egypt since before the 1952 revolution. Still, the opposition charged that the NDP "forged" the results, and the true strength of the opposition is much greater than election results showed.[11] The published figures revealed that the opposition attracted 27 percent of the total votes cast. Equally important, but difficult to interpret with any certainty, is that only 43 percent of registered voters actually voted. The largest turnout was in rural Egypt, where 61 percent of those registered voted, while in Cairo, presumably the most literate, sophisticated, and politicized area of the country, voter turnout was only 20 percent. In Giza it was 28 percent and in Alexandria 24 percent. The low turnout may indicate considerable cynicism and widespread malaise, and was anticipated.[12] The national vote, by party, was as follows:

Party	Valid Votes	Percent of Total
National Democratic Party	3,756,359	72.99
New Wafd Party	778,131	15.12
Socialist Labor Party	364,040	7.07
Nationalist Unionist Progressive Party	214,587	4.17
Liberal Party	33,448	0.65
	5,146,565	100.00[13]

The NDP list contained many people who identified themselves as social democrats and some who would be inclined to join a Nasserite party if one were available. Nasserites and social democrats could also be found on the SLP and NUPP list. By contrast, some people who could be identified as "Sadatists" were dropped from the NDP list. Thus, Rawya Attia, a social democrat first elected to parliament in 1957, replaced Farkhounda Hassan, a close friend of Mrs. Sadat's, as the NDP women's representative for Giza. Party membership does not imply complete acceptance of a party's platform, and each of the legal parties contained representatives from various portions of the political spectrum. Even the NUPP list contained anomalies, as Marxists shared billing with sheikhs.

The oddest coalition was the basically secular New Wafd, composed largely of people the left refers to as secular right wing, prerevolutionary, neofeudalists; and the Muslim Brotherhood, which advocates an Islamic state and opposes the excesses of capitalism and hereditary privilege. Although the other parties were, to some degree, created by the regime, the New Wafd was a revival of the prerevolutionary Wafd. The "new" secretary-general of the party, Fuad Serag al-Din, held that post when the "old" Wafd was made illegal in 1954. In February, 1978, soon after the changes in the law in 1977, the Wafd resurrected itself. It lasted only four months before it ceased political activity, charging that harassment from the Sadat regime made it impossible for the New Wafd to continue.[14] At the time, it was thought the party had dissolved itself and was no longer a legal entity. Thus, when Serag al-Din tried to revive it again in 1983, anticipating the forthcoming elections for parliament, the government tried to block him, claiming the Wafd no longer existed. A complicated legal battle followed, the details of which need not be recounted here, and the Egyptian courts decided finally that in 1978 all the necessary legal steps to dissolve the New Wafd had not been taken.[15] Therefore, in the fall of 1983, the New Wafd resumed its political activities and, in February, 1984, two of its principal leaders, Fuad Serag al-Din and Ibrahim Farag, won a case in court against the government, which had sought to prohibit them from participating in politics because of their pre-1952 political activity.[16]

Shortly after this case was decided, a de facto electoral alliance between the New Wafd and the Muslim Brotherhood was announced.[17] Thus, the National Democratic Party, which represented continuity and claimed credit for all the achievements of both Nasser and Sadat, was challenged in the 1984 elections by a coalition of organizations with genuine grassroots political support and considerable organizational skill. The NDP won a decisive victory, but the New Wafd gained roughly 15 percent of the popular vote and fifty-eight seats (13 percent) of the 448 chosen by the voters. Although the Wafd platform did not differ markedly from that of the NDP,[18] its list of candidates did, as the Wafd nominated a large number of people from Egypt's most prominent prerevolutionary families and people associated with or supported by the Muslim Brotherhood.

The Egyptian political spectrum is sui generis, and observers should not expect anything more than superficial resemblance to patterns found elsewhere. Nasserites, Sadatists, Marxists, Wafdists, and feminists are mixed with Muslims who seek to establish an Islamic state, Christians who wish to protect minority rights, and humanists who find new injustices to confront with alarming regularity. Women participate in the political process not only as leaders of women but as women leaders, and sixteen of them, representing a cross-section of women in the political opposition, will be discussed now that we have identified salient features of the milieu within which they operate.

WOMEN IN THE POLITICAL OPPOSITION[19]

Formative Years and Family Life

In the elections for parliament in 1984, over 140 women were candidates for office. Roughly 75 percent of these women competed on behalf of an opposition party, but only two were successful, both representing the New Wafd. Olfat Kamel, a veteran Cairo politician and incumbent parliamentarian, and Rizqah al-Balashi, a veiled social worker from Alexandria whose candidacy was supported strongly by the Muslim Brothers, joined the thirty-three NDP women elected to the Majlis al-Shaab. These two women have little in common although they are members of the same party, and they help to illustrate the diverse and sometimes paradoxical position of women in the opposition in Egypt. One attracted votes from one of Cairo's slums, the other from mainly male Islamic fundamentalists. Both added strength to a liberal party headed by a genuine pasha. However, they are not the only significant women in the political opposition, and running for office is not the only important activity for politically active people in Egypt, many of whom consider writing and organizing to be more meaningful than running for office.

Most of the leading women in the political opposition have the same types of family and educational background as the parliamentary women discussed in chapter 2. Some, in fact, served in parliament at some time between 1957 and 1982 and were included in that chapter. The discussion of the formative years of the opposition women will be brief, because the story is similar to that of the more politically orthodox group. The majority come from upper-class or upper-middle-class families, were encouraged by their families, particularly their fathers, and educated. However, some features of the early lives of these women are different from those who serve in parliament.

Most of the female opposition leaders discussed in this chapter come from urban areas. Only 37 percent have clear rural or provincial capital origins, compared with 44 percent of the parliamentary women. Like their parliamentary counterparts, the majority learned "proper," that is, classical, Arabic but are even more likely than parliamentary women to know a foreign language. Eleven of the sixteen are fluent in either English or French, and seven know both languages. In general, women opposition leaders are even better educated than their parliamentary counterparts, 43 percent of whom have university degrees compared to 63 percent of the opposition women. Advanced degrees are also more common among this group, as 38 percent have earned doctorates or masters degrees, whereas only 10 percent of the women who have served in parliament, but who are not included in this group of opposition women, have done so.

Additional significant differences appear when comparing the marital and professional life of these women with those of the establishment. Divorce is almost more common than is a single stable marriage. 38 percent of the opposition women have been divorced at least once. Also, although there is professional diversity among women in the political opposition, virtually all are, or have been, academics, writers, journalists, or leaders of unions or interest group associations. Both their professions and their politics have been central to the lives of these people, helping to account for the relatively high divorce rate and the smaller family size. Even though two members of the group have had four children, the average number of children is below two. Very few are likely to agree with a leading female parliamentarian who said "My house first, then political activity."[20] For most of these women, life has never been as uncomplicated as that. If it were, they would not have become rebels, a role which some were inclined to adopt even as children, but which others picked up much later in life.

Becoming Rebels

For a variety of reasons, the political left has more magnetism for opposition women than has the right. Nearly two-thirds of those discussed in this section are on the left, possibly because the left calls for extensive economic reforms, and women, who are clearly among the poorest of the poor, would benefit from those reforms.[21] Most opposition women also consider themselves to be feminists, and, as most feminists see tradition as part of the source of women's problems, they move leftward politically because the left represents, for them, a challenge to tradition and more hope for women. The right also attracts women, although in fewer numbers, because it offers opportunity for individuals based on ascription or achievement. Whether attracted to the right or the left, many politically active Egyptian women are more inclined to be drawn to the opposition than to the government, but this is not because the government has been against women or has done nothing for them. As indicated in earlier chapters, the reverse is true. Especially since 1952, the Egyptian government has done a great deal to improve the status of women in Egypt. Nevertheless, a number of other factors have impelled women to oppose the government.

Women move toward the opposition for the same kinds of reasons that attract men: ideological conviction or the pull of a particular leader. They are also moved to join the opposition as women, because no matter how much has been done to improve the lot of women in Egypt, it is easy to reach the conclusion that in many ways they are still second-class citizens. Not only is their right to vote or hold office still questioned by many influential people,[22] but aspects of the Personal Status Laws, even after recent reforms, permit men to have up to four wives at a time and make divorce easy for a man but quite difficult for a woman. They place women in such a disadvantageous position that those who do not withdraw from politics out of despair are likely to be drawn toward the forces of change.

This could be illustrated in many ways, but the following item from Egypt's leading newspaper will suffice. In February, 1984, it was reported that a man had gone to court to ask it to force his wife into *bayt al-taah* (house of obedience), that is, return to his house and submit to his authority. He had beaten her and mistreated her in other ways and then thrown her out of the hut in which they lived, which was adjacent to, and even had the same address as, a public toilet. Having expelled her, he then went to court to have the police force her to return and be obedient to him. The judge demurred, but only on the grounds that a public toilet was not a legal home.[23] The case could have gone the other way. If women, particularly poor women, must face even the remote chance of having to submit to such an in-dignity, it is easy to understand why so many politically active women are inclined toward opposition to the regime in power, regardless of how well-intentioned toward women that regime may be.

The story related above portrays the plight of women, and also highlights the special vulnerability of the poor, a traditional concern of the left. The combination of an ideological inclination to support a particular cause, plus some specific triggering event, helps to ex-plain how and why these opposition women became rebels against rather than supporters of the regime in power.

One leftist woman, whose background is quite different from that of most of the women mentioned in this book, is Shahenda Mogled, a member of the general secretariat of the NUPP and the leader of the peasant's section of that party. In 1976, 1979, and again in 1984, she was an unsuccessful candidate for parliament from Tala, the place where Jihan Sadat started her first social welfare project. In 1984, she was placed second on the regular list of candidates rather than for a woman's seat. She is well known in her district because of her in-volvement in the notorious Kamshish affair. On May 1, 1966, her hus-band, Salah Hussein was murdered, as the party newspaper put it, "by the feudalist Fiqi family."[24] He had been a minor ASU official, active on behalf of the interests of the rural poor, and his murder did little more than stimulate a series of investigations.[25] The abuses re-mained and Shahenda Mogled, left with three children to support, continued her husband's work. Her life was not easy. In 1971, she was ordered by the Sadat government to leave Menoufia province, in which Tala is located. She was arrested because of her political ac-tivities in 1975 and again in 1981. In 1984, she stated her chief interest in running for parliament was to try to do more to protect the rights and enhance the prospects of tenant farmers and women.[26] As she is still well under fifty years of age, it is likely she will be active in Egyptian politics for the forseeable future. Before her husband's mur-der, Shahenda Mogled was interested in helping poor peasants. Radi-calized by the murder, she was at loggerheads with the government soon after the event. Although more traumatic than others, her entry into opposition politics is typical in that she did not start out to oppose the system. She got involved in a particular political activity and in the course of that activity, something happened to cause her to decide to rebel rather than seek accommodation.

Trying to discover whether the regime was initially against these women, or whether they started to object and the regime responded, is another version of the familiar dispute concerning the chicken and the egg. Fortunately, there is no need to resolve the dispute. What is important is that all reached a point where they had to decide whether to stand against the government or for it, and all chose opposition rather than capitulation or accommodation. Furthermore, this stance was maintained for an appreciable period of their lives rather than being confined to the particular time associated with the triggering event.

For many members of this group, the pattern of rebellion against authority began when they were still children. Nawal al-Saadawi, for example, has been rebelling against what she calls the patriarchal class system since early childhood. Everywhere she looked, she saw injustice, particularly discrimination against females, and her parents permitted her to think and talk about what caused injustice and what could be done about it. This freedom led her to challenge the conventional values and institutions of the society in which she was raised, including male authority, religion, and capitalism. As a young girl, she was subjected to ritual clitoridectomy, and the lingering memory of that event, as well as of other childhood traumas, alienated her permanently. She doubted God's justice, and even God's existence, and in one of her nineteen books, reflects on the way God is typically thought of as a man. Why couldn't God be a woman?[27] She concluded, as an adult, that the problem of justice and male domination of society was not created by religion, particularly Islam, but by capitalism. As her opinion is shared by many leftist feminists in the Arab world, it is worth quoting at length and helps explain why many opposition women are attracted to the left.

> Economic factors and, concomitantly, political factors are the basis upon which such customs as female circumcision have grown up . . . Many . . . are not able to distinguish between political and religious factors, or . . . [they] conceal economic and political

motives behind religious arguments in an attempt to hide the
real forces that lie at the basis of what happens. . . . It has very
often been proclaimed that Islam is at the root of female circum-
cision, and is also responsible for the underprivileged and back-
ward situation of women in Egypt and the Arab countries. Such
a contention is not true. If we study Christianity it is easy to see
that this religion is much more rigid and orthodox where women
are concerned than Islam. Nevertheless, many countries were
able to progress rapidly despite the preponderance of Christianity as a religion. . . .

That is why I firmly believe that the reasons for the lower
status of women in our societies, and the lack of opportunities
for progress afforded to them, are not due to Islam, but rather
to certain economic and political forces, namely those of foreign imperialism operating mainly from the outside, and of the
reactionary classes operating from the inside. These two forces
cooperate closely and are making a concentrated attempt to mis-
interpret religion and to utilize it as an instrument of fear, oppression and exploitation. [28]

Discrimination against women, the tyranny caused by what she
and others regard as false interpretations of Islam, the domination
of society by privileged and exploitative classes, and the evils of imperialism are part of a package. In 1981, Nawal al-Saadawi's political
activity was of a high enough profile that she was among the roughly
1500 opposition figures arrested in September of that year. Released
by President Mubarak after Sadat's assassination, she continued to
be active in politics and, in 1983, tried unsuccessfully to form a new
women's group which might later have been turned into a political
party. [29] Her perspective is shared by many women and men in Egypt's
political opposition, and her path to rebellion is not unique. Neither
is hers the only view, as illustrated by the case of Zeinab al-Ghazali,
a vehement opponent of secularism and an advocate of a society based
on Islamic law.

Zeinab al-Ghazali al-Gebali established the Muslim Women's
Association in 1937. She was barely twenty years old at the time. Raised
in a wealthy and religious family and educated at home by tutors
from al-Azhar, religion was the center of her life from early childhood. The association she established grew and, in the late 1930s Hassan al-Banna, the founder of the Muslim Brotherhood, urged her to

merge it with his organization. She refused, opting for continued independence. In 1948, the Brethren were under intense pressure from the government. Zeinab al-Ghazali again met with Hassan al-Banna and, still keeping the Muslim Women's Association independent, swore personal allegiance to him.[30] Her active political involvement did not become major until after the 1952 revolution, when she and the Muslim Women's Association, which by now had 119 branches, provided food, medical care, and other services to needy members of the Brotherhood. She kept her association with the Ikwan secret in order to protect the Muslim Women's Association from government harassment. Thus, even though the Brotherhood was disbanded by law in 1953, the Muslim Women's Association was recognized officially by the Ministry of Social Affairs in 1957.[31]

At an early age, this organizer for a holy cause had rebelled against secular society. This early rejection led her, as it did Nawal al-Saadawi, toward a life of dedication to a cause. In the late 1950s, she and Abdel Fattah Ismail, another member of the Ikhwan, gained permission from Hassan al-Hudeibi, the leader of the Brotherhood at that time, to organize an essentially underground revival of the Brotherhood.[32] The details of her involvement in this activity need not be related here,[33] but they led to her arrest in 1965 in what she regarded as, "the fake case of the Muslim Brotherhood."[34] Although the prosecutor asked for the death penalty, she was sentenced to only twenty-five years in jail. Some of her fellow activists, including Sayyid Qutb, who had become the leading religious leader of the covert group, and her colleague, Abdel Fattah Ismail, were executed on charges of attempting the violent overthrow of the government. Zeinab al-Ghazali denied the Islamic legitimacy of these charges then, and has continued to do so since. While in jail, she suffered considerably and at one point two of her jailers tried to rape her. In her autobiography she describes how she defended herself by biting one of the would-be rapists on the neck until he died.[35]

The case of Zeinab al-Ghazali illustrates that the way in which these women became rebels does little to predict the eventual consequences of involvement in opposition politics in Egypt. Like other women from wealthy families, she began by organizing a private voluntary social organization. Because of the Islamic character of that association, she made no distinction between the world of religion and the world of politics, and became involved with the Muslim Brotherhood.

It is easy to understand how she came eventually into serious conflict
with the essentially secular Arab nationalism of Gamal Abdel Nasser,
but she had been active in Egyptian political life for nearly thirty years
before she was tried and convicted of attempting to subvert the government. Although sentenced to twenty-five years, she served less than
six. In 1971, she and several others arrested at the same time were
released by the new president, Anwar Sadat, who wished to come to
terms with, rather than destroy, the leadership of the Islamic trend.
Zeinab al-Ghazali's period of intense organizational activity was over,
and except for her opposition to the 1979 and 1985 changes in the
Personal Status Laws, which she regarded as un-Islamic, she has not
been conspicuous in opposition politics since that time.

Some political violence is planned or organized, but at other times
it is almost random, and the possibility that force might be used in
politics is something of which most Egyptian politicians are aware.
In the spring of 1984 an event took place which both male and female
politicians are likely to remember. In May 1984, Niemat Hassan Muhammad Ali was the Labor Party candidate for the women's seat in
the first district of Qena, in upper Egypt. Known simply as Niemat
Hassan, she had been a member of the NDP in the 1970s and, before
that, a member of the Socialist Youth Organization. She was a social
worker in her district and, as a candidate for parliament, advocated
the establishment of day care centers for the children of working
mothers, feminist associations which would provide homes for elderly
women, and special programs to combat illiteracy among rural women
and teach them such practical skills as sewing and knitting.[36]

Programmatically, her ideas did not differ substantially from those
expressed by the majority of the women in parliament or from those
of the presidential wives discussed earlier in this book, but policies
are not always the most important issues in politics. Active in the Socialist Labor Party since shortly after its formation, she had switched
from the NDP to the SLP as a reaction against the corruption she
saw in government, corruption for which she held the ruling party
responsible. She was also impressed by the leadership of Ibrahim Shoukry, the head of SLP. In the 1984 election she was a vigorous cam-
paigner and, a few days before the election, accused the NDP of trying to bribe her to switch parties. She declined the alleged bribe and
accused the current and previous governor of Qena of corruption, contributing to the heated atmosphere of the campaign.

On the whole, the 1984 parliamentary election was orderly, especially by third world standards, but such a general statement was of little consolation to her family. On election day, in an incident which was not explained fully in the Egyptian press at the time, Niemat Hassan was shot in the head and killed by a cousin of a male NDP candidate for parliament from the same district. He was caught by the police and charged with first-degree murder.[37] Electoral violence such as this is rare in Egyptian politics,[38] but in upper Egypt many people are armed, and the 1984 election was one in which hopes, and tempers, ran high. Although there is no evidence that Niemat Hassan was shot because of her sex, it is also clear that male chivalry did not protect this mother of four from a politically inspired killer.

Not all entries into an opposition stance were as traumatic as that of Shahenda Mogled, as early as Nawal al-Saadawi's, or culminated as violently as that of Niemat Hassan's. Some opposition women evolved into an opposition posture gradually and some were, at one time, part of the regime rather than antagonistic to it. Afaf Mahfouz, a French-trained political scientist, was Egyptian cultural attaché in Washington, D.C., in the mid-1970s. Disenchanted by violations of basic human rights, she had not had much to do with Egyptian politics in the 1960s, most of which she spent in graduate study in France. Although she had rebelled against paternal authority as a teenager, and been offended by "excesses" of both Nasser and Sadat, she worked on behalf of the government from 1974 until 1978. Ambassador Ashraf Ghorbal "let me be free in organizing my business at the Cultural Office."[39] It was only after she returned to Egypt in 1978 that she became involved in opposition politics, focusing on objecting to the terms of the Camp David Treaty, Egypt's growing dependence on America, and the lack of freedom, equality, and justice she found in Egypt. She did not join a political party, preferring to maintain maximum personal and political independence. Her most conspicuous role in the opposition has been helping other people and groups to organize, and encouraging opposition people to be aware of their own limitations while they are critical of others. The role of independent humanist is particularly lonely, and occasionally puts Afaf Mahfouz at odds with friends as well as political allies, but many of the members of the opposition in Egypt have chosen to remain independent rather than join a political party or association.

Like Afaf Mahfouz, Mona Makram Obeid is another opposition woman who could easily have worked with the government rather than join the opposition, but her family background impelled her toward the New Wafd. Her father was a Wafdist parliamentarian before 1952, but the major influence on her early life was her uncle, Makram Obeid, one of the major Wafdist leaders of prerevolutionary Egypt. Rebellious as a child, she changed schools four times, but she remembers her uncle as always being supportive of her. Always interested in politics, she remained aloof from direct involvement until 1978, when she joined the New Wafd. A few years later, as a graduate student at Harvard, she enjoyed working as a student representative at the J.F.K. School. Upon returning to Egypt, she joined a new independent political organization modeled after the British Fabian Society. She probably would have continued to be independent of any party but when the New Wafd was revived in 1983, she reactivated her membership. As she put it in an interview, "The Wafd is my home."[40] In the 1984 parliamentary elections, Mona Makram Obeid ran for the woman's seat in Shubra, her father's former constituency. As an articulate Coptic woman from a distinguished political family, she attracted voters and attention in heavily Coptic Shubra, but the woman's seat for that district went to the NDP. She learned from the experience and plans to be active in the Wafd in the future, helping to prepare it and herself for the next electoral challenge to the government.

ACCOMPLISHMENTS AND ROLES OF OPPOSITION WOMEN

The roles undertaken by women in the political opposition in Egypt can be thought of as falling into two fairly distinct categories. One could be called "consciousness raising" and the other, "organizational creation or innovation." The latter is the most concrete and, hence, the easiest to discuss.

Women have been active and conspicuous members and leaders of opposition political parties and movements, especially since 1977, when political parties were legalized. Not only have nearly all of the members of the group studied been active in such parties or movements, but several have served in leadership capacities. Laila Takla, who broke with President Sadat over Camp David, was deputy leader of the Socialist Labor Party for nearly five years, and Olfat Kamel had the same post in the Liberal Party until 1984, when she joined the New Wafd. Hekmat Abu Zeid, who began criticizing President Sadat in the mid-1970s, later became a leader of the Egyptian National Front. This organization, based outside Egypt, called for the overthrow of the Sadat government. As a consequence of its activities, the leaders, including Dr. Abu Zeid, were stripped of their right to participate in Egyptian politics. [41]

Another type of opposition activity which has attracted women has been working with unions or voluntary associations. Over the past several decades, the government of Egypt has tried to control these organizations, [42] and union leaders such as Amina Shafiq and Shahenda Mogled have been active in the process of resistance to government encroachment on union and associational autonomy. At least as far as these women are concerned, the government has not been successful in securing their compliance.

Chronic opposition to the government from within parliament has been unusual in Egypt, and few people have sustained this role for any appreciable period of time. One notable exception is Olfat Kamel, who bills herself as "Egypt's Thatcher."[43] Tough, independent, and forceful, she is one of Egypt's most respected politicians and was elected to parliament in 1984 on the Wafd ticket. It is likely that she will have some type of leadership role in that party in the future.

The role of women in the political opposition in Egypt can also be considered as an exercise in consciousness raising. That is, by what they do and how they do it, women who criticize or reject government or societal demands, or who offer alternative ideas or plans, help change conventional notions of behavior regarding a wide range of issues, particularly issues of special interest to women. Women interviewed for this study were aware of this role, but also conscious that it is hard to measure or evaluate the significance of this type of activity. By engaging in organizational work, half of the opposition women studied have tried to change what people in Egypt *do*, to influence behavior directly. Two-thirds, however, have worked to change how and what people *think*, to influence ideas, and through ideas to alter future behavior. In addition to writing, roughly 30% of them have taught at the university level and influenced students directly by modeling new roles and, more importantly, by providing students with encouragement to think on their own.

Additionally, opposition women may have contributed to changing political consciousness in Egypt as a consequence of themselves being victims of violence or oppression. One has been widowed, one murdered, and five have been sent to jail for political reasons. Several have been divorced by men who could not coexist with a wife active in opposition politics. There are few secrets in Egypt, and the circumstances surrounding these divorces are well known among politically conscious people. Research has not been done to determine what effect such events have on public opinion at large, or opinion among the most politically relevant strata in the country, but it is reasonable to assume that many of these women became at least minor heroines particularly because of their jail records and in general, because of the difficulties they have faced. Politicians in Egypt do not conceal these events from public scrutiny. President Sadat was proud of his jail experience, and many opposition women have reason to be proud of theirs and have written about the event to make sure it becomes part of the recorded history of Egypt.[44]

Perhaps the most specific achievement which can be claimed by women in the political opposition is the passage of new Personal Status Laws in July of 1985. Prior to their approval by parliament, a consensus on their terms was reached by a broad coalition of Egyptian political leaders. This coalition included a number of opposition women who were conspicuous in and essential to a process which created a climate of opinion in which new laws were perceived as both possible and necessary. Nawal al-Saadawi, for example, was especially prominent in this brief and effective movement, as were several other women mentioned in this chapter. Others, like Zeinab al-Ghazali, felt the new laws were against Sharia. Those favoring reform, however, carried the day and both governmental and opposition leaders may share credit for the reforms made in the Personal Status Laws in 1985, when "Jihan's Laws" were replaced by rules created and supported by a cross-section of Egyptian political leaders including the president, parliamentarians of both sexes, and opposition women.

CONCLUSION

In the years since the Free Officers' Revolution, the political opposition in Egypt has grown in complexity and size. By 1984, it included five legal political parties and a formally banned religious movement among its most prominent elements. One of the most conspicuous aspects of the opposition considered as a whole has been the presence in it of significant numbers of women. This chapter has presented salient information about and perspectives on a selective sample of leading women in that opposition. While their early background did not appear to differ markedly from the parliamentary women studied in chapter 2, their marriage and family circumstances did. Partly as a result of the political and professional careers they have led, opposition women have a high divorce rate relative to parliamentary women, as well as smaller families.

The women studied got involved in opposition politics in a variety of ways. Most had an early start as youthful rebels against parental, usually paternal, authority, but the actual entry into the opposition typically was triggered by some fairly dramatic event or a major change in government policy. They became interested and involved in politics and were committed to a fairly specific set of policies or programs. Steadfast attachment to those ideas led them toward an opposition stance.

As members of the opposition, women have been significant as leaders in virtually all of the various components the opposition has developed. With the possible exception of the underground groups involved in such activity as the assassination of President Sadat, women have been important role models, organizers, and consciousness raisers. Opposition women have demonstrated that not all women are compliant or reserved, and that women as well as men are ready to share the risks, and if successful, the rewards, of opposition politics in contemporary Egypt.

Future prospects for women dissidents and rebels depend on the overall prospects for freedom for interest groups and political parties to organize, and for individuals to exercise freedom of speech, press, and assembly. While individual rights are important, the history of the women's movement in Egypt illustrates the centrality of organization. The women studied showed a marked preference for legal as contrasted to underground political activity, and are likely to use the opportunities afforded them by the Mubarak regime, but the signals relative to democracy and freedom to organize emitted by that regime have been ambiguous. On the positive side, the opposition press has been able to publish and criticize policies and personnel associated with the regime. Also, the 1984 parliamentary elections resulted in significant electoral success by the Wafd and the Muslim Brothers. On a more negative note, not all who wished to form parties were free to do so. Interest groups remained under considerable pressure to conform to the government line, and the electoral rules were stacked against minority parties. Furthermore, the man selected in June, 1984, to be the new speaker of the People's Assembly, and a potential future prime minister, Dr. Rifaat Mahgoub, is a well-known Nasserite, former head of the ASU, and is on record as having opposed the original shift from a one-party to a multi-party system.[45] On balance, however, in mid-1985, the ability of the opposition to continue its role in Egyptian politics appeared relatively secure, guaranteed by law, presidential support, and its own enthusiasm for the game of democracy.

So far, this book has dealt with the roles of women in the political elite. From this consideration of political women, we move to examine the role of women in business. Once again the focus will be on an elite, this time a small group of entrepreneurs whose business operations are national in scope. As we shall see, political and economic women share many characteristics, but there are important differences as well. If anything, the entrepreneurs are even more accomplished and have overcome greater obstacles than have Egyptian women in politics.

Women in Business

D OING BUSINESS in Egypt has an effect on participants similar to that of riding an untrained horse on a muddy field in a jumping competition. It is exciting, dangerous, frustrating, and exhilarating. If you finish the course or make the sale you feel as if you have won, even if others are in ahead of you. At that moment nothing else matters. As you ride, both horse and ground slip from under you; as you try to do business, the rules change. When the ride is over, or the investment proves profitable, you are convinced you are both blessed and skilled. Riders of recalcitrant horses, and Egyptian entrepreneurs, emerge from their respective experiences believing they can do anything if they devote their entire being to the task.

Entrepreneurial talent can operate in virtually any field. Witness Othman Ahmad Othman, Egypt's leading entrepreneur, who as head of the largest construction firm in Egypt controlled what was legally a public sector enterprise before he turned some management tasks over to other family members in the late 1970s and early 1980s. For the most part, however, entrepreneurs gravitate toward areas where there is greater freedom, where one can not only make a profit but can, in Schumpeter's words, "found a private kingdom."[1] This kind of opportunity is more likely to be in the private sector. In Egypt, however, the structural links between the two are so important that the private sector cannot be understood in isolation from the public sector. Furthermore, Egypt's economy is subject to considerable political influence.[2] Therefore, before we can understand how entrepre-

neurs function in Egypt, we must consider some of the major features
of the changing political and economic environment within which they
must operate.

THE EGYPTIAN ECONOMY SINCE 1952[3]

When Nasser and the Free Officers came to power in 1952, they were
favorable rather than hostile to free enterprise. They seemed to prefer
a liberal economy and strong ties with the west but wanted the terms
of trade to be more in Egypt's favor than had been the case under
the monarchy. Also, they wished to Egyptianize the economy while
at the same time reducing the power of the old landed aristocracy.
Thus, in 1952 individual ownership of land was limited to a maximum of 200 feddans, and following the Suez War of 1956, French
and British assets were sequestrated. In general, the economic role
of foreigners resident in Egypt was diminished. From 1957 on, the
position of the state in the economy expanded and the public sector,
which accounted for 18 percent of gross capital formation in 1952,
was responsible for about 74 percent of gross capital formation by 1960.
By 1976, the public sector accounted for approximately 50 percent
of gross domestic product. In 1952 it had contributed only about 13
percent.[4] In 1960 and 1961, nationalizations took property from about
700 individuals (some for political reasons) and all or most of the capital of over 300 private firms.[5] To say the least, these events sharply
discouraged enthusiasm for private investment. This was followed by
the 1962 National Charter, which proclaimed socialism as the guid-
ing principle for Egypt's future development. "Private property was
not abolished, but the opportunities for private economic activity and
decision-making, especially in investment and production, were severely circumscribed."[6]

　　Egypt experienced considerable economic growth during this
time, especially during the period of the first Five Year Plan, 1960–65.
But other things grew as well — bureaucracy, population, school enrollment, the army, and the number of goods and services that were
subsidized. Appointment to public sector management positions came
to be based more on loyalty than on technical competence.[7] In general, the forced march of planning ended in 1965 and has not been

resumed in quite the same way since that time. Two years later, Nasser and Egypt were humiliated and defeated in a short, vicious war with Israel. Physically and psychologically, the results of the war were devastating for Egypt. The Sinai was occupied by Israel, the Canal was unusable, and Egypt sank into despair. The military leadership was purged, and the process of resupplying and retraining the army, air force, and navy began. Soon, the "War of Attrition" started, with the Suez Canal area becoming the major battle zone. This period was marked by widespread dissatisfaction with the regime. President Nasser responded by combining repression of some elements of society with efforts to co-opt or placate others. In 1968, he proclaimed the March 30 Program in which there was an effort to stimulate the economy, make the Arab Socialist Union more democratic, reform the public sector, and at least marginally, encourage the private sector.

> The net result of the policy was that the public sector became bogged down in a morass of conflicting interests while the private sector became a magnet for quick and (economically) counter-productive profits. . . . Anti-regime violence was reduced, but the bickering and jockeying for political position went on. The regime lurched chaotically along with bitter debates occurring repeatedly in all arenas of politics.[8]

That was roughly the situation in 1970 when Gamel Abdel Nasser died and Anwar Sadat became president. The economy Sadat inherited was overwhelmed by military burdens as well as the weight of the welfare programs of the 1960s. The late 1960s and early 1970s even saw some years of negative growth. October 1973, however, marks the beginning of a period of change for the economy at least as important as the two decades which preceded it. Following the psychological victory of the October War of 1973, President Sadat promulgated his October Paper of 1974 in which he enunciated his plans for the future development of Egypt. One key to this program was *al-Infitah* (The Open Door), which was designed to help develop Egypt by stimulating foreign and private investment and foreign aid. Exports dropped briefly but imports surged, funded in part by massive foreign aid and in part by growing remittances from Egyptians who had left Egypt to find work abroad.

During the 1960s, many people of proven or potential entrepreneurial talent left the country, mostly to the West. Later, this brain drain turned into a minor hemorrhage, with many university graduates and, still later, skilled and unskilled laborers as well, leaving Egypt to find work in Arab countries. This was true especially after 1974 and the sharp increase in the price of oil. The Canal was reopened, the economy stimulated, peace pursued, and optimism and enthusiasm were palpable. Not everyone agreed with everything that was done, but virtually everyone in Egypt joined in the scramble for prosperity which took place. People changed jobs, careers, residences, spouses, styles of clothing, ideologies. Inflation, from which Egypt in the 1960s was relatively shielded, surged and annual rates of inflation of 15 percent and more became common. Rates of about 8 percent real growth, however, made this somewhat easier to manage for the largely urban minority who received most of its benefits, especially contractors, speculators, and merchants dealing in imported goods. Income distribution became less equal, but the entrepreneurial elite prospered.

Between the 1950s and the 1980s Egypt switched from free enterprise to socialism to a mixed economy. Politically, it saw the end of monarchy, the establishment of a bureaucratic authoritarian state, the birth and decline of Arab nationalism, and the beginnings of a controlled multiparty political system. It helped give birth to nonalignment, then became a de facto Soviet ally, and later changed allegiance from East to West. It fought five wars (Suez, Yemen, June War, War of Attrition, October War) and merged with other states twice (Syria, Libya), only to separate soon after. It made peace with Israel and experienced Western acclaim and Arab ostracism. What was both legal and encouraged one year was forbidden the next, with ex post facto punishment possible. Hundreds of people occupied cabinet posts in a game of political musical chairs. To thrive through all of this required luck, flexibility, patience, optimism and, in many cases, a haven in which to wait out a political or economic storm.

With change as the pattern, it helps to be able to put some elements of the situation in perspective. Tables 5.1 and 5.2, located in the appendix at the end of the book, summarize major issues of special importance for the economy. Reflection on the overall significance of the data they contain, summarized here, is crucial if we are to understand the environment within which entrepreneurs function.

One of the most obvious things about Egypt is that it is experiencing rapid population growth. By mid-1983, Egypt was estimated to be adding more than 100,000 new people per month to its overall population, which by 1984 exceeded forty-five million. An increasing percentage of these people are urbanites, or at least urban residents, and the image of Egypt as an agricultural country with a largely peasant population is no longer valid. Furthermore, urban sprawl has probably cost Egypt 400,000 of the 900,000 feddans it has reclaimed from the desert.[9] Infant mortality remains high, especially for the poor, but life expectancy at birth improved almost 24 percent over the past two decades, largely due to better nutrition and health care. Additionally, the population is more likely to be educated now than then, and school enrollment at all levels has increased significantly. Greater numbers of both males and females attend school, although females still lag far behind, especially in rural areas and poor urban slums. While adult literacy has increased dramatically, the majority of the people of Egypt are still illiterate and, for those in school, the quality of education has probably declined, although this is difficult to measure or prove.

Another important difference between Egypt in 1960 and 1980 is reflected in the dramatic increase in per capita consumption of energy. Much of this was made possible by the completion in 1970 of the Soviet- and Egyptian-financed High Dam at Aswan. However, American-financed thermal generation plants built after 1974, while less dramatic, probably produce more electricity. The High Dam, however, is significant for other reasons. A World Bank study published in 1980 concluded that:

> Construction of the High Dam, together with completion of a system of dams and barrages along the Nile, allowed perennial irrigation through a vast network of canals and considerably intensified farming in the "old land." Unfortunately, the plentiful supply of water and the absence of any user charge led farmers to overirrigate, causing a serious drainage problem. . . . Investment in extending irrigation and service infrastructure into marginal soils on the desert fringes had by mid-1976 added 0.9 million feddans of "new land" to the existing 5.6 million feddans of old land.[10]

For good or ill, and frequently both, the High Dam has changed Egypt fundamentally, contributing to industrial and agricultural growth, pride, hope, and, paradoxically, such major problems as increasing salinization of the soil. The Soviets may have financed much of it, but Egyptians built it and it symbolizes achievement, utility, and hope for a better future. Egypt without the Dam was a different country from what it is now.

Between 1960 and 1980, Egypt's gross domestic product increased roughly 440 percent, which is much more dramatic than population growth. By 1980, the service sector contributed more to production than either industry or agriculture alone, reflecting, among other things, "the population explosion, the indiscriminate expansion of education and the unsatisfactory performance of agriculture and industry."[11] Most of the economic activities of Egypt's female entrepreneurs have been associated with the service sector, although some are in construction or industry. Nevertheless, by the late 1980s, the situation was changing and the industrial portion of the economy was growing more rapidly than any other. The contribution of agriculture, however, declined in relative terms, accounting for only 13 percent of total production in 1980, down from 30 percent in 1960. The most attractive opportunities for entrepreneurs have been in the industrial and service sectors, with most private firms consisting of what economists classify as small-scale enterprises having between ten and fifty employees.[12]

Egyptian industry produces both for internal consumption and export. Since 1960, agricultural exports declined in relative terms while textiles and clothing more than doubled their share of the market. At least as important, however, as a result of new discoveries and the recovery of the Sinai, Egypt became a petroleum exporting country in the 1970s. At an impressionistic level, this post-1974 development affected Egypt almost as much as the construction of the High Dam.[13] By the early 1980s, sale of petroleum constituted one of Egypt's major sources of foreign currency, where before the cost of petroleum imports had constituted a drag on the economy. Table 5.3 illustrates the balance of payments situation for fiscal years 1979–80 and 1980–81, and shows the importance of oil exports for contemporary Egypt. Even more important, it illustrates the significance of another factor along with oil that was not notable in 1960: remittances from Egyptian workers abroad.

These two things, both of which depend upon events outside Egypt's control, suggest in a small way how Egypt has become, since 1960, more integrated into the world market and consequently more

vulnerable to its vagaries while enjoying its largess. Oil prices go down
as well as up, and oil is a depletable resource. (By 1983, Egypt's proven
reserves were only 3.1 billion barrels.) Worker remittances depend on
at least tacit cooperation from Arab host countries, most of whom
severed formal relations with Egypt when it signed the peace treaty
with Israel. Remittances and oil continued to flow, however, thus helping buoy the environment of optimism in Egypt. While remittances
reduced debts and financed purchases, the fact that perhaps as many
as 3.5 million Egyptian workers were out of the country in 1983[14] contributed to a highly unstable domestic labor market. It also meant
that many Egyptian firms had either to compete with wages in Saudi
Arabia or somehow live with training workers who then migrated rather
than staying to serve the company.

Although people seem to be Egypt's most significant export, conventional analysis excludes them from export data. When considering such issues as the destination of merchandise exports, Table 5.2
shows how dramatically Egypt's trade patterns have been adjusted over
two decades. In 1960, Egypt's merchandise exports went mainly to
other developing countries and to nonmarket industrial economies.
The West received only 26 percent of Egypt's merchandise exports
in 1960, but by 1980, due mainly to oil and the foreign policy of President Sadat, 51 percent of those exports traveled to the West, while
trade with the eastern bloc and with the developing world declined
sharply in relative terms. Furthermore, in 1960 much of the trade with
the eastern bloc was financed by aid. By 1980 Egypt received most
of its aid from the West and from such international organizations
as the World Bank. Most notable was the American AID program,
the largest nonmilitary foreign aid program in the world. Also important, however, were the West German, French, British, Canadian,
Japanese, and even Chinese aid programs to Egypt, all a result of the
response to Mr. Sadat's diplomacy and its continuation by President
Mubarak.[15]

Although Cairo was awash with money from remittances, aid,
oil, tourism, the Suez Canal, and trade, it was also the capital of a
country with a growing burden of external public debt, which by 1980
approached $12 billion. By 1984, it was nearly $20 billion. The drop
in oil prices in the early 1980s did not alter Egypt's pattern of trade
but it did make imports harder to finance. Although not in the same
debtor league with Mexico, Brazil, and Poland, the volume of foreign

debt and domestic subsidies constituted major limiting factors for both her economy and her polity. This, plus the fact that the bulk of new investment was applied to maintenance, replacement of plants and equipment, and repair, imparted a special flavor to doing business in Egypt and meant that there were numerous but changing pockets of opportunity for entrepreneurial exploitation.

ON BEING AN ENTREPRENEUR

According to specialists on the topic, entrepreneurial activity differs from other business conduct in a variety of important ways. Managers can be thought of as those who insure that a firm operates at maximum efficiency and profitability. Entrepreneurs, on the other hand, look for new ideas and make them operational and profitable.[16] A review of the literature on the topic reveals a variety of perspectives on entrepreneurship and its role in business as well as its importance for developing economies.[17] Reflection upon this wealth of ideas enabled me to develop a comparatively simple working definition of entrepreneurs which I used in order to identify prospective members for a study group of female entrepreneurs in Egypt.

People with recognized entrepreneurial talent might be employed by someone else, but to be included in this study one had both to own and operate the business. Preference was given to those who also started the firm, but if they had not done so, they had to have contributed to it in such a way as to have "made it what it is today." Thus, businesswomen must own, operate, and start or substantially alter a business firm to have qualified for consideration for inclusion in this study. The problem then became identifying the elite within the rather sizable number having these characteristics. In order to narrow the group further, the first consideration was number of employees; the second was reputation. To be considered among the elite a businesswoman had to have a firm with at least ten employees, the minimum number economists use to distinguish between artisanal and small-scale industrial firms. Second, to be considered in the business elite either the entrepreneur, or the firm itself, had to be identified as elite by leading members of the business and financial community in Egypt. Numerous bankers and business people, both Egyptian and foreign, were consulted on a confidential basis and a tentative list of names to be considered was drawn up in the summer of 1982. Some individuals were suggested repeatedly and interviews with them revealed a few more people who had to be considered. As might be expected given the nature of the problem, the number of women ultimately identified as constituting the female business elite in Egypt is small, an even dozen. Thus, the entrepreneurial elite was roughly one-fourth the size of the political elite. The business world has no functional equivalent of reserved seats, nor is anyone appointed to elite status in business in recognition of achievement in another field. Even though it turned out that virtually all came from privileged backgrounds, success in business was earned in a highly competitive and risky environment, even by those who had a head start.

WOMEN IN THE ENTREPRENEURIAL ELITE IN EGYPT[18]

According to official figures, by 1976 only 1.7 percent of the female labor force in Egypt occupied executive, administrative, or managerial positions. Modest as it is, this figure represented an increase from 0.9 percent in 1961.[19] Not too much should be made of this, however, because the figures are bloated by the inclusion of women in sex-typed jobs, particularly in the fields of health, education, and social service. Egyptian law forbids discrimination in hiring on the basis of sex, but virtually all business people consulted in the course of this research indicated there is considerable resistance in all sectors to hiring female executives, managers, and administrators. This is due mainly to the extreme discomfort felt by most Egyptian men regarding being seen to be supervised by a woman. If this is a problem in businesses in which women executives are employees, how do women who own and operate a firm cope with it? Virtually all have been forced to deal with this issue, often by trying to play down the fact that they are women. Additionally, some have made their authority as inconspicuous as possible by using a "front man" to make it appear as if a male is in charge. This ruse of a man at the top and up front calmed nervous employees and facilitated initial contacts with customers and bankers. The type of business some firms are engaged in made this tactic impossible to use, but in one way or another this issue, along with other start-up problems, had to be handled by all of the women in this group. Perhaps they were successful in this regard because prior to this point in their life they all had extensive experience in dealing with people.

In 1983, the average business woman studied was fifty-four years old and had been in business for herself for roughly twelve years. Put in comparative terms, she was six years older and more than twice as experienced as her sisters in the political elite. However, for most of her life, activities other than seeking markets, products, capital and personnel had occupied her attention. It is worth taking a brief look at those earlier years, in the hope that we might find some clues to the later success in business of this unusual group of twelve Egyptian women.

FORMATIVE YEARS

The families into which today's female entrepreneurial elite were born were almost all upper-class and urban. One, Ina Maggar, the head of the General Motors franchise, was raised in Assiut, a provincial capital in upper Egypt, but all of the others are from Cairo or Alexandria. The youngest was born in 1942, the oldest in 1916. Only four reported their parents were particularly supportive of the idea of them having public careers. All but two of the fathers had university degrees. The mothers tended to have married young, before finishing secondary school, as was the general custom in Egypt at the time. Virtually all come from business or political families, but a few fathers were in medical or health fields. Most come from Muslim families, but one was raised as a Jew and three are Christian. Regardless of religion, however, all the families were westernized to a considerable degree. One manifestation of this is that all but one sent their daughters to "language" schools, usually French, where instruction was in a language other than Arabic. Arabic was taught, however, as was at least one other foreign language, and all of the women in this group have a working knowledge of French and English as well as Arabic. A few know as many as six languages.

The old adage that it takes money to make money is true in the case of all but one of these women. However, very few are in businesses which required a great deal of personal start-up capital. The way in which wealth helped them most was probably that it provided a substantially different kind of early life from that experienced by most Egyptians, male or female. As little girls during the 1930s and 1940s, when most of them were growing up, they learned languages, traveled, went to movies and parties, and wore fashionable clothes. Their families were involved in interesting and important aspects of life in Egypt at that time. The mothers of two were colleagues of Hoda Sha'rawi; three of the fathers were active in politics and served in the cabinet or as governors. Apart from personal tragedies — half had a parent die during their childhood — they were shielded from most material problems and grew up self-confident and optimistic about the future.

For virtually every member of the group, formal education stopped, at least temporarily, with the completion of secondary school. Marriage while still a teenager was the norm. The average age of the first marriage was nineteen, but one out of every four of these marriages ended in divorce. Only two members of the group went directly to university from secondary school, but one paused briefly to get married first. For the most part, secondary education was considered enough for girls of their class at that time. Marriage to a man from a "good family" was of prime consideration. But informal education, in some cases, was also part of their early life. At least one member of the group was taught by her father to manage the property and money she inherited from her mother when she was fourteen. Also, one future company president, Niemat Alexane, the head of Nestle in Egypt, got a job as a secretary-receptionist at age eighteen, largely for the experience. She did not need the money but continued working until she married, at age thirty, and did not work again until after her husband's death. But that is getting ahead of the story.

MARRIAGE AND FAMILY

All of the women in the entrepreneurial elite have been married at least once. Three of the twelve have been divorced at least once. All but one have had children, an average of two, and spent appreciable periods of their lives as housewives. However, for over half of these women the life of an upper-class housewife was boring and confining and, even at the risk of marital discord they insisted on joining the world of work outside the home. This caused some divorces and in other cases divorce was threatened, but all who wished to work insisted on doing so, suggesting the early development of strong personalities and stubborn wills. A statement from Soad al-Sowaf, one of the most important members of this group, gives some of the flavor of this period of life for most.

> I was supposed to go to the U.K. to study medicine. For personal reasons I found that I was just scared (at age 18) to be alone in England. So I got married and my husband didn't approve of me continuing my studies. For four years I was sitting at home, doing nothing, being bored. But then I learned German, I learned Italian, I learned sewing. I tried to get busy, the way women get busy. My temperament is not for wasting time. I tried to play bridge and I found that I hated my life; I hated myself. I like to feel that I'm doing something constructive, adding knowledge. When I had the boys [the first of whom was born four years after marriage, the second, one year later]. . . it was all right; they changed my life. But once they went to school the gap started again and I'm not for morning coffees . . . reading is all right but I wanted a target for whatever activity I'm in so I went to the American University (to apply for admission) . . . I had a younger sister who was already in business with my brother, so she said, "Why do you want to go to university? Why don't you come and join us?" And it was *something* — not just gossip, you know — constructive![20]

That was the beginning for one; others had similar experiences; two reported being content as housewives for most of their lives.

Only two future entrepreneurs engaged in extensive private voluntary social service before going into business. Both were continuing a family tradition, as their mothers had worked with Hoda Sha'rawi and raised their girls to be active and assertive. However, even in the absence of this direct link to the roots of the Egyptian feminist organization, all but one of these women were products of an age and a class which contained conflicting notions regarding proper public roles for women. Volunteer social work was generally acceptable by the 1940s or 1950s, and those who were not involved in it refrained by their own choice. But they were restless. Four went to university some time after getting their children started in school, a pattern observed in previous chapters in this book. The question of timing was important. As one respondent explained: "It is important to choose the time when one starts to work. For me, I would not like to have started earlier. Otherwise I would have been an unsuccessful mother. And, even when I went back to school, it was because I was free, with no responsibilities toward my husband, who worked abroad at the time."

The men these future entrepreneurs married may, in many ways, have been as important as were their parents regarding career development. Virtually all married businessmen, and in marriages that survived for any appreciable period of time, the women learned a great deal about business from their husbands. As one said, "He showed me everything." Starting usually as lawyers, engineers, or accountants, most of the spouses turned to business even though, after the nationalizations of 1961, several became public sector managers. Sometimes teaching a wife about business was unintentional. One woman, who did not come from a business family, established her first business in 1958 in spite of government policies constraining the private sector. She was thirty years old at the time and, when interviewed, explained how she knew how to start and run a business: "All through these years [of marriage] I was sitting every dinner or almost every dinner in a business surrounding. My husband was talking business morning, night and day, and in the evening we were either entertaining businessmen or listening to business talk anyway."

Intentionally or not, several husbands served as informal tutors for their wives, and three explicitly helped them get started in business. Others helped simply by giving them permission to go into business or cooperating with the idea in order to keep a peaceful home. Some husbands also placed limits on the kinds of things their wives could do. For example, sometimes it is necessary to travel with a prospective client in order to visit a potential work site in a remote area. Most of the married women in this group would send a male representative on such a trip rather than risk trouble at home. By 1984, however, half of the group were either widowed or divorced and did not have to concern themselves with this problem, and three of the others had husbands who would not object to their spouses going on such trips.

GETTING STARTED

Following a fairly typical upper-class childhood, most of Egypt's future female entrepreneurial elite married young and began to run a household and raise a family. About half started a career in business about ten to twelve years later; for others the time elapsed was significantly longer—thirty-five years in one case. This meant roughly half of the women in this group went into business while their children were still young. Most of the others waited until the children were grown. None went into business with a preschool infant at home. Thus, at least in some sense, home and family came first, and for most it remained the top priority from an emotional point of view, even if not in terms of the time they actually spent with their families.

The question of the passage of time between first marriage and going into business helps us understand the relationship between business and personal life. The married women in this group expressed pride in their roles as wives, mothers, and business women and believed they could manage all three successfully. This requires cooperation and commitment on the part of both husband and wife as well as an atmosphere of mutual respect. Furthermore, as one woman put it, "I never try to be stronger at home." Implied in her statement was the possibility that she could be more decisive than her husband, but chooses not to be so in order to help preserve a stable and satisfactory marriage. In one form or another this sentiment was expressed by all except the divorced members of this group. Commitment, mutual respect, and perhaps wifely forebearance help to explain the durability of the marriages which lasted. For those marriages which ended in divorce, all of the women said it was because the man could not cope with the multiple roles played by the wife, not because she had failed. This, of course, is an obviously subjective and personal view, but it reflects the characteristic attitude toward marriage expressed by each of these women.

All the women in this group reached a stage in life where it was clear they had achieved success in business. In that way they are similar, but not all had the same kind of introduction to the role of top executive. A few stories of how they got started may help to explain why this is important.

One of these women is a planner. Armed with a master's degree in management from the American University in Cairo, Zeinab al-

Naggar studied Egypt and the market and concluded that, after Sadat consolidated his position in the May 1971 "Corrective Revolution," the business environment was ripe for change. Her study of the market also led her to conclude there was room for a firm to sell small-to-intermediate-size "appropriate technology" computers for use in business planning and management. After locating an American company which manufactured such computers, she became their agent in Egypt, and over a year before the announcement of the Open Door Policy of 1974, went into business. She succeeded, and she did so by investing her own capital and time and by introducing what was essentially a new product into what she estimated correctly to be an expanding market.

This is almost textbook entrepreneurship, but some of her colleagues have a different story. One, for example, was a housewife until her husband was arrested as part of the crackdown on the business and upper classes in 1961. As a supposedly temporary measure, Hoda Abou Seif, better known as Lula Zaglama, took over a small advertising firm her husband had just opened. Following his release from jail three months later, he took a low-profile, low-paying job with a public sector company and she and her partner kept the business, starting essentially from zero. As she put it:

> I was left with two children, a newly established advertising company and no money. I had to manage my life. My family are from upper Egypt. No woman ever worked [outside the home] before. My oldest brother . . . and my sister . . . did not appreciate my work. They rejected [the idea of my] working, meeting people and traveling. But I had to earn a living by any means.

She too succeeded. Over the next ten years she competed against subsidized, public-sector firms in what was, to say the least, a thin market for advertising. Adding public relations to the repertoire of the company, she learned the craft on the job and from whatever courses she could take. When the climate for business changed, she and her company were ready. Personable, trilingual, attractive and aggressive, she persevered. Her firm, which lost all of its customers in 1961, became one of the largest and most successful of its kind in Egypt by the early 1980s.

These two stories illustrate one of the most telling differences among women in this group. Some planned, thought it out, and took a calculated risk. But the majority were more or less thrust by special circumstances into an executive role, becoming entrepreneurs on the job. Divorce and widowhood are the most common "special circumstances" but, as the story above indicates, Egyptian politics also served this function. Imagine the glee of someone who has learned about swimming from reading a book or by watching others and then, after being thrown into the water, discovers "I can swim!" Some such people never want to leave the water. They have something in common with the women in Egypt's entrepreneurial elite. Even those who are reserved and modest about their achievements, as the widows tend to be, are self-confident and proud of what they have done.

In addition to capital or access to capital, the chief assets of women who started a business, or altered one substantially, seem to be knowledge and certain qualities of personality. Those who expanded existing businesses did so mainly because they had an idea about how to take new advantage of old opportunities or how to exploit new markets. The same is true for those who started their own firm. Nine of the twelve members of the female entrepreneurial elite discussed in this chapter are in this latter category. What kind of businesses do they have? What personality traits help account for their success? What problems did they face as women in business in Egypt?

WOMEN IN BUSINESS

U.S. Steel's "man in Egypt" is a woman. The same can be said of such major multinational enterprises as General Motors, Alcoa, and Nestle. However, while most of the businesses owned by the female entrepreneurial elite have an international flavor of some kind, the businesses they run are Egyptian owned and managed. The firms involved are mainly in the services sector, but include some investments in construction and industry. Covered were the following categories of businesses:

- Public Relations, advertising, marketing
- Restaurants
- Import and sale of consumer nondurables

- Office equipment
- Automobile agencies
- Tourism
- Beauty parlors, health spas
- Business management
- Manufacturing of consumer nondurables
- Construction
- Import of capital goods
- Export of Egyptian textiles

Each is a leading example of its type in Egypt. Financial statistics on commercial firms in contemporary Egypt are not readily available for a variety of reasons. However, it is clear that all of these businesses are profitable. One medium-sized firm, for example, apparently made sales of over 30 million £E in its 1982 fiscal year. Another started a business in the late 1960s with an initial investment of 500 £E. By 1982, the firm was profitable, had outstanding bank loans of over 1 million £E, and was expanding rapidly, with at least two new branches about to open when research for this book was being completed.[21]

One measure of the size of a business is the number of people it employs. Here the differences are quite striking, ranging from as few as thirteen for Dorra Fiani's public relations firm to over seven thousand for Hoda Abdel Meneim's construction company. However, some types of businesses (restaurants, construction) are more labor than capital intensive, so these figures do not indicate as much as they would if all respondents were in the same fields. Furthermore, some of our study group own, operate, and manage more than one type of business. Conspicuous by its absence is extensive investment in manufacturing, but in 1983 several of these women, as well as a few others who were considered for this study group but not included because they did not fit all the criteria, had plans for such investments. Apparently, many Egyptian entrepreneurs felt sufficiently secure after nearly a decade of the Open Door Policy that they were willing to risk more capital in manufacturing than they were at first, when they tended to concentrate in fields with low capital requirements and/or relatively short periods before showing a profit. Should a follow-up study be done a decade from now it is likely that the size of the busi-

ness elite group would be larger and more would be engaged in manufacturing, particularly in such sectors as leather goods, ready-to-wear
clothes, woodworking, and packaged food. Judging from plans current in 1983, it seems that most of these new industrial enterprises
will be producing for local consumption more than for export.

Anyone doing business in Egypt for the foreseeable future must
cope with major personnel problems. Some of the difficulty is due
to Egyptian labor laws, which make firing an employee difficult if not
impossible, even in the private sector. Thus, virtually every firm is
stuck with at least some workers whose productivity is marginal. But
while the least talented or poorly motivated workers are almost frozen
in place, at the other end of the spectrum capable and adventurous
people leave Egypt in droves. By 1983, roughly 3.5 million were living
and working abroad.[22] For Egyptians, the boundaries for the market
for their labor are not coterminous with the boundaries of their country. While this is true for many nationalities, the effect it has on Egypt
is remarkable. For example, although she was a member of Egypt's
parliament, one of the members of the political elite group missed
most sessions of parliament in 1982–83 because she lived and worked
in another Arab country. Two others were actually residents of another Arab country at the time of election. These incidents serve to
illustrate that the mobility of labor of all kinds, but especially for the
educated and talented, is one of the chief features of contemporary
Egypt.

Private sector companies face competition for employees with
the private sector and from at least two additional major areas. First
is the low-paying governmental and public sector. However modest
the pay may be, such jobs frequently offer respectability, security, important contacts and often a relatively light work load. Second, and
perhaps more important, is the competition from Arab countries, particularly Saudi Arabia and the small oil-rich states on the Arabian
Gulf. In many cases, salaries and other perquisites are so enticing that
no firm in Egypt can even begin to compete. The following example
illustrates the problem. In 1983, a recent graduate from an Egyptian
university could be hired by a local private sector company at a starting salary greater than that of a cabinet minister. Such a person might,
however, acquire some work experience and additional training with
the Egyptian firm and then leave for Saudi Arabia or Kuwait to take
a job paying five to ten times what he could make in Egypt.

Private sector companies compete with each other, with the Egyptian government, and with foreign countries for labor. Learning how to function in such a volatile labor market is a problem with which all employers in Egypt must cope, whether male or female. It is probably more difficult for women than for men, however, because many find it harder to recruit employees in the first place due to the reluctance of some to work for a woman. Some, as mentioned before, cope with it by having a male who serves as a front man, specializing in personnel and customer relations as well as handling negotiations with some male bank officers who are more comfortable dealing with fellow men. These women are careful, however, to retain real executive authority.

Egyptian employees, customers, clients, and banks all present problems for women in business that their male counterparts do not have to confront. Many women in the entrepreneurial elite try to de-emphasize sexuality by dressing modestly and conservatively and avoiding coquettish behavior. An agent for several foreign firms which supply Egypt with capital goods states: "What I do, at least consciously, is try not to make them [the men] feel it is a woman present. It's just another presence there." Women who are most successful at this tactic are often given the backhanded compliment of being told they are just like men. Each of those who reported this experience also reported resenting it.

> When I am told, "You are a man" I say, "I'm not a man. It takes a real man to see the woman in me." I don't feel I'm not feminine and I don't approve of or accept being told I'm a man. I just don't see why a man's success or know-how is not a quality of . . . a human being! . . . I don't see where sex has anything to do with it.

A leading public relations executive on the other hand, does not try to downplay the fact she is a woman, while another feels that "a businesswoman must look and act feminine" in some respects but must "usually think and act like a man." In the Egyptian context, what does this mean?

Looking and acting feminine, to some, seems to be a matter of both dress and demeanor. For example, many young women dress and act as if they are advertising for a spouse. There is a lushness and overt sensuality about them which they do not bother to hide.

Many men, confronted with this, are bound to think of possibilities other than business. Although one or two occasionally use related tactics in business, the majority of this group disapprove, believing that success should be due to having a better idea, plan or product, not to the chemistry of male-female relations. They think of themselves as decisive and logical and most describe themselves as "aggressive" but "straight." Eschewing flashy clothes, bright colors, and plunging decolletage, they dress modestly but well and avoid wearing much jewelry. Women in this group wish to be treated as professional equals by men and do not wish clothes or other incidentals to distract anyone from the business at hand.

Without exception, Egypt's leading female entrepreneurs take the business of being in business seriously. Their biggest problem has been to get others to take them seriously as well, to be regarded as equals. Their competitive tendencies are honed to a fine edge because to be regarded as equals, they must repeatedly prove themselves to be superior. At least that is their almost unanimous subjective perception. An especially analytical and observant member of this elite identified the biggest problem she and her colleagues faced. In her opinion it is:

> Credibility. For a woman in business, maybe in other things but especially in business, credibility is very hard to prove. You have to be ten times as good as a man to convince people that you are good or that you are even viable. I keep my promises religiously, scrupulously. Any promise. If it's something given, any benefit of the doubt goes to the person, customer, employee, whatever, just to prove to everybody that the word I say is as good as a contract. Many men can get by with less than that. They can promise things they forget at once. Nobody will accuse them of being unreliable — right? They are taken for granted. Women are not. . . . They must keep proving themselves.

Even allowing for the somewhat self-serving nature of this statement, the point is clear and, according to my observations as well as those of my male informants in the business elite, valid.

As employers as well as competitors, the women interviewed believe they are part of a meritocratic elite. One manifestation of this is their general unwillingness to give preference to female job candidates, especially for managerial or professional positions. Above all, most want their business to succeed, and will hire people who are likely to contribute to that end. Ironically, they, like most other business executives in Egypt, fear that women will not be able to overcome widespread bias and stereotyped images and consequently prefer to hire men. The woman owner of one large and multifaceted company, for example, has sixty professional employees. Only five are women. The sole exception to this pattern is that some of the members of the study group try to recruit female relatives, especially daughters, into the family business. This, however, does not always work out.

Fathers the world over often try to recruit children or other relatives into the family business. The Egyptian example suggests that mothers are likely to do the same, as long as children understand that, at work, mama is the boss. Apparently for this reason, several reported that their children, especially daughters, were unwilling to go to work for them. Sons or sons-in-law are somewhat more likely to be willing to work in a firm owned and managed by the matriarch of the family. But in all cases it had to be recognized that, while authority can be delegated, there is room for only one boss. With family members in particular, there can be no subterfuge, no disguise, no "front man." In some cases, the situation presents no visible problems. Amina Zaghloul, for example, runs several businesses, each through her current husband or one of her sons. The son of another woman, however, had to leave his mother's company and start his own because of a dispute over how to run the mother's business. Clearly there are powerful emotions at work here, and it is not likely that the full complexity of the relationship between the entrepreneurial matriarch and her family can be unravelled without a well-designed and executed case study. Even then, certain enigmatic questions are likely to remain. But even this brief consideration of the topic suggests that, in order to understand what these women do we must try to comprehend why they do it.

The most obvious motive for entrepreneurial activity, and one clearly present in each of these cases, is profit. However, every woman interviewed deemphasized this aspect of her work. Some pointed out that if money were the issue they would have quit business long ago, as they have all the money they will ever need. When it was suggested there is no such thing as too much money, they smiled and said that there are other values to be considered, prime among which was the personal satisfaction gained from doing something important and worthwhile. The format of the interviews, especially those which were recorded on tape, lent itself to probing questions, and it became clear that this was a subject about which each woman had thought a great deal. When asked what drives them a few gave quick and blunt answers. One divorced woman, for example, said that at first her motive was survival, but now it is "to build a career, a name, and a future of my own." One corporate executive's marriage has survived in spite of the fact that she brings her troubles home from work and is more successful in her career than her husband is in his. She stated that her work was like another child to her, part of her being. Moreover, it was her work that gave her equal status at home with her husband, as well as being her source of dignity and identity. She was set in her ways and would not change; her husband could either accept her as she was or leave. He stayed.

Several of the women studied reported they enjoy taking risks, but qualified this to say they enjoy *calculated* risks and do not like to gamble. Lottery tickets and race horses hold little interest for them, but the prospect of capital gains is a powerful lure. They also enjoy competition and winning, but for some an even more important issue is the sense of satisfaction derived from their belief that they are doing something important for Egypt. Feminism in Egypt has been associated with nationalism, and many of these women believe they are doing more good for Egypt than are women in politics. Two stated they would make more money in other types of business activity, but engaged in their particular field because of the added satisfaction of knowing their success also helped Egypt by contributing to its industrialization and improving the efficiency of business operations. This, in addition to other motivations, made entrepreneurial risk taking especially rewarding for them.

Most of the women studied enjoy what they do to the point where it has become an end in itself. Perhaps the clearest example of this is an executive who considers her craft artistic and creative and often works twelve-hour days, six and sometimes even seven days a week. Two stated they enjoy their work but feel motivated primarily by family considerations, and look forward to the day they can hand the company over to one of their children. They want not only to establish a private kingdom: they wish to see it pass to a worthy heir. Even in cases where this was not the major reported motive, women interviewed said they would derive intense satisfaction if what they had built could be passed on to a child or other relative sufficiently like themselves to be able to carry on in the same tradition. A few may be one-dimensional professionals, but most seek to strike a balance between work and other aspects of life. In one way or another, family played a big part in their lives. Soad al-Sowaf, who is married, has two sons and is probably Egypt's leading businesswoman, made an extemporaneous statement to me on this topic which is worth repeating.

> My philosophy is that work and career fill your time. They never fill your life. Companionship is very necessary for the human being. You end your day's work and you go back home and if you don't have the companionship, then what have you done during your life? Made money, made success. . . . I am talking to you and remembering the fate of the man in the grey flannel suit. . . . I've been telling my sons, enjoy life and don't make money a target in itself. Don't be slaves to success but use success to enjoy life and be happy. I see many of the young girls concentrating on their careers and forgetting that they are human beings. I see men who do that. My philosophy in life is very different. We do not work in the afternoon. I've encouraged both of my sons to have time for their families, for sport, for life. And after 3:00 p.m. we close the shop. There's no point in making more money than you have time to spend. . . . We don't like to be slaves. . . . I've seen tycoons who go at 9:00 a.m. to their offices, and at 9:00 p.m. they're still after money-making, and it's unfortunate. . . . I've seen women waste their lives in just fulfilling part of it, and this is the career. But life is not just a career. To me it's not just a career. No. It's a family. Maybe again it's my oriental upbringing. I feel it's up to the woman to make that. And at the end it's very rewarding for the woman because the home means [she has] everybody around her. If she loses that she'll end up by being lonely and success in the career will not fill that gap. [23]

SUMMING UP

Over the past thirty years the climate for private business in Egypt has been erratic in the extreme. During this period, private enterprise had its status changed three times by the regime in power. First, it was to be the main engine of Egypt's economic development, but after a short time it was proscribed and Arab socialism became the official ideology of the system. This was followed, in 1974, with a partial rehabilitation of the private sector. A decade later it had a somewhat ambiguous position as a junior partner in Egypt's economic development.

In Egypt, women have had the right to work outside the home longer than they have had the right to vote. Furthermore, the right to own and manage their own property is a long-established prerogative protected by the state and Islamic law and, in effect, is a key part of the foundation of a woman's ability to go into business for herself. It is only within recent decades, however, that women have exercised this tacit right by engaging in large-scale entrepreneurial activities. By 1983, at least a dozen women had joined the growing but still small group of men who constitute Egypt's entrepreneurial elite.

The women selected for inclusion in this study turned out to have certain things in common. All but one come from a privileged background, and most developed a strong and assertive personality while young. Except for a few members of religious minorities, they tended to marry while still teenagers and most had only two children. Marriage was not peaceful in all cases. Three were divorced and others were threatened with divorce. Some worked before marriage and then stopped, while the majority did not work outside the home until about ten or twelve years after marriage. With few exceptions, family obligations came first, and these women did not go into business without somehow managing the multiple roles of wife, mother, and career woman.

All of the women in this group enjoy taking calculated risks and relish the satisfaction and profit from successful business ventures. Self-assured, optimistic and confident, they are proud of what they have done and look forward to future successes. A minority got started in business entirely on their own volition, often with little or no support from anyone. For over half, however, divorce, widowhood, or some other tragedy helped thrust them into business. Rather than rely on family, find a conventional job, or remarry, they struck out on their own. Regardless of how they got started, all stayed because they liked the work. One of the most interesting differences between them pertains to motivation. In all cases, they do what they do for complex reasons. Some, however, live to work. What they do has become who they are. Others, who seem to be the most successful, have a more balanced life and enjoy family time, hobbies, friends and nonbusiness-related travel. Whether they live to work or work to live, this is an impressive and productive group of individuals, each distinctive and significant in her own right and way.

Women in Egypt's Political
and Economic Elite

WOMEN IN PUBLIC LIFE

T HE BIAS against women playing a prominent or significant role
in politics or economics is virtually a cultural universal. Nevertheless, many are tempted to believe the prejudice found in the Islamic world presents a special barrier to change. Michael Gilsenan,
one of the most astute students of contemporary Islamic communi-
ties, has described the traditional attitude toward women in the following terms.

> Women are the center of a family's sacred identity. For the males
> of the family the women are both the embodiment of purity and
> also a source of danger and defilement. Their sexuality, which
> their natures can never totally control, may bring dishonor and
> destruction unless father or husband or brother jealously guards
> the shrine. Women may only exist in the private domain, in a
> socially closed space. They have no public and open life.[1]

If, as Gilsenan says, women in Islam "have no public and open
life," what are we to make of the Muslim women who form the overwhelming majority of the seventy-four subjects of this book? Are they
simply violators of tradition, to be swept away if the defenders of the
faith gain a stronger hold on power? Alternatively, are they helping
to transform and transcend tradition? Or, is some of what they do

151

carried on within traditional delimitations? Gilsenan suggests how this might be when he points out that, even in a traditional community, women engage in politically important work as intermediaries between families, tribes, and other groups. Cynthia Nelson makes the same point in her work on bedouin women.[2] Gilsenan contends these women are able to carry out these necessary and important tasks because everyone *acts as if they were invisible.* This creative pretense enables them to perform jobs which require at least some public activity without a loss of honor. In short, they engage in politics *within* the tradition, not in defiance of its code.[3] We shall see, in discussing the hypotheses which follow, how some of the roles of women in our elite group can be considered as being loosely within the rules rather than clearly outside them.

The honor code of traditional Egypt is not the only ideological barrier to be overcome by women who seek political or entrepreneurial lives. The Western world contains biases that are, potentially at least, as formidable as those of Egyptian tradition.[4] Westernization is not a guarantee of emancipation for women. As Egypt modernized it took ideas from the West, and some male leaders were no doubt comforted by the symmetry between East and West regarding the dominant prejudice against women. Nevertheless, the West and other parts of the world have increasing numbers of women in prominent positions in politics, business, the professions, and the arts and also have strong feminist movements, and interested Egyptians can find multiple sources of new ideas regarding roles for women and relations between the sexes.[5]

These are some of the themes and issues with which we must cope as we try to understand the information we now have regarding the participation of women in Egypt's polity and economy. In assessing the evidence for these options we should expect to find some support for each. The challenge is to determine whether a dominant trend can be identified. In attempting to locate this trend, we will reflect on the ways in which these elite women have dealt with the culture into which they were born, and the political and economic environment within which they have worked. If, as Saad Ibrahim suggests, Egypt is a society which accumulates and recycles customs from its long history, it is also a country capable of adding to its traditions.[6] Therefore, the rules of the political and economic system and the values of the social order should be kept in mind as we review the evidence relevant to the hypotheses and research questions identified in the Introduction, which formed the framework for this research. Rather than rephrasing hypotheses retrospectively in light of the evidence, each will be reproduced exactly as it was written in 1982, when the study started. In this way, readers may share with the author something of the flavor of excitement of intellectual discovery, as well as the pained feeling one gets when supposedly intelligent guesses miss the mark. Each hypothesis will be discussed in turn. Then, we shall examine the evidence relative to the research questions.

SUCCESS AND FAMILY BACKGROUND

1. *Women who succeed in national political or entrepreneurial careers come from a privileged social and economic background.* This hypothesis is suggested in part by aspects of previous work on the role of women in the development of Egypt.[7] It is not startling to suspect that success will breed success or that the rich will get richer. However, in 1952 Egypt experienced a revolution. More than thirty years later, is the current Egyptian elite part of the "new class" of officers and technicians created by the revolution, or is it rooted in the prerevolutionary upper-middle class and upper class? This hypothesis suggests that prerevolutionary privilege is one of the hallmarks of the women in Egypt's current political and economic elite. To the extent this is proven true, what accounts for the durability of privileged birth as a political and economic asset? To the extent it is not true, what other factors explain the political or business success of those not blessed with an upper- or upper-middle-class background?

Evaluation of the data gathered for this research suggests that approximately 74 percent of the women in Egypt's current economic and political elite come from families which were considered privileged prior to the 1952 revolution. That is, the families were highly respected and had income levels substantially above average. The data, as well as the criteria used to place an individual in a specific class, are shown in Table 6.1. All but one of the women in the business elite have upper-class or upper- middle-class backgrounds, as do at least 86 percent of the urban women and 71 percent of the rural women in the parliamentary political elite. If the political elite is taken as a whole (parliamentary, presidential, and opposition), 71 percent have upper- or upper-middle-class origins. This does not mean their current privileged status was simply inherited. As indicated in the data cited in chapter 2 pertaining to education and professional background, most political women worked hard for several years before achieving elite status, and the majority have earned distinction in at least one field other than politics. Furthermore, in order to prosper politically, those with prerevolutionary privileged backgrounds often had to demonstrate loyalty to the new order repeatedly, to overcome the political stigma of their family background. The new regime came to need the skills and talents of members of prerevolutionary elite families willing to express loyalty to the new system. In spite of the revolution, privileged birth gave those men and women who enjoyed it certain obvious material advantages, especially education, capital, and contacts, as well as a legacy of confidence and optimism upon which they could draw as they struggled to get ahead.

While noting that the rich and reasonably well-born continue to do well in postrevolutionary Egypt, the most significant finding relevant to this hypothesis is that at least eleven women not so blessed have managed to attain elite status in politics. They represent fifteen percent of the total group studied. While there are no peasants or even former peasants among the women in parliament, three are the educated daughters of bedouin leaders. These families, involved in trade and animal husbandry, had high status in their own community but not in Egypt at large, except possibly insofar as they had a reputation for being mavericks. Their income was not comparable in any way to that of the pashas, cotton brokers, and professionals of the upper class or upper-middle class. Four more come from essentially lower-middle class or working class backgrounds. For example, the father of one was a cook and another was a plumber. In prerevolutionary rural Egypt these jobs were neither high-status nor high-income positions, but these men, like their bedouin counterparts, encouraged their children to be educated, optimistic, self-confident, and to think in terms of upward mobility, not by social climbing, but by work. The same general pattern holds for nonprivileged opposition women. In a small minority of cases parental encouragement was absent, but the girls were bright and decided when still young they were not going to settle for the same kind of life their mothers had. By then, women prominent in public life were available as positive role models for their youthful aspirations. The most important clue to explain the success of this small group of women, however, is age. These women are products of Egypt's revolution, educated in schools built by a government which set out to increase dramatically the number of children who had the chance to go to school. This group of women struck me as being unusually independent and strong-willed, but these personality traits would not have carried them to prominence had not educational and work opportunities existed in the relatively poor or remote areas in which most of them grew up. Furthermore, six of the parliamentary women without privileged background would not have been in parliament were it not for the creation in 1979 of reserved seats for women. In short, the nonprivileged women now in the political elite tend to be the beneficiaries of systemic, regime-created opportunities, more than of private, family-created opportunities. They represent tangible evidence of marginal, but still meaningful, social mobility in contemporary Egypt.

If there are a small but significant number of women in the political elite who lack a privileged background, why is this not true of women in business? Clearly, this question requires further investigation, particularly in research with a policy focus. If women of middle- and lower-middle-class backgrounds have been able to succeed in politics due partly to regime-created opportunities, how can similar opportunities be created for women in business? What did the family provide for the privileged that the state or some other entity can offer to the nonprivileged? One inference from this study is that those in the current elite acquired knowledge about how to run a business from fathers or, in some cases, husbands. In addition, and probably more important, as young girls and young women they became acculturated into the folkways of the business world. Thus, they reached a point where they were comfortable dealing with bankers, accountants, suppliers, and lawyers. Workshops, or even social clubs, which could bring successful women entrepreneurs together with female management employees and those having viable small businesses might be partial but productive surrogates for privileged birth.

THE ROLE OF EDUCATION

2. *Women in Egypt's political and economic elite will tend, on average, to be well educated, probably significantly better educated than their male counterparts.*

In contemporary Egypt, men may reach the top with a variety of coping techniques, but for a woman, education is a necessary (but not sufficient) condition for success. A recent study of women in the labor force indicates that virtually all growth in female employment in Egypt since 1960 is accounted for by one variable: education.[8] Thus, we should expect to find that all, or nearly all, of the members of the study group have received at least a secondary school education or its equivalent, and many will have university degrees. Any exception to this rule will require explanation and investigation.

This hypothesis is confirmed beyond doubt. Education is an unambiguous good as far as these people are concerned. Most come from educated families, but those who do not used education as the chief and first means to achieve upward mobility, particularly those women who are now in parliament or members of the political opposition. The education of women in business is symbolized by the pattern of trilingualism. Approximately 25 percent of the parliamentary group have doctorates, earned in such fields as chemistry, literature, medicine, and dentistry. In Majlis al-Shura, women account for only 3.3 percent of the membership but 8.1 percent of the doctorates. While complete statistics are not available, it is clear from observation that the pattern of education among men in the political elite is not equivalent to that of the women. In this respect, women in the parliamentary elite are not equal to men: they are superior. Presidential wives and opposition women also tend to be well educated. Mrs. Nasser is trilingual, both Mrs. Sadat and Mrs. Mubarak have advanced degrees, and nearly two-thirds of the opposition women could best be described as intellectuals. Even more than privileged birth, education is the hallmark of successful women in Egypt today.

POLITICIANS AND ENTREPRENEURS AS WIVES AND MOTHERS: AMBITION DEFERRED

3. *Women in the political and economic elite will not always have been involved in a major way in politics or business. Most will be married, have children, and postpone or interrupt careers for significant periods while being occupied almost exclusively with roles of wife and mother.*[9] Traditional values indicate clearly that woman's place is foremost in the home. Women who wish

to have a career outside the home typically must fulfill wife and mother duties first. Analysis will focus on the impact this expectation has had on the lives of women in the study group. Are women who meet this expectation more successful or visibly happier than women who do not?

This hypothesis is also confirmed. The importance to these women of being a wife and mother is clear from the evidence. In all interviews conducted, only one political woman expressed the opinion that her role in parliament was more important to her than her roles of wife and mother. Women in the business group spent an average of twelve years as housewives before going into business. Women from all groups whose husbands had jobs in other countries resigned their own positions or took leaves of absence in order to travel with the husband and keep the family together.

Of the seventy-four women about whom we have data, only two were never married and only fourteen divorced. Seven of those who were divorced remarried. The marriages of the parliamentary group were especially stable, but one-fourth of the entrepreneurs and a little over one-third of the opposition women have been divorced. Future parliamentary women tended to marry much later than future business women, and seem to have taken care to select mates who would be amenable to the idea that they would have a career outside the home. Women in the opposition, who lead the least conventional lives of any of those studied, account for one-half of the divorces, but most have found new husbands prepared to share their unconventional lives. Marriage, rather than the single life, remains the norm.

It is impossible to be certain about impressions of happiness, but women whose marriages worked seemed both proud and happy of the fact. None expressed regret about the "loss" of professional or business experience due to the need to spend time with children. Those who managed careers and raised children simultaneously, however, often reported their children felt deprived because they did not receive as much maternal attention as did friends whose mothers did not work. My impression is that this was a fairly widespread problem, but it is difficult to gauge its seriousness. In many societies, the parental claim "I did the best I could" is often counterposed to the child's lament; "Where were you when I needed you?" Further research, perhaps by social psychologists, might help illuminate some of the darker corners of the relationships between elite Egyptian mothers and their children. What can be said now is that this group seems to be handling these problems in a fairly successful way, and I could detect no cases of the extreme alienation which sometimes exists in such families in the West.

WOMEN BEHIND MEN

4. *Women perform a significant and necessary role behind the scenes as mediators and sources of pressure on "their" men to effect changes in public policy pertaining to women, and to relax or suspend the application of social mores which proscribe or limit roles for women.* This hypothesis is suggested by the research of Cynthia Nelson, who points out in her study of bedouin women that they have a crucial but "private" role in the politics of desert tribes.[10] We shall try to find out if women in the study group play, or played, similar roles in national politics, especially with regard to recent attempts to change laws or rules pertaining to women. Do public women exert power publicly, or do they still function mainly behind the scenes?

The situation in regard to this hypothesis is straightforward. Mrs. Sadat, although she held no formal national office, did exercise influence while her husband was president. The changes in the Personal Status Laws in 1979 and the provision of reserved seats in parliament for women in the same year were not entirely her work, but she was involved in producing these changes. However, she was not really "behind the scenes" or invisible. The role she played was unofficial but quite public and, although her efforts remained controversial, in 1985 her achievements stood relatively intact, except for the issue of the Personal Status Laws, despite the "de-Sadatization" which has taken place since 1981.

Virtually all business women surveyed believed that in politics the wives of important men probably have more political power than do women who hold office in their own right. The political women disagreed. For example, almost all parliamentary women surveyed believed that, since 1979, circumstances have changed and women who hold office have more real power than those who simply have powerful husbands.

From a traditional point of view, it is legitimate for an Egyptian woman to have power by virtue of her influence with "her men," that is, a father, husband, son, or other close relative. The problem arises when she is *seen* to exercise this power. Mrs. Sadat was perceived to have violated the norm, and she and her husband were subjected to criticism accordingly. Other presidential wives have not exercised power publicly, and women in business have often used "front men" routinely to on their behalf, concealing and thereby protecting their own power and profits. This is a common ploy in business, but not a universal phenomenon, and no general rule can be deduced.

In contemporary Egypt, women exercise influence through men, and by virtue of the office they hold or business they run. Egyptian women have not discarded their former quiet tactics, but have added the public use of power to the roles they may play. It is reasonable to conclude that women have earned the right to own and operate a business, or hold public office, without gross violation of social norms. Women who do not hold office in their own right, however, are still held accountable to the code and exercise power only if they remain discreetly behind the scenes.

ENTREPRENEURIAL PERSONALITIES
IN BUSINESS AND POLITICS

5. *Egyptian women entrepreneurs (and perhaps some female politicians) will exhibit the same psychological characteristics attributed in standard studies to entrepreneurs in general.* [11] Specifically, they will tend to be iconoclastic, individualistic, domineering, and the type of person who wishes, in Schumpeter's terms, "to found a private kingdom . . . to prove oneself superior to others" who enjoys "success itself" and who "seeks out difficulties, changes in order to change, [and] delights in ventures."[12] Testing this hypothesis will be subjective and impressionistic, but it is important to know if Egyptian female entrepreneurs share the same personality traits as the entrepreneurs, virtually all of whom are male, who have been the basis of the standard works on the subject. Also, how do people with such characteristics fit into and relate to what is regarded commonly as a nonentrepreneurial society? Finally, how do the politicians in the group differ from the entrepreneurs?

Some of the women in Egypt's entrepreneurial elite seem to have no internal limits to their ambitions. Others do, believing, as stated so eloquently by one woman, that wealth has no real value if it is acquired at the cost of such things as health and family. But they do "delight in ventures" and seek "a private kingdom," and they place a considerable premium on personal independence. They are cosmopolitan but still part of Egyptian society. Notable for being inconspicuous, some shield entrepreneurial activity from prying eyes because they do not want their businesses to suffer, which they fear will happen if people know a woman is in charge. A few of the rural women in politics stated they believed business was an inappropriate career for a woman. This may reflect class bias more than anything else, for in the areas these people come from, the most visible women in business are peasants who barter, buy, and sell in the souk. The business women defended their careers, but some suggested that politics is too public and too dirty for women.

My general impression is that many political women shared personality traits found among the entrepreneurs. They certainly "delight in ventures" and in demonstrating superiority, and they relish success. For them, politics is another venue for entrepreneurial activity. No successful business women have gone into politics, but some politicians have gone into business. For the most part, however, these seem to be mutually exclusive careers for women in Egypt, though the same is not true for men. Among the entrepreneurs, whether in business or politics, specialization is the norm for women, and they tend to stay as close as possible to a field in which they have developed expertise. To step out of one's area is, for many, an uncomfortable gamble. While they will take a calculated, hedged risk, virtually none of the women in this group of political and business elites will chance the plunge into the unknown. Like their more successful male colleagues, they do not tend to enjoy risk taking as a goal in itself, but take a risk if there is good reason to believe it will be profitable.

WOMEN LEADERS AND LEADERS OF WOMEN

6. *Successful women will tend to know other successful women, be reasonably well-informed about the history of the women's movement in Egypt, and will perceive a close, positive, and reciprocal link between national development and progress for women.* In short, the women in the contemporary economic

and political elite will tend to agree with Egypt's pre-1952 feminist movement with regard to the link between feminism and national progress.[13] Continuity with Egypt's feminist past is thus assumed. The degree to which it is not found must be explained and discussed.

One of the most striking features of women in the political and economic elite of Egypt is that very few regard themselves primarily as leaders of women rather than as women leaders. Furthermore, fewer than 20 percent of the whole group defined themselves as feminists. However, even women who did not consider themselves to be feminists, or did not act as leaders of women, tended to be in accord with the major values of the prerevolutionary feminist movement. This suggests that, even in the absence of an organized feminist movement, many of the values of that movement have been adopted by most educated Egyptian women. For example, all but one of the parliamentary women favored the 1979 changes in the Personal Status Laws, and all who responded to the question agreed that women had a right to work outside the home. All but a few considered education necessary for girls, and roughly 20% of the whole group believed that education is more important for girls than for boys. Urban women in politics were especially prone to hold this view.

Women in both political and economic careers represent direct links to the roots of feminism in Egypt. Some, like Amina Said, worked with Hoda Sha'rawi, while others were carrying on a tradition begun by their mothers. Furthermore, many of these women have tried to make the case that the development of Egypt and progress for women to hand in hand. Some Egyptian women leaders believe women should be given *extra* rights. Others believe women should be treated exactly like men, while still others advocate developing a special public sphere for women, protected by both religion and secular custom.[14] All three views have echoes in Egypt's feminist past. By the early 1980s, the tendency among women in the political and economic elite, except for women in the opposition, was to stress the exercise of existing rights rather than fight for additional perquisites for women. Opposition women, especially those on the left or those who defined themselves as feminists or secularists, tended to be quite critical of the status quo, even after the 1979 changes in the laws. They wanted more rights for women. However, the rights in question were essentially the same as those put forward by the founders of feminism in Egypt in the early part of this century. Thus, disagreement among the elite on the next steps to take does not obscure the impressive continuity with the past regarding what is at stake.

It is clear that women in the current business and political elite have a great deal in common. Roughly three-quarters come from an upper-class or upper-middle-class background, but not even this has produced ideological agreement regarding future policy and action relative to women in Egypt. In fact, the absence of consensus regarding steps to be taken in the future is one of the most striking features of this group. Most of the political women (as well as most concerned male politicians) take one general approach, while the entrepreneurs (regardless of sex) ascribe to another, more conservative stance.

For the most part, the leading business women in Egypt do not favor special treatment or consideration for women. They are merito-cratic egalitarians, believing that if women are to succeed they must do so on their own. The general view among the Muslim women in the group, who constitute all but nine of the total, is that Islam gives women the right to inherit and own property and, therefore, gives them the possibility of financial independence, the "room of one's own" that Virginia Woolf said women needed most. To the entrepreneurs in our group, it is *all* they need. The rest they can earn as individuals by hard work. Most of the political women, who view the problem in general rather than personal terms, see the issue as more difficult than this, complicated particularly by class.

Although their class origins are similar to that of the business women, women in parliament and in the political opposition tend to believe that what contemporary women need from the government differs according to class. Thus, urban working women need such things as access to prepared foods and day care centers. Although they work outside the home, the responsibility of household management is still theirs. Peasant women need education and better health care. All women, according to the leadership, need to be made more aware of their rights. On these issues, opposition women, presidential wives, and parliamentary women share similar views and as individuals have acted to involve political parties, labor unions, private voluntary associations, and the government of Egypt in efforts to help women. They do so, however, against considerable opposition from traditionalists, who do not approve of the changes which have already taken place and who continue to resist additional efforts in that direction.

THE FUTURE OF WOMEN IN EGYPTIAN PUBLIC LIFE

The strict sexual division of labor, characteristic of the not too distant past, can no longer be used as "proof" that women are incapable of performing important political, economic, or technical tasks. The evidence that women can do these jobs is now part of everyday experience. For many traditionalists, however, this does not make women's public roles any less controversial. For them, seeing women work is not proof that women can do these tasks, but proof that society is perverted and organized improperly. Thus, for some Egyptians, the fact that the sexual division of labor has changed makes the public role of women more controversial rather than less. Even in the face of evidence to the contrary, they doubt the capacity of women to do important public work *and* deny the propriety of it when it is done.

Although it is impossible to tell how many people hold such views, or how powerful they are or may become, this hard core opposition to women's emancipation is likely to remain a force to be contended with in Egyptian public life. In the early 1980s, it seemed to be held in check, but no one can say for certain what the future will hold. Women who attempt to function in the public arena as agents of change will not succeed without overcoming an enduring challenge to the legitimacy of their role. Viewed from another perspective, those who oppose the participation of women in politics and business will not succeed in reversing existing trends unless they can overcome women in parliament, women married to powerful men, women in numerous organizations and associations, and women entrenched in the professions, active in all political parties, and successful in business. This is not to imply women are alone in perceiving that society as a whole is likely to benefit from expanded roles for women. Many men sympathize with this view and are prepared to lend active support, but much of the leadership, resistance to retrogressive change, and pressure for progressive change is likely to come from women.

In order to assess the future prospects for women in Egyptian public life, it will be helpful to consider the issue in the context of the research questions identified in the Introduction to this book. First, we asked about the relative importance on the careers of women in the current Egyptian elite of six factors: (1) the household, (2) patron-client relationships, (3) presidential leadership, (4) private voluntary associations, (5) the state as an agent of change, and (6) foreign influence. Second, we asked about evidence that women have functioned as agents of change on the national level. The responses to these queries should help explain how the Egyptian elite came to include women in the past and, by implication, suggest general principles relevant to the future. These principles are not guarantees, however, because history is sometimes a poor teacher, and its lessons are seldom learned, partly because they are often so ambiguous. Hopefully, the following conclusions about the role of women in Egypt's modern history are sufficiently clear to warrant consideration.

Women as Agents of Change

Egyptian women have been agents of change, helping to transform social customs as well as laws and, through work, contributing to increased production. By concentrating in such fields as health, education, and welfare, they have also helped improve the overall quality of life in Egypt. Individual women who have been agents of change include Hoda Sha'rawi, Doria Shafik, and Jihan Sadat, but other less conspicuous people, especially the parliamentarians discussed in chapter 2, have also accomplished a great deal for Egypt and for women. Women in public life serve as ambiguous role models, stimulating opposition and discomfort as well as emulation. Women who hold public office in their own right can function as effective and respected public leaders. Women married to powerful men may exercise considerable influence. There is a risk, however, that the legitimacy of their achievements and the honor of their spouse may be threatened if these women are *seen* to exercise power.

Given the tendency of the system to compromise and accommodate when necessary, but come down hard on opposition which is perceived as a serious threat, women who worked as reformists within the system achieved more change than those who challenged that system totally. Occasionally, however, more radical confrontationalist tactics, such as those employed by Doria Shafik, have been quite successful. Regardless of tactics, however, women in the opposition have helped shape the public debate about what is to be done in Egypt and are likely to have greater influence in the somewhat more liberal and

democratic polity which seems to be evolving in the mid-1980s. Although some women have had successful careers in politics and business, there is no evidence to suggest the dominant bias against such
roles for women has been replaced by a more supportive ethic. Instead, what exists now is a set of competing notions regarding women's
roles in society, both of which have substantial numbers of important
supporters. Slowly and irregularly, change has occurred, but women
who seek education, wish to work outside the home, or enter politics
still encounter opposition, although, due to factors discussed below,
that opposition is less formidable than it was a few decades ago.

The Role of Organization

Although many women have succeeded in their chosen fields as
individuals, women have exercised considerable influence as a result
of being organized. Women's organizations, discussed in every chapter
of this book, have provided a separate sphere in which women can
work, achieve goals, and gain experience. They have also served as
points of entry, enabling women to participate in the mair ·ream of
Egyptian public life. Other organizational activity has also been important for women. Bint al-Nil was at least partly responsible for getting women the vote in the 1950s. Political parties and pressure groups
have been helpful venues for political women, as have work-related
organizations and professional associations. As pointed out in chapter 2, these have been important for the career development of more
parliamentary women than has experience in private voluntary agencies. However, many of these organizations have been vital components
of social action and welfare in Egypt, and through them women have
helped improve the quality of life for many Egyptians and, in the process, demonstrated that organized women can contribute to the welfare of their country.

Patron-Client Relationships

Although women in the Egyptian elite have benefited from patron-
client relationships, political women appear to have placed more reli-

ance on ordinary political coalitions than on political shillal. The evidence suggests that a relationship with a particular shillal may, in the long run, damage a political career more than it helps it. For example, women who were especially close to Mrs. Sadat in 1979 tended to be among the first people dropped as candidates by the party in 1984. Women who had a more independent and flexible political base have tended to be more durable over time. The formation of relatively short-term coalitions, typically with men, seem to be the most successful tactics employed by women who have achieved distinction in Egyptian politics or business. This tactic is consonant with the traditional ideology of Egyptian feminism, according to which women should seek collaboration with and support from men, rather than viewing men as the enemy who must be overcome. In most cases, benefits for women have been linked to family and national wellbeing, and have not been pursued as part of a "zero-sum game" in which women's gains are men's losses. Rather, the Egyptian feminist position, as represented by the feminist movement and most of the women in this book, suggests that progress for women will yield increased welfare for everyone in Egypt.

Supportive Households

Family background, education, facility with language, and personal drive are the most obvious determinants of success for women in Egypt's current elite. Evidence suggests that, in this regard, women do not differ significantly from men, but have to struggle harder, longer, and more continuously to prove themselves than do men. The role of parents, especially fathers, in providing early support and encouragement, is notable, as was the related supportive role of the marital household. It is difficult for anyone to succeed in contemporary Egypt, doubly so for women. Without the support of the family, it is doubtful if any but a few lucky and hardy women would have much of a chance for a public life in politics or business. Given the importance of education for women, the initial key issue seems to be whether girls go to school or not. For most urban middle-class families, education for girls is now the norm. Whether this pattern is continued or extended to the rest of society may depend on economic factors and political leadership more than anything else.

Presidential Leadership and the State
as an Agent of Change

All of Egypt's presidents have taken positive actions to support the general cause of women's interests. Specific examples of presidentially supported issues include granting the franchise, appointing women to high office, creating reserved seats for women in parliament, reforming the Personal Status Laws, and trying to increase female enrollment in schools. Presidential support is not a sufficient condition for progress on these fronts, but it is probably a necessary one. Legal alterations, although essential, are not sufficient in themselves to bring about substantial social change. These caveats aside, the record of the twentieth century shows that the state has been a major agent of change and, since 1952, presidential leadership has been an important element in changing the rules pertaining to the roles and status of women. For women who do not come from an upper-class or upper-middle-class background, education and other regime-sponsored programs have been the most important factors (along with such intangible qualities as luck and personal drive) accounting for upward mobility.

The state-dominated economy has also been an important influence on the roles and status of women. State encouragement for the private sector has meant growing opportunities for many women, particularly those discussed in chapter 5, who, along with entrepreneurially oriented men, have prospered under the Open Door Policy. Economic factors affect other women as well. As anthropologist Andrea Rugh has pointed out in a recent book, such economic forces as inflation have recently driven many women into the job market out of necessity. They often relate their outside jobs in a positive way to their roles as wives and mothers. That is, their job means more resources to support the family. [15] Furthermore, it seems that, especially in urban areas, educating girls makes them more attractive as potential wives because it improves their ability to get a socially acceptable job outside the home. [16]

Thus, an economy which makes working outside the home necessary for many women, plus a welfare-oriented state which provides free education, guaranteed jobs, and other rights for women, combine to encourage people to support the legitimacy of that which has become necessary. Numerically, women are now minor components of a labor force and national elite into both of which they have only recently gained access. But the fact they are there at all and their numbers are growing, stimulated by economic forces, state policy, and regime leadership, suggests the direction of change favors continued and growing importance for women in Egyptian public life.

Foreign Influence

Throughout the period under review, Egypt has been a major international crossroads for commerce in ideas as well as goods. In some ways, foreign ideas may have hindered women in the exercise of political or economic functions (for example, capitalism in the nineteenth century caused women to lose status and diminished their economic roles), while in others they helped stimulate the feminist movement, (for example Qasim Amin and Hoda Sha'rawi both took some of their inspiration from abroad). More recently, Mrs. Sadat got the idea for reserved seats for women in parliament from the Sudan, demonstrating that not all foreign ideas have come from the West. As clear as foreign ideas are in the history of the advancement of women in Egypt, it cannot be said that the whole issue is simply a foreign notion. The outside world serves as a source of ideas for some Egyptians, but those ideas are quickly adapted to local needs and "Egyptianized." Some women in the elite are more cosmopolitan than others, but they are no less Egyptian for it. The vast majority of these women are at home in their own culture, not alienated from it. There is evidence of a strong "khawaga complex" in Egypt, whereby some people love all things that are foreign while others abhor them. However, no president has proposed legal changes *because* he wished to copy a foreign custom, and families do not decide to educate their girls *simply* to be like foreigners. Decisions such as these are complex and multi-dimensional and, as indicated above, often have strong economic as well as political motivations. As shown in chapter 1, the Egyptian feminist movement adopted a distinctly Egyptian character from the moment of its founding in 1923. Foreign notions are capable of influencing events in Egypt, as they are in most countries, without compromising Egypt's integrity. Furthermore, the impetus to reform the rules pertaining to women's status and roles has emanated from Egyptian nationalists and patriots who hoped to strengthen Egypt by their efforts to improve conditions for women. It is also important to recall that some of what is seen as "new", such as, women managing a business, can be thought of as traditional and authentic, in that it was common among the Egyptian elite in the eighteenth century. In part, as Egypt "modernized" it returned to an earlier tradition.

CLOSING THOUGHTS AND DIRECTIONS FOR FUTURE RESEARCH

Reflection on the significance of these conclusions can serve as a starting point for an attempt to derive lessons from history. These ideas can also serve as an agenda for future research. They suggest part of history must be rewritten to include the important but misunderstood role of women. It is also clear that micro- and macro-level research on the participation of women in Egypt's political and economic decision-making systems enables us to learn about Egypt's polity and economy as we learn about women. This research, for example, demonstrates that Egyptian public life has both a personalist and an institutional dimension and that ignoring either would result in a flawed view of Egypt. It also illustrates some of the complexity of such social structures as family, polity, and economy as well as showing some of the ways in which they are interrelated.

Research-oriented readers of this book should find several topics which merit attention for future investigation. Specific projects, which seem to me to be the most promising, could include research on any of the categories of women listed in the Introduction but not covered extensively in this book. For example, each of the following groups deserves a monograph of its own: women who have small businesses; the large number of women who have become active in local politics since 1979; women in the professions; women who own and manage agricultural land; and women in private voluntary agencies. Additionally, a biography of Doria Shafik, without whose activity and organization women might not have gained the vote, would be in order, as relatively little is known about her at this time.

The attitudes and behavior of women *and* men in their twenties and thirties deserves special attention, in order that we might have a clearer picture of what to expect when that generation begins to assume prominent roles in public life.[17] Also, studies which focus on peasant and labor union activity as well as detailed studies of women who have had especially long careers in politics or business would help illuminate some of the ways women cope with adversity. Another way of getting at the same issue would be to study women who have failed, or more positively, not yet succeeded, and compare them with a similar group of men.

Comparative studies of women in other third world and Arab countries in circumstances similar to the women in this book would be especially helpful.[18] Arab women who do research in this field have an obvious comparative advantage over other scholars, and they may wish to consider maximizing this advantage by concentrating on action-research programs, aimed at helping specific target groups of women — budding politicians, organizers, or entrepreneurs—as they try to solve practical problems. Another important question has to do with the changing attitudes and behavior of men with regard to the roles and status of women, and researchers of both sexes could do useful work in this area.

The women who were the subjects of this book were neither out of the public eye nor unimportant. They have legitimate and important roles to play in the public life of contemporary Egypt. For them, and the increasing numbers of women who emulate them, tradition is in the process of being transformed. Research on that transformation, especially that which involves direct interaction between researchers and agents of change, has a way of becoming part of the process. To the degree that is the case with this study and any work it helps stimulate, I hope the effect proves, on balance, to help improve the quality of life for all involved. This book provides a rough topographical sketch of how things have gone thus far and some projections regarding the future. It may induce others to produce a more accurate and finely detailed perspective than this brief overview allows. In any case, the interaction between thought and action will continue.

Appendices

CHRONOLOGY OF MAJOR EVENTS, 1873–1985

1873   The first government primary school was opened for girls.

1892   The magazine *Al-Fatah,* the first women's magazine published in Egypt, was started in Alexandria by Hind Nawfal, a Syrian Christian.

1899   Qasim Amin published *Tahrir al-Mar'a (Women's Emancipation).*

1901   Qasim Amin published *Al-Mar'a al-Jadida (The New Woman).*

1908   Fatima Rashid started the first women's magazine to be published in Egypt by an Egyptian Muslim, *Majallat Tarqiyat al Mar'a.*

1911   Malak Hifni Nasif presented ten demands to the Egyptian Legislative Assembly. All were rejected.

1914   The educational Union of Women was founded in Cairo.

1919   Hoda Sha'rawi led demonstrations of veiled women in support of the Egyptian nationalist cause. These were the first demonstrations of their kind in Egypt.

1920   Founding of Bank Misr (the Bank of Egypt) by Talat Harb.

1921   The first government secondary school was opened for girls.

1923   Hoda Sha'rawi attended the meeting of the International Alliance for Women in Rome. She, and the rest of the Egyptian delegation, returned to Egypt unveiled. Many other women began to follow their example.

171

The Egyptian Feminist Union was established in Cairo by Hoda Sha'rawi in March.

1924   The new constitution was approved. It included the principle that elementary education was to be free and obligatory for both sexes. The 1924 constitution did not give women the right to vote.

1925   The first Egyptian girls to be sent abroad by the government for advanced degrees, Soad Farid and Fardus Helbawi, left for England.

L'Egyptienne magazine, edited by Ceza Nabarawi, was published in French by the Egyptian Feminist Union. It continued publishing until 1940, when the war made its continuation impossible.

1925   Rose al-Youssef, which came to be the leading weekly political magazine in Egypt, was founded in Cairo by Fatma al-Yussef, a former actress.

1928   The first female students entered Cairo University.

1935   The Egyptian Feminist Union for the first time advocated equal political rights for women.

1937   Al-Masreyya, a fortnightly periodical, was published in Arabic by the Egyptian Feminist Union. The first editor was Mrs. Fatma Neimat Rashed.

1938   The Eastern Feminist Conference was held in Cairo. The chief issue was the question of Palestine.

1939   The Egyptian Ministry of Social Affairs was established.
World War II began.

1944   The Arab Feminist Union was founded in Cairo. Hoda Sha'rawi was elected president.

1945   United Nations was founded, with Egypt as a founding member.
World War II ended.

The League of Arab States was founded, with Egypt as a founding member.

Prime Minister Ahmad Maher was assassinated in August.

1946   Former minister Amin Othman was assassinated in January.

1947   An epidemic of cholera started in September.

On December 12, 1947, Hoda Sha'rawi died at the age of 68.

1948   A woman's political party, Bint al-Nil, was established in Cairo by Mrs. Doria Shafik.

Egyptian troops entered Palestine, attempting to prevent the establishment of Israel.

1949   Legalized prostitution was abolished, culminating a 35-year cam-
          paign by Egyptian feminists.

          Hasan al-Banna, Supreme Guide of the Muslim Brethren, was
          assassinated.

1950   Parliamentary elections were held.

1951   In January, mobs burned many sections of Cairo.

          Members of Bint al-Nil briefly occupied parliament demanding
          representation for women.

          Wafdist Minister of Education Dr. Taha Hussein made education
          free through the secondary level.

1952   The Free Officers' Revolution succeeded. The constitution was
          abolished and political activity in general was circumscribed.

1953   All political parties were made illegal on January 16, 1953.

1956   The new constitution was promulgated giving women the right
          to vote for the first time in the history of Egypt.

          The Suez Canal was nationalized. Shortly after this the Suez War
          broke out, with France, Britain, and Israel invading Egypt. Due
          in major part to American and Soviet diplomatic intervention, the
          foreign forces withdrew, and Egypt assumed ownership and con-
          trol of the canal.

          French and British interests in Egypt were nationalized after the
          Suez War.

1957   Parliamentary elections were held. The first women were elected
          to parliament.

1961   Most of the private sector of the Egyptian economy was nation-
          alized.

          A decision was made by the government to make higher educa-
          tion free.

1962   The National Charter was promulgated.

          Dr. Hekmat Abu Zeid was the first woman appointed to the cabi-
          net, as she became the minister for social affairs, serving until 1965.

1964   Parliamentary elections were held.

1967   Egypt, Syria, and Jordan were defeated by Israel in the June War.

1968   The March 30 Program was promulgated as an effort to encour-
          age the private sector and reform the public sector.

1969   Parliamentary elections were held.

1970   Anwar Sadat replaced Gamal Abdel Nasser as president of Egypt following Nasser's death from natural causes.

1971   Dr. Aisha Rateb became the second woman appointed to the cabinet as minister of social affairs.

A new constitution was promulgated, following the May 1971 "corrective revolution," by which President Sadat purged Ali Sabri and others for allegedly planning to kill him. The new constitution is perceived by many as more conservative as it emphasized women's role in the family.

A fifteen-year Treaty of Friendship and Cooperation was signed between Egypt and the Soviet Union.

Elections for Majlis al-Shaab were held.

1973   The October War was fought with Israel. Both Egypt and Israel claimed victory, and the United States became involved heavily in Middle East diplomacy.

1974   Arab oil-exporting countries boycotted the United States and the Netherlands. Oil prices increased dramatically. The boycott was lifted following the Second Disengagement Agreement with Israel.

The United States and Egypt renewed formal diplomatic relations, and the United States began making substantial aid transfers to Egypt.

The "Open Door" economic policy was promulgated in President Sadat's "October Paper," in which he outlined his plans for postwar Egypt.

1976   The fifteen-year treaty of friendship between Egypt and the Soviet Union, signed in 1972, was abrogated unilaterally by Egypt on March 15.

Parliamentary elections were held using the political "platforms" of right, left and center, permitted by law since November 1975. The center, government, platform won 82% of the seats.

1977   In January, the government announced cuts in subsidies for such basic staples as bread and cooking oil. Riots ensued and the subsidies were restored.

In a cabinet shuffle in February, Aisha Rateb was replaced as minister of social affairs by Dr. Amal Othman, who thus became the third woman to serve in that post.

In November, President Sadat went to Jerusalem and spoke at the Knesset.

1978 President Carter invited Prime Minister Begin and President Sadat to Camp David in September. Basic agreements were reached regarding a peace treaty between Israel and Egypt.

1979 March 1979: The Camp David treaty between Egypt and Israel was signed. Most Arab states broke off formal diplomatic relations with Egypt. An Israeli embassy opened in Cairo and an Egyptian embassy opened in Tel Aviv. In addition to development assistance, Egypt now began to receive military aid from the United States.

The law was changed to provide for 30 reserved seats for women in the Majlis al-Shaab. The law of local government was amended to provide that 10% to 20% of the seats on all local councils must be reserved for women.

Parliamentary elections were held. Four legal political parties, plus numerous independents, contested elections. The government party, the NDP, won nearly 90% of the seats in Majlis al-Shaab.

The Personal Status Laws were amended, reforming rules pertaining to divorce, alimony, and child custody.

Dr. Aisha Rateb became the first Egyptian woman to be appointed ambassador.

1980 The Majlis al-Shura was formed with 7 women among its 210 original members.

1981 President Sadat ordered over 1500 people arrested for political as well as domestic security reasons. Several women were included in the group.

In October, President Sadat was assassinated. Hosny Mubarak became President of Egypt, proclaiming his commitment to the continuation of Sadat's basic policies.

1984 Parliamentary elections were held, with the (government) Hezb al-Watani party winning 87% of the seats in the Majlis al-Shaab.

1985 In May, the Higher Constitutional Court declared the 1979 amendments to the Personal Status Laws unconstitutional on procedural grounds.

In July, Majlis al-Shaab passed new amendments to the Personal Status Laws which were almost identical to the 1979 amendments.

TABLES FOR CHAPTERS 2, 5, AND 6

TABLE 2.1. LOCATION DURING YOUTH

	total urban	rural (I)	rural (W)	total rural	TOTAL
N =	25	12	9	21	46
Urban	24	1	1	2	26
Provincial capital	1	5	6	11	12
Village	—	6	2	8	8
No response	—	—	—	—	—

I = Islamic dress

W = Western dress

TABLE 2.2. DEATH OF A PARENT

	total urban	rural (I)	rural (W)	total rural	TOTAL
N =	22	12	9	21	43
Father died	5	3	2	5	10
Mother died	1	3	—	3	4
Both died	—	—	—	—	—
Two parent family	11	6	7	13	24
No response	5	—	—	—	5

TABLE 2.3. MOST SUPPORTIVE PARENT

	total urban	rural (I)	rural (W)	total rural	TOTAL
N =	22	12	9	21	43
Father	6	4	2	6	12
Mother	3	1	1	2	5
Both	3	2	4	6	9
Neither	4	2	1	3	7
Other	—	3	1	4	4
No response	6	—	—	—	6

TABLE 2.4. FATHER'S EDUCATION

	total urban	rural (I)	rural (W)	total rural	TOTAL
N =	22	12	9	21	43
Illiterate	—	2	—	2	2
At home	1	—	2	2	3
Primary only	1	3	1	4	5
Secondary highest	1	2	3	5	6
University highest	14	4	3	7	21
Post-grad. degree	—	—	—	—	—
No response	5	1	—	1	6

TABLE 2.5. MOTHER'S EDUCATION

	total urban	rural (I)	rural (W)	total rural	TOTAL
N =	22	12	9	21	43
Illiterate	1	3	3	6	7
At home	3	5	1	6	9
Primary only	3	2	2	4	7
Secondary highest	9	1	3	4	13
University highest	—	—	—	—	—
Post-grad. degree	—	—	—	—	—
No response	6	1	—	1	7

TABLE 2.6. HIGHEST EDUCATION RECEIVED

	total urban	rural (I)	rural (W)	total rural	TOTAL
N =	22	12	9	21	43
Primary	—	—	—	—	—
Secondary	5	5	2	7	12
University	6	7	7	14	20
Post-grad.	11	—	—	—	11
No response	—	—	—	—	—

TABLE 2.7. LANGUAGE ABILITY

	total urban	rural (I)	rural (W)	total rural	TOTAL
N =	22	12	9	21	43
"Good" Arabic plus "good" foreign lang.	12	2	2	4	16
Other	9	10	7	17	26
No response	1	—	—	—	1

TABLE 2.8. MARITAL STATUS*

	total urban	rural (I)	rural (W)	total rural	TOTAL
N =	25	12	9	21	46
Married	16	11	8	19	35
Widowed	2	1	1	2	4
Divorced*	4	—	—	—	4
Single	3	—	—	—	3
No response	—	—	—	—	—

*This refers to the marital status when the data for this study were gathered. One woman was divorced and remarried and is listed here as married.

TABLE 2.9. AGE AT MARRIAGE

	total urban	rural (I)	rural (W)	total rural	TOTAL
N =	14	10	4	14	28
15–19	1	3	1	4	5
20–29	12	5	2	7	19
30–39	1	1	1	2	3
40–49	—	—	—	—	—
50–59	—	1	—	1	1
Mean	25.4	25.0	26.5	25.4	25.4

TABLE 2.10. NUMBER OF CHILDREN

(excludes nonresponses and single respondents)

	total urban	rural (I)	rural (W)	total rural	TOTAL
N =	19	12	9	21	40
0	4	2	2	4	8
1	—	—	1	1	1
2	8	1	2	3	11
3	6	5	3	8	14
4	1	2	1	3	4
5	—	1	—	1	1
6	—	1	—	1	1
Mean	2.0	3.0	2.0	2.6	2.3

TABLE 2.11. PROFESSIONAL BACKGROUND

	total urban	rural (I)	rural (W)	total rural	TOTAL
N =	25	12	9	21	46
Educational administration	2	5	2	7	9
University level teaching/research	8	—	—	—	8
Housewife	4	2	2	4	8
Law	2	1	1	2	4
Writer/journalism (includes radio and television)	4	—	—	—	4
Medicine/dentistry	1	—	2	2	3
Social work	1	1	1	2	3
Teacher	—	1	—	1	1
Military	1	—	—	—	1
Agricultural engineer	—	1	—	1	1
Politician	1	—	—	—	1
Entertainment	1	—	—	—	1
Accounting	—	—	1	1	1
Landlord	—	1	—	1	1

TABLE 2.12. SPOUSE'S EDUCATION

	total urban	rural (I)	rural (W)	total rural	TOTAL
N =	22	12	9	21	43
Illiterate	—	—	—	—	—
At home	—	—	—	—	—
Primary only	—	—	—	—	—
Secondary highest	1	2	—	2	3
Univ. highest	10	9	8	17	27
Post-grad. degree	8	1	—	1	9
No response	1	—	1	1	2
Single	2	—	—	—	2

TABLE 2.13. PROFESSION OF SPOUSE
(excludes single respondents)

	total urban	rural (I)	rural (W)	total rural	TOTAL
N =	20	12	9	21	41
Law	4	2	2	4	8
University level teaching/research	5	—	—	—	5
General civil service	2	4	1	5	7
Medicine/dentistry	2	1	1	2	4
Senior national civil service	2	—	1	1	3
Private business	2	1	—	1	3
Educational administration	—	3	—	3	3
Agricultural engineer	—	—	2	2	2
Other engineering	—	1	1	2	2
Writer/journalism (includes radio and television)	1	—	—	—	1
Military	1	—	1	1	2
Politician	—	—	—	—	—
Entertainment	—	—	—	—	—
Accounting	—	—	—	—	—
Social work	—	—	—	—	—
Landlord	—	—	—	—	—
Teacher	—	—	—	—	—
No response	1	—	—	—	1

TABLE 2.14. AGE AT FIRST ENTRY INTO PARLIAMENT

	total urban	rural (I)	rural (W)	total rural	TOTAL
N =	25	12	9	21	46
Between 20–29	1	—	1	1	2
Between 30–39	7	4	3	7	14
Between 40–49	8	4	2	6	14
Between 50–59	4	1	2	3	7
Between 60–69	4	3	1	4	8
Between 70–79	1	—	—	—	1
Mean	47.7	45.8	41.7	44.0	46.0

TABLE 2.15. POLITICAL ASSETS

	total urban	rural (I)	rural (W)	total rural	TOTAL
N =	20	12	9	21	41
Prominent local family*	4	6	7	13	17 (41%)
Social activities	6	7	6	13	19 (46%)
Previous political activity	14	7	5	12	26 (63%)
Connections due to profession	14	7	5	12	26 (63%)
Broad name familiarity†	3	—	—	—	3 (7.3%)
No response	2	—	—	—	2
Mean number of assets	2.05	2.25	2.55	2.33	2.33

*Self identification of "prominence" plus data on respondents' families were both used to produce this measure. The result was checked with party insiders. "Local" refers to the specific electoral district.

†Broad name familiarity is a category not mentioned by party leaders as a political asset. However, three parliamentarians have extensive media experience and as a result are well known. They believed this factor helped them win popular support but it is unclear as to whether or not it helped them win the Party's nomination.

TABLE 2.16. VOLUNTARY SOCIAL SERVICE AND POLITICAL SUCCESS

	total urban	rural (I)	rural (W)	total rural	TOTAL
N =	24	12	9	21	45
Social service main key to success	4	1	2	3	7
Social service plus other work was key	7	6	5	11	18
Social service unrelated to political success	13	5	2	7	20

TABLE 2.17. PARTY EXPERIENCE PRIOR TO ENTRY INTO PARLIAMENT

	total urban	rural (I)	rural (W)	total rural	TOTAL
N =	24	12	9	21	45
Little or none	4	1	3	4	8
Moderate	2	—	—	—	2
Extensive	16	5	6	11	27
Ran as independent	—	3	—	3	3
Opposition party	1	—	—	—	1
No response	1	3	—	3	4

*Party experience means active involvement in at least one of the following organizations: National Union; ASU; Misr Party; Hezb al-Watani al-Democrati (NDP); a legal opposition party.

TABLE 2.18. PRINCIPAL PARLIAMENTARY COMMITTEE MEMBERSHIP:
1982-83*

Majlis al-Shaab

	total urban	rural (I)	rural (W)	total rural	TOTAL
N =	25	12	9	21	46
Planning	—	1	—	1	1
Economy	—	—	—	—	—
Legislative/Law	—	1	1	2	2
Proposals/Complaints	—	—	—	—	—
Arab Affairs	—	1	—	1	1
Foreign Affairs	2	—	—	—	2
Industry and Energy	—	1	—	1	1
Agriculture and Irrigation	—	2	2	4	4
Social, Awqaf and Religious Offices	7	—	1	1	8
Health	1	—	2	2	3
Youth	1	—	1	1	2
Education and Science Research	1	5	1	6	7
Culture, Information and Tourism	1	—	—	—	1
Transportation	—	—	—	—	—
Housing	2	—	1	1	3
Labor	—	—	—	—	—
Public Security and Mobilization	—	—	—	—	—
Local Government and National Organizations	—	—	—	—	—
No response	3	1	—	1	4

Majlis Al-Shura: 1982-83

	total urban	rural (I)	rural (W)	total rural	TOTAL
Services	4	—	—	—	4
Foreign Affairs	1	—	—	—	1
Production	—	—	—	—	—
Economic Affairs	—	—	—	—	—
Legislation	—	—	—	—	—
No Response	2	—	—	—	2

*Committee assignments are for 1982–83 for the women in parliament at that time. For the women included in this study, because they served in earlier parliaments, committee assignments refer to their principal assignment at that time.

TABLE 2.19. ROLE DEFINITION: Local vs National Issues

	total urban	rural (I)	rural (W)	total rural	TOTAL
N =	22	12	9	21	43
Local issues/ constituent service	6	7	6	13	19
National issues/ elected to Shaab	4	5	2	7	11
National issues/ appointed or in Shura	11	—	—	—	11
No response	1	—	1	1	2

TABLE 2.20. PERSONAL STATUS LAW: Attitudes toward Further Changes

	total urban	rural (I)	rural (W)	total rural	TOTAL
N =	21	12	9	21	42
Oppose: too conservative	1	—	—	—	1
Oppose: too liberal	—	1	—	1	1
Support: don't change	4	6	6	12	16
Support: also would support more change	6	3	2	5	11
Support: no comment on further change	9	2	1	3	12
No response	1	—	—	—	1

TABLE 5.1. CHANGES IN THE QUALITY OF LIFE IN EGYPT: 1960–80

	1960	1980
Population (in thousands)	25,832	42,289
Urban population (% of total)	38	45
Life expectancy at birth	46	57
Enrollment in primary schools (% of age group)		
A.) Total	66	76
B.) Male	80	89
C.) Female	52	63
Enrollment in secondary schools (% of age group)	16	52
Enrollment in higher education (% of age 20–24)	5	15
Adult literacy rate (%)	26	44 (B)*
Energy consumption per capita (kilograms of coal equivalent)	299	595

TABLE 5.2 ECONOMIC CHANGES IN EGYPT: 1960–80

	1960	1980
Gross domestic product (GDP) (In millions: U.S.$)	3,880	23,110
Distribution of GDP (%)		
A.) Agriculture	30	21
B.) Industry	24	38
C.) Services	46	41
Destination of merchandise exports (%)		
A.) Industrial market economies	26	51 (A)*
B.) Developing countries	39	24 (A)
C.) Nonmarket industrial economies	33	21 (A)
D.) Capital surplus oil exporters	2	4 (A)
Fuels, minerals and metals (% of total merchandise exports)	4	67
Textiles and clothing (% of total merchandise exports)	9	9
External public debt (In millions: U.S.$)	1,644	11,409
GNP per capital ($U.S.)		480 (A)

*A = 1979; B = 1976

Sources for Table 5.1 and Table 5.2: World Bank, World Development Report 1981, 1982, 1983; Central Agency for Public Mobilization and Statistics, Statistical Yearbook (July 1981) Arab Republic of Egypt.

TABLE 5.3. BALANCE OF PAYMENTS (U.S.$ billions)

	FY 1979–80	FY 1980–81
Exports	3.4	4.3
(of which oil products)	2.1	2.7
Cotton and cotton products	0.7	0.6
Imports	7.2	8.6
Trade balance	– 3.8	– 4.3
Services receipts	4.9	5.4
(of which tourism)	0.9	1.1
Suez Canal	0.7	0.8
Workers' remittances	3.0	3.0
Services payments and transfers	1.9	2.4
Current account balance	– 0.8	– 1.2

Source: (London) *Financial Times Survey,* June 7, 1982, p. II.

**TABLE 6.1. CLASS ORIGINS OF WOMEN IN THE POLITICAL
AND ECONOMIC ELITE OF EGYPT**

	Parliamentary Women*		Pres. Wives	Opp.*	Business	TOTAL
	urban	rural				
Upper class[1]	6	1		2	8	17 (22.9)
Upper-middle class[2]	13	14	2	6	3	38 (51.3)
Middle class[3]	1	6	1		1	9 (12.2)
Working class[4]				2		2 (2.7)
Peasant[5]				1		1 (1.4)
Not reported	2			5		7 (9.5)

*Three urban women who are in both the parliamentary group and the opposition group are counted here as opposition rather than as parliamentary, thus reducing the size of the latter category from 25 to 22.

1. "Upper class" includes people whose father fits into at least one of the following groups: titled before 1952; cabinet member before 1952; governor before 1952; part of the Talat Harb group or other *major* capitalist activity; self-reported high family income; major land holding, had land taken in the immediate aftermath of the 1952 coup; sequestrated in 1961.

2. "Upper-middle class" includes people not included under "upper class" whose father fits into at least one of the following groups: professional, for example, physician or lawyer, before 1952; successful in business, but not part of the top national capitalist group; self-reported above average family income; owner of at least 50 feddans but less than 200 feddans; holder of a major civil service position.

3. "Middle class" includes people not included above whose father fits into at least one of the following groups: small tradesman; minor civil service; bedouin leader; village headman; owner of between 5 and 49 feddans.

4. "Working class" includes people not included above whose father fits into at least one of the following groups: manual laborer; nonfarm; craftsman.

5. "Peasant" includes people not included above whose father fits into at least one of the following groups: owner of less than 5 feddans; farm laborer.

Notes

A s THIS is a book about Egypt, Arabic words have, for the most part, been transliterated into English in an attempt to suggest the way they are pronounced in Egyptian colloquial Arabic rather than classical Arabic. Thus, the first name of President Nasser is written Gamal rather than Jamal. I tried to follow this rule consistently, but some names are spelled the way the individual in question prefers to have it written in English rather than the way it is pronounced in Egyptian colloquial. For example, the name of the minister of social affairs is written Amal Othman rather than Amal Osman, and Amina al-Sayyid's name appears as Amina Said. There is no English alphabet equivalent for some letters in Arabic, for example, the *ayn*. When necessary to render this letter in order to replicate Egyptian pronunciation, an apostrophe has been used.

The Egyptian currency, commonly called the pound, has changed in value considerably during the period of history covered by this book. Prior to July 1947, Egypt was part of the Sterling Zone. Some illustrative real market rates for the Egyptian pound since then are:

> 1948   £E 1 = $2.87
> 1962   £E 1 = $2.30
> 1982   £E 1 = $1.00
> 1985   £E 1 = $ .75

Land in Egypt is measured in a traditional unit called a *feddan*.

> 1 feddan = 1.038 acres = .42 hectares

189

INTRODUCTION

1. In addition to works cited in this volume, readers may wish to consult the following bibliographies. A. al-Qazzaz, *Women in the Middle East and North Africa: An Annotated Bibliography* (Austin: Middle East Monograph No. 2, Center for Middle Eastern Studies, University of Texas, 1977); Soha Abdel-Kader, "Survey of Trends in Research on Women," in: UNESCO, *Social Science Research and Women in the Arab World* (Paris, London, and Dover, N.H.: Frances Pinter Publishers for UNESCO, 1984), pp. 139–75.

2. Abdel-Kader, *"Trends in Research on Women,"* p. 154.

3. For example, see: Afaf Lutfi al-Sayyid Marsot, "The Revolutionary Gentlewomen in Egypt," in *Women in the Muslim World*, ed. Lois Beck and Nikki Keddie (Cambridge and London: Harvard University Press, 1978), pp. 261–76; Thomas Philipp, "Feminism and Nationalist Politics in Egypt," in *Women in the Muslim World*, pp. 277–94; and the forthcoming study of Hoda Sha'rawi by Margo Badran.

4. Cynthia Nelson, "Changing Roles of Men and Women: Illustrations from Egypt," *Anthropological Quarterly* 41 (April 1968): 57–77; and "Public and Private Politics: Women in the Middle Eastern World," *American Ethnologist* 1 (August 1974), 551–63.

5. Kathleen Howard-Merriam, "Egypt's Other Political Elite," *Western Political Quarterly* 34 (March 1981): 174–87.

6. Abdel-Kader, "Trends in Research on Women," pp. 148–54, mentions some examples of work of this type. Ideology may have something to do with the paucity of studies on women in business and entrepreneurship, in general, has been a relatively neglected topic in social science until quite recently.

7. See Abdel-Kader, "Trends in Research on Women," pp. 151–54, for citations of works in these categories.

8. For example, see: Renate Duelli Klein, "How To Do What We Want To Do: Thoughts About Feminist Methodology," in *Theories Of Women's Studies*, ed. Gloria Bowles and Renate Duelli Klein (London and Boston: Routledge and Kegan Paul, 1983), pp. 92–93; and UNESCO, *Research and Women in the Arab World*, pp. vii–viii, Preface; and Amal Rassam, "Introduction; Arab Women: The Status of Research in the Social Sciences and the Status of Women," esp. pp. 1–2, in UNESCO, *Research and Women in the Arab World*; Maria Mies, "Toward a Methodology for Feminist Research," in *Theories of Women's Studies*, pp. 117–39.

9. Rassam, "Introduction," pp. 2–4.

10. One recent example of an excellent book which uses the public-male/private-female concept is Michael Gilsenan, *Recognizing Islam: Religion and Society in the Modern Arab World* (New York: Random House, Pantheon Books, 1982). This model is not unique to studies of the Arab world and can be seen in Western society and thought as well. For a discussion of this issue in Western political theory see Jean Bethke Elshtain, *Public Man, Private Woman* (Princeton: Princeton University Press, 1981).

11. Amal Rassam, "Toward a Theoretical Framework for the Study of Women in the Arab World," esp. pp. 125–27, in UNESCO, *Research and Women in the Arab World*, argues for a similar focus in an essay published approximately two years after this research started. For an interesting discussion of patriarchy in the Arab world from a Marxist perspective, see Rosemary Sayigh, "Roles and Functions of Arab Women:

A Reappraisal," *Arab Studies Quarterly* 3 (Autumn 1981), 258–74; Khalil Nakhleh, "Commentary," *Arab Studies Quarterly* 4 (Autumn 1982), 254–55; Rosemary Sayigh, "Response," *Arab Studies Quarterly* 4 (Autumn 1982), 256–60.

12. For the rationale behind this method, see: Barbara Du Bois, "Passionate Scholarship: Notes On Values, Knowing and Method in Feminist Social Science," pp. 105–16, in Bowles and Klein, *Theories of Women's Studies*; Marcia Westkott, "Women's Studies as a Strategy for Change: Between Criticism and Vision," pp. 210–18, in *Theories of Women's Studies*.

13. Nelson, "Public and Private Politics," p. 561. The idea of being "true" to the subjects of research is a major issue in social research but seems to me to be especially intense in women's studies. Some points relevant to this issue are discussed in: Maria Mies, "Towards a Methodology for Feminist Research," pp. 117–39; and Toby Epstein Jayaratne, "The Value of Quantitative Methodology for Feminist Research," pp. 140–61, both in Bowles and Klein, *Theories of Women's Studies*.

When this book is published, I expect to be living in Egypt. The book will be available there and many of its subjects can be expected to read it or hear about it. Whereas many social scientists write about subjects whom they will never see again, that is not the case with this study, and I have tried to represent them so that they will see an accurate reflection of their lives and attitudes in this book. It may be that some will not be pleased with that reflection, but I have done my best to see that the reflection will be their own.

14. Sayigh, "Response," 259–60. Ms. Sayigh considers herself to be a Marxist feminist with a perspective different from that of either traditional Marxists or traditional feminists. Marxists often tend to see the exploitation of women as a subsidiary problem to be solved after the root problem of class exploitation and dominance is dealt with. Feminists, on the other hand, tend to see the exploitation of women as primary, related to class inequality but not subordinate to it. Feminists and Marxists often join hands in common cause, but I have often noticed considerable tension between them regarding the issue of priorities. Ms. Sayigh is concerned about such issues as patriarchy in the party and too much trust being placed in the force of modernization, and is trying to effect a synthesis of Marxism and feminism.

15. For example see: Amos Perlmutter, *Egypt: The Praetorian State* (New Brunswick, N.J.: Transaction, 1974); Robert Springborg, *Family, Power and Politics in Egypt: Sayed Bey Marei — His Clan, Clients, and Cohorts* (Philadelphia: University of Pennsylvania Press, 1982); R. Hrair Dekmejian, *Egypt Under Nasser* (Albany: State University of New York Press, 1971); Shahrough Akhavi, "Egypt: Neo-Patrimonial Elite," in ed. Frank Tachau, *Political Elites and Political Development in the Middle East* (Cambridge, Mass.: Schenkman, 1975), pp. 69–113.

16. Springborg, *Family, Power, and Politics*, esp. pp. 105–14.

17. An excellent discussion of corporatism as it pertains to Egypt can be found in Robert Bianchi, "Changing Patterns of Interest Group Representation in Modern Egypt," the American University in Cairo, 1984, unpublished paper. Also see Leonard Binder, *In a Moment of Enthusiasm: Political Power and the Second Stratum in Egypt* (Chicago: University of Chicago Press, 1978), esp. pp. 1–32.

18. John Waterbury, *The Egypt of Nasser and Sadat: The Political Economy of Two Regimes* (Princeton: Princeton University Press, 1983), p. xiii. Waterbury also points

out that the minister of defense has not always been in the top group because not all presidents have always granted that power to all defense ministers (p. xiii). The fact that the minister of defense has not always been among the few most important leaders of the country does not imply he has ever been unimportant. A conception of the elite which recognizes its depth is essential if we are to understand how the Egyptian system works.

19. Leonard Binder's book, *In a Moment of Enthusiasm*, also uses a similarly broadened and deepened concept of the Egyptian elite in his study of the role of the rural middle class, or "second stratum" in Egyptian politics. To some degree, I take as given what he described at great length. Also see Raymond A. Hinnebusch, "Political Participation and the Authoritarian-Modernizing State in the Middle East: Limited Institutionalization and Political Activism in Syria and Egypt" (paper presented at the 1983 Annual Meeting of the Middle East Studies Association, Chicago). Another book which has a partly analogous focus is Clement Henry Moore's study of Egyptian engineers, *Images of Development: Egyptian Engineers in Search of Industry* (Cambridge, Mass.: MIT Press, 1980).

20. Waterbury, *The Egypt of Nasser and Sadat*, pp. 3–20, elaborates on these themes and concepts. Also see Bianchi, "Changing Patterns of Interest Group Representation."

21. Waterbury, *The Egypt of Nasser and Sadat,* p. 10.

22. The phrase is borrowed from the title of an article by Fouad Ajami, "The Struggle for Egypt's Soul," *Foreign Policy* 35 (Summer 1979), pp. 3–30.

23. Waterbury, *The Egypt of Nasser and Sadat*, esp. pp. 21–40.

24. Fadwa el-Guindi, "Veiling Infitah With Muslim Ethic: Egypt's Contemporary Islamic Movement," *Social Problems* 28 (April 1981): 465–85; and "Veiled Activism: Egyptian Women in the Contemporary Islamic Movement," *Femmes de la Mediterranee Peuples Mediterraneens* 22–23 (January–June, 1983), pp. 79–89. Professor el-Guindi also has a book forthcoming, tentatively entitled *Islamic Feminism.*

25. The level of analysis framework is one used frequently in the study of international relations. See J. David Singer, "The Level of Analysis Problem in International Relations," in ed. J. N. Rosenau, *International Politics and Foreign Policy: A Reader in Research and Theory* (New York: Free Press, 1969), pp. 20–29.

26. There is a general paucity of research on women as agents of change. See Sylvia Hale, "Women as Change Agents: A Neglected Research Area," pp. 42–46, in E. A. (Nora) Cebotarev and Frances M. Shaver, *Women and Agricultural Production* (Toronto: Resources for Feminist Research, Volume 2, No. 1, March 1982); and Sue Ellen M. Charlton, *Women In Third World Development*, (Boulder and London: Westview Press, 1984).

27. At that stage, the four groups not well represented, out of the fifteen mentioned above, were: (1) business women who own and manage such enterprises as coffee shops, groups of taxis, etc.; (2) agriculturalists, who own and manage agricultural land; (3) public sector managers; and (4) politicians active via their husbands' positions. Adding presidential wives to the study group added category number four, and adding opposition women gave better representation to women in the political opposition, women in local politics, journalism, and education.

28. Roughly the same result might have been achieved by a chapter on, for example, women in journalism or the fine and performing arts, but opposition women

(many of whom are journalists) were in direct juxtaposition to parliamentary women and seemed to me, several parliamentary women, and most of the Egyptian social scientists whom I consulted at the time to be a better choice.

CHAPTER 1—THE PUBLIC ROLE OF WOMEN IN MODERN EGYPT

1. Baheega S. Rasheed, *The Egyptian Feminist Union* (Cairo: Dar El Maamoon, 1973), pp. 6–7.
2. Saad Eddin Ibrahim, *Egypt in a Quarter of a Century (1952–1977)* (Beirut: Arab Promotion Institute, 1981), pp. 43–44. (In Arabic).
3. Ceza Nabarawi made this point several times in a May 1979 interview with the author.
4. Baheega Arafa, *The Social Activities of the Egyptian Feminist Union* (Cairo: Elias Modern Press, 1954). Also see: Nancy Adams Schilling, "The Social and Political Roles of Arab Women: A Study in Conflict," in *Women in Contemporary Muslim Societies*, ed. Jane I. Smith (Lewisburg: Bucknell University Press, 1980), pp. 100–145; Kathleen Howard-Merriam, "Egypt's Other Political Elite," *Western Political Quarterly* 34 (March 1981): 174–87; Laila el-Hamamsy, "The Changing Role of the Egyptian Women," *Middle East Forum* 33 (1958), p. 24; Laila el-Hamamsy, "The Role of Women in the Development of Egypt," *Middle East Forum* 33 (1958), pp. 592–601.
5. The forthcoming book by Nancy Gallagher covers this topic in detail. See "Helping Others: Epidemics, Medical Aid, and the Struggle for Power in Egypt, 1940–1950" (Santa Barbara, Calif.: manuscript in progress, 1985).
6. Arafa, *The Social Activities of the Egyptian Feminist Union*, p. 1.
7. Kathleen Howard-Merriam, "Women, Education, and the Professions in Egypt," *Comparative Education Review* 23 (June, 1979), pp. 256–70.
8. Soha Abdel-Kader, *The Status of Egyptian Women 1900–1973* (Cairo: American University in Cairo, Social Research Center, 1973); Earl L. Sullivan, "Women and Work in Egypt," in *Women and Work in the Arab World* by Earl L. Sullivan and Karima Korayem, Cairo Papers in Social Science 4 (Cairo, December 1981).
9. Nada Tomiche, "The Situation of Egyptian Women in the First Half of the 19th Century," in *Beginnings of Modernization in the Middle East*, ed. William Polk (Chicago, University of Chicago Press, 1968), pp. 171–84. Also see Judith Tucker, "Decline of the Family Economy in Mid-Nineteenth Century Egypt," *Arab Studies Quarterly* 1 (Summer 1979), pp. 245–71.
10. Cynthia Nelson, "Public and Private Politics: Women in the Middle Eastern World," *American Ethnologist* 1 (August 1974), p. 551ff.
11. Enid Hill, *Mahkama: Studies in the Egyptian Legal System* (London: Ithaca Press, 1979), p. 73.
12. Tomiche, "The Situation of Egyptian Women," p. 177.
13. Afaf Lutfi al-Sayyid Marsot, "The Revolutionary Gentlewomen in Egypt," in *Women in the Muslim World*, ed. Lois Beck and Nikki Keddie (Cambridge and London: Harvard University Press, 1978), pp. 261–76.
14. Amina Said, "The Arab Woman and the Challenge of Society," in *Middle*

Eastern Muslim Women Speak, ed. Elizabeth Furnea and Basima Q. Bezirgan (Austin: University of Texas Press, 1977), pp. 374–90.

15. Ruth F. Woodsmall, *The Role of Women: A Study of the Role of Women, Their Activities and Organizations in Lebanon, Egypt, Iraq, Jordan and Syria* (London and New York: The International Federation of Business and Professional Women, 1956), p. 24. For those who wish a useful overview of social and political events in modern Egypt, see P. J. Vatikiotis, *The History of Egypt*, 2nd ed. (Baltimore: Johns Hopkins University Press, 1980).

16. Qasim Amin, *Tahrir al-Mara* (Cairo, N.P., 1899) and *Al Mara al Jadida* (Cairo, N.P., 1901). On Qasim Amin see the excellent article by Juan Ricardo Cole, "Feminism, Class and Islam in Turn-of-the-Century Egypt," *International Journal of Middle Eastern Studies* 13 (November 1981), pp. 387–405.

17. Thomas Philipp, "Feminism and Nationalist Politics in Egypt," in *Women in the Muslim World*, Beck and Keddie, p. 278.

18. Albert Hourani, *Arabic Thought in the Liberal Age, 1798–1939* (Cambridge: Cambridge University Press, 1983), esp. pp. 67–102; 130–60.

19. John L. Esposito, *Women in Muslim Family Law*, (Syracuse: Syracuse University Press, 1982), p. 50.

20. Ibid.

21. Philipp, "Feminism and Nationalist Politics," p. 279.

22. Cole, "Feminism, Class and Islam," p. 404.

23. Ibid, p. 286.

24. Arafa, *Social Activities of the Egyptian Feminist Union*, p. 2.

25. Mohammed Nowaihi, "Changing the Law on Personal Status Within a Liberal Interpretation of the Sharia," in *Law and Social Change*, ed. Cynthia Nelson and Klaus F. Koch (Cairo: Cairo Papers in Social Science, Volume 2, No. 4, 1979).

26. Arafa, *Social Activities of the Egyptian Feminist Union*, p. 3.

27. Philipp, "Feminism and Nationalist Politics," p. 289.

28. Arafa, *Social Activities of the Egyptian Feminist Union*, p. 4.

29. Ibid.

30. Nadav Safran, *Egypt in Search of Political Community* (Cambridge: Harvard University Press, 1961), pp. 141–64.

31. Rasheed, *The Egyptian Feminist Union*, pp. 46; 55.

32. Hourani, *Arabic Thought in the Liberal Age*, p. 171ff. On Ahmad Lutfi al-Sayyid, see Afaf Lutfi al-Sayyid-Marsot, *Egypt's Liberal Experiment: 1922–1936* (Berkeley and Los Angeles: University of California Press, 1977).

33. The leaders of the Egyptian feminist movement were surely aware of these issues, as they participated regularly in international feminist conferences and, in general, were alert to what was going on in the world at that time. In the early 1920s, American feminists were concerned about birth control. Margaret Sanger founded the National Birth Control League in 1917, and international conferences were held on the topic regularly, starting in 1927. Perhaps Margo Badran's forthcoming book on Hoda Sha'rawi will shed more light on the reaction of early Egyptian feminists to these issues.

34. Amina Said in an interview with the author, April 1983, stated that self-respect was the first thing Hoda Sha'rawi taught her.

35. Arafa, *Social Activities of the Egyptian Feminist Union*, pp. 9–11.

36. Esposito, *Women in Muslim Family Law*, pp. 53–60.

37. Carolyn Fluehr-Lobban, "The Political Mobilization of Women in the Arab World," in *Women in Contemporary Muslim Societies*, ed. Jane I. Smith (Lewisburg: Bucknell University Press, 1980), pp. 245–46.

38. Audrey Chapman Smock and Nadia Haggag Youssef, "Egypt: From Seclusion to Limited Participation," in *Women: Roles and Status in Eight Countries*, ed. Janet Z. Giele and Audrey C. Smock (New York: John Wiley and Sons, 1977), p. 67.

39. Doria Shafik, "Egyptian Feminism," *Middle Eastern Affairs* III (August–September 1952), p. 234.

40. *Al-Ahram*, March 20, 1954, p. 1.

41. Khalid Ikram, *Egypt: Economic Management in a Period of Transition* (Baltimore and London: Johns Hopkins University Press for the World Bank, 1980), p. 110.

42. Sullivan, "Women and Work in Egypt," pp. 14–16.

43. Amal Othman, minister of social affairs, stressed this point repeatedly in a March 1983 interview with the author and in an undated and unpublished paper, "The Legal Status of Women in Egypt," which she gave me during the interview.

44. Helmy Tadros, *Social Security and the Family in Egypt* (Cairo: Cairo Papers in Social Science, Vol. 7, No. 1, March 1984).

45. Sullivan, "Women and Work in Egypt," p. 10.

46. Ibid., p. 26.

47. Ibid., p. 32.

48. Amal Othman, Egyptian minister of social affairs, in a March 1983 interview with me stated that the latest government figures available to her showed that women constituted roughly 15% of the formal labor force. The degree to which the issue of women working outside the home remains controversial is illustrated by an article appearing in a leftist Egyptian weekly newspaper which quotes a leading fundamentalist as saying that any woman who works outside the home is sinful and her sin is shared by her husband and all her male relatives. See "Sheikh Sha'rawi and the Sinful Women," *Al-Ahali*, July 3, 1985, p. 8 (in Arabic).

49. Sullivan, "Women and Work in Egypt," p. 35.

50. Ikram, *Egypt*, p. 130.

51. Amal Othman, in her March 1983 interview with me stated that she believed that "in the future" Egypt would have women judges, but she declined to speculate on how soon that change might come about.

52. Mahmoud Shaltout, "Women are Eligible to be Judges," *Rose al-Youssef*, December 17, 1962, p. 36. (In Arabic) Other Islamic countries, such as Algeria and Indonesia, have women judges.

53. *Al-Ahram*, July 4, 1980, p. 7.

54. Ragai Abdullah, "Case #520 That Stopped the Application of the Personal Status Law," *Al-Mussawar*, March 9, 1984, pp. 20–25, 72. (In Arabic)

55. On the constitutional law case, see "Personal Status Laws Not Valid," *Al-Ahram*, May 5, 1985, p. 1. For the Personal Status Laws passed by Majlis al-Shaab in 1985, see "Majlis al-Shaab Agrees With Majority in Principle," *Al-Ahram*, July 1, 1985, pp. 1, 11; "Majlis al-Shaab Agrees in Principle About Law of Personal Status," *Al-Akhbar*, pp. 1, 4. On page 4 of *Al-Akhbar*, July 1, 1985, there is a photo of eight

women members of Majlis al-Shaab, five of whom are veiled, participating in the debate on the new laws. For some of the political background to the new laws, see Judith Miller, "Egypt Divided by Court's Abolition of Law Guarding Rights of First Wives," *New York Times*, June 10, 1985, p. 4Y; and "Egypt Tries to Curb Fundamentalists," *New York Times*, July 7, 1985, p. 3Y.

CHAPTER 2—PARLIAMENTARY WOMEN

1. Rawya Attia, "Rawya Attia Talks," *Rose al-Youssef*, July 22, 1957. (In Arabic)

2. *Akher Saa*, April 1, 1964; *Al-Ahram*, January 8, 1969. (In Arabic)

3. Robert Stephens, *Nasser: A Political Biography* (London: Penguin, 1971), p. 331.

4. Raymond William Baker, *Egypt's Uncertain Revolution Under Nasser and Sadat* (Cambridge and London: Harvard University Press, 1978), p. 162.

5. Ibid.

6. Clifton O. Lawhorne, "The Egyptian Press: An Official Fourth Estate" (paper presented at the Annual Convention of the Association for Education in Journalism, Athens, Ohio, July 1982).

7. This view was expressed to me by several male and female members of the Majlis al-Shura in interviews conducted between 1982 and 1984 while doing research for this book.

8. The group studied consists of 46 women, who constitute 92% of the total number of women who have served in Egypt's parliament between 1957 and 1983. It includes forty-one of the forty-two women serving in parliament in 1983. One rural woman attended parliament very seldom and could not be located for an interview. Five women who served in previous parliaments were also included in the total group, but only one was interviewed. Also see note 13, below. The women parliamentarians about whom this chapter is written are: Soheir al-Qalamawi, Zeinab al-Sobky, Akila al-Samaa, Nawal Amer, Olfat Kamel, Faida Kamel, Amal Othman, Buthayna al-Tawil, Imtithal Ali al-Deeb, Farkhounda Hassan, Habiba Ali Sahlib, Sawsan Ibrahim Ali, Aleya Refaat, Hamida Hamam, Soraya Khalifa, Bahiya Baradah, Wagiha al-Zalabani, Enayat Aboul Yazid, Safiya Ali Hegazi, Fatma Abdel Meneim Anan, Aisha Kassem Hassenein, Esmet Namiq, Samaa Alewa Adham, Kamla Megahid Kamel, Saidiya Hassan, Rawhiya Bakir Mahmoud, Amal Abdel Karim, Niemat Yadim, Soad Hassenein, Fatma al-Gamal, Soheir Gilbana, Gilila Gomaa Awad, Mary Salama, Janet Kamel Saad, Shafika Nasser, Nabila al-Ibrashi, Safiya Mohandis, Nahouth Abdullah, Hemet Mustafa, Amina Said, Iris Habib al-Masri, Aisha Rateb, Laila Takla, Rawya Attia, Amina Shoukry, and Hekmat Abu Zeid.

9. Raymond A. Hinnebusch, "The Reemergence of the Wafd Party: Glimpses of the Liberal Opposition in Egypt," *International Journal of Middle Eastern Studies* 16 (March 1984), pp. 99–121.

10. On leftist parties in Egyptian politics, see Berties Hendricks, "The Legal Left in Egypt," *Arab Studies Quarterly* 5 (Summer 1983), pp. 260–75; and Layla A. Kassem, "The Opposition in Egypt: A Case Study of the Socialist Labor Party" (M.A. Thesis, American University in Cairo, 1983).

11. Stephens, *Nasser*, p. 323.

12. Leonard Binder, *In a Moment of Enthusiasm: Political Power and the Second Stratum in Egypt* (Chicago: University of Chicago Press, 1978), passim.

13. Unless otherwise noted, information about women who have served in Egypt's parliament is based on interviews done in 1982 and 1983 by this writer or one of his research assistants. Forty-two of the forty-six women were interviewed at least once, each interview lasting approximately forty-five minutes to an hour. Four were not interviewed, but colleagues or family members were consulted for relevant information about them. Eight members of the group were interviewed at greater length, at least twice. In addition to these interviews, some information is based on newspaper reports or personal observations made by the author.

14. In spite of her prominence, perhaps partly because of it, Dr. Qalamawi, along with a number of other women who had been associated closely with Mrs. Sadat, were dropped from the NDP list and not elected to parliament in 1984.

15. Stereotypes persist, and women in politics are often subjected to unfair criticism. For example, a cartoon appeared in *Al-Ahram* on April 6, 1984 (p. 24) showing a married couple arguing about politics. Both husband and wife held large cigars and sported huge mustaches. The caption below the cartoon had the woman say to her silent husband: "You are no better than I am. I am running in the elections just like you."

16. Binder, *In a Moment of Enthusiasm*, p. 62.

17. Mark Neal Cooper, *The Transformation of Egypt* (London and Cambridge: Croom Helm, 1982), p. 213.

18. In 1984, Nawal Amer was elected to parliament but not to a reserved seat for women. She and three others, Amal Othman, Olfat Kamel, and Rezqah al-Balashi, were the only women elected to unreserved seats in 1984. Amal Othman and Nawal Amer represented the NDP, while Olfat Kamel and Rezqah al-Balashi were on the Wafd list.

19. Of the thirty-three women elected to Majlis al-Shaab in 1979, only eighteen were reelected in 1984. Approximately 50 percent of the NDP women from the 1979 parliament were not nominated by their party in 1984. Also see note 13 above.

20. To the best of my knowledge, there are no published accounts of this event. In addition to interviews with participants, one of my research assistants happened to be in the parliament building at the time and became an eye-witness to the proceedings. The background to the issue was provided in my March 1983 interview with Dr. Amal Othman.

21. *Rose al-Youssef*, September 16, 1957.

22. In 1984, Salah Abu Ismael became the parliamentary spokesman for the New Wafd Party and the party's liaison with the Muslim Brotherhood.

23. Although she was one of the most successful members of the parliament elected in 1979, Farkhounda Hassan was not nominated by the NDP for parliament in 1984. Her place was taken by Rawya Attia, who had first been elected to parliament in 1957. In 1985, Farkhounda Hassan was appointed to Majlis al-Shura by President Mubarak.

24. Earl L. Sullivan, "Health, Development and Women" (Cairo: Cairo Papers in Social Science, Volume 1, No. 1, 1977).

25. *Al-Ahali*, April 25, 1984, p. 3.

26. The minimum age for entry into parliament is thirty, and one woman was barely old enough to qualify when she took her seat in 1979. Thus, the age range is from the low thirties to the low eighties.

27. As noted in table 2.8, four women are listed as divorced but the actual number is five if the woman who has remarried is counted as divorced rather than, as the table lists her, married because she had remarried when the data for this study was gathered.

28. Sullivan, "Women and Work in Egypt," p. 36; also, John A. Williams, "Veiling in Egypt as a Political and Social Phenomenon," in *Islam and Development*, ed. John Esposito (Syracuse: Syracuse University Press, 1980).

29. The Koran (XXIV:31) enjoins women to veil, but not all Muslim women believe that a woman *must* be veiled to be a good Muslim. The fundamentalist movement in Egypt has been trying to change the climate of opinion on this subject and, even at such a "Western" enclave as the American University in Cairo the number of veiled female students has increased considerably between 1973 and 1984. No university-wide figures are available, but in one of my spring 1984 classes, roughly 20% of the Egyptian female students wore Islamic dress. In 1974, none of my students was so attired.

30. Although about 50 percent of the NDP female parliamentarians were not renominated by the party in 1984, none of those who led the effort to keep the reserved seats for women in the desert fringe areas was purged.

CHAPTER 3 — PRESIDENTIAL WIVES

1. Derek Hopwood, *Egypt: Politics and Society, 1945–1981* (London: George Allen and Unwin, 1982) p. 88. Nasser was not the only person responsible for extending the franchise to women. President Neguib made the promise to do so in 1954, as a result of political action by Bint al-Nil and a threatened "fast unto death" by Doria Shafik. See notes 39 and 40 for chapter 1 of this book.

2. Woodsmall, *The Role of Women*, esp. pp. 22–37.

3. Soheir al-Qalamawi stated this in an interview in July, 1982. She was involved in the ASU at the time and tried to get that organization to support changes in the Personal Status Laws. She remembers Nasser intervening personally to quash this effort and was left with the impression that Nasser did not understand how deeply women felt about such problems as polygamy.

4. Amina Said, who has been involved with this cause for over fifty years, stated in an interview in April 1983, that she did not support the 1979 changes in the laws because they did not go far enough, particularly regarding polygamy, which she feels should be abolished.

5. Ragai Abdullah, "Case #520 That Stopped the Application of the Personal Status Law," *Al-Mussawar*, March 9, 1984, pp. 20–25; 72 (in Arabic) Contains an excellent discussion of the arguments for and against the 1979 changes in the Personal Status Laws.

6. Mustafa Kamel Said, "The Executive Branch in Egypt: Power in One Hand

and Veto in the Other," *Al-Ahram Al-Iqtisadi*, August 8, 1983 (in Arabic), pp. 36–39, esp. pp. 38–39, where he argues that the *only* basis of legitimacy for the Mubarak regime is respect for the law.

7. Tahia Kazem did not wish to be interviewed but delegated the task to her oldest daughter, Hoda, who was interviewed at length in May 1984. Unless otherwise noted, data for this section on Tahia Kazem was derived from that interview. Secondary sources are cited only to support or confirm information gathered from primary sources.

8. P. J. Vatikiotis, *Nasser and His Generation* (New York: St. Martins Press, 1978), p. 37.

9. Ibid., p. 24.

10. J. Lacouture, *Nasser*, trans. by D. Dofstadter (London: Secker and Warburg, 1973), p. 212.

11. Peter Mansfield, *Nasser's Egypt*, (Harmondsworth: Penguin, 1969), pp. 39–40.

12. Jihan Sadat was interviewed at length in May, 1983 and again in April and May of 1984. Unless otherwise noted, information for this section was derived from these interviews. Readers may also wish to consult her forthcoming autobiography, tentatively entitled *My Life with Sadat.* Secondary sources are cited only to support or confirm information gathered from primary sources, In cases where a discrepancy exists the version obtained from the primary source is cited. For example, in interviews with me, Mrs. Sadat stated her mother was English. Other people, such as Mohamed Heikal, claim she was Maltese but affected British background (*Autumn of Fury*, p. 38). At issue is status: to be of British background was considered of higher status than being Maltese. However, I saw little point in trying to sort out this discrepancy, as the fact of foreign parentage was clear. Moreover, Agnes Raouf evinced a pro-British attitude during World War II, injecting political diversity into family discourse, as her husband was pro-German, and conducted herself as if she were British even in the confines of her own home. Faced with a choice between believing Mrs. Sadat, as a primary source, or Mr. Heikal, a secondary one, I decided to accept the version of Mrs. Sadat.

13. David Hirst and Irene Beeson, *Sadat* (London: Faber and Faber, 1981), p. 71.

14. Anwar Sadat, *In Search of Identity: An Autobiography* (London: Fontana/Collins, 1978), pp. 94–96. Sadat never directly says that he was thinking of another, more suitable wife, when he decided to divorce his first wife. It is clear from the context, however (p. 95), that the thought of another wife had crossed his mind. Also, he proposed to Jihan little more than a month after his release from jail and did not actually divorce his first wife until March 1949, a little more than six months after he proposed to Jihan and only two months before their marriage in May, 1949.

15. Mohamed H. Heikal, *Autumn of Fury: The Assassination of Sadat* (London: Andre Deutsch, 1983), p. 27.

16. *Rose al-Youssef*, August 19, 1957, pp. 16–19. (In Arabic)

17. Sadat, *In Search of Identity*, p. 213.

18. Heikal, *Autumn of Fury*, p. 38.

19. Jihan Safwat Raouf, *Shelley in Arabic Literature in Egypt* (Cairo: Dar El Maaref, 1982) (in Arabic).

20. Heikal, *Autumn of Fury*, p. 38.
21. Hirst and Beeson, *Sadat*, p. 244.
22. *Playgirl*, June 1978.
23. Hirst and Beeson, *Sadat*, pp. 342–43.
24. If there are any actual surveys of public opinion on this topic, I am not aware of them, but I have lived in Egypt for over a decade (1973–84) and know numerous Egyptian academics from many specialties. Among them, opinion is almost unanimous that televising Mrs. Sadat's oral defense was unnecessary. Most, whether male or female, expressed opinions considerably stronger and more negative than the consensus view reflected above. The only strong opinion I heard in favor of what happened came from an elderly man whose mother had been a colleague of Hoda Sha'rawi.
25. Suzanne Saleh Sabet was interviewed twice at length. The first formal interview was in January 1983, the second in April 1984. Unless otherwise noted, data for this section was derived from these interviews or from my personal knowledge of her as a student at the American University in Cairo. Secondary sources are cited only to support or confirm information gathered from primary sources.
26. Suzanne Saleh Sabet, "Social Action Research in Urban Egypt: A Case Study of Primary School Upgrading in Bulaq" (M.A. thesis, American University in Cairo, 1982).
27. While these women were growing up, Egypt was a colonized country. Although nominally independent, Egypt was not fully self-governing and even in families without foreign parents, children, especially those of middle- and upper-middle-class families, would have grown up with non-Egyptian points of reference, as was the case with a majority of the women discussed in this book.

CHAPTER 4—OPPOSITION WOMEN

1. The standard work on the Brethren is Richard Mitchell, *The Society of Muslim Brothers* (London: Oxford University Press, 1969).
2. P. J. Vatikiotis, *Nasser and His Generation* (New York: St. Martins Press, 1978), pp. 30, 67–84. Also see Layla A. Kassem, "The Opposition in Egypt: A Case Study of the Socialist Labor Party" (M.A. thesis, American University In Cairo, 1983).
3. Ali al-Din Hillal (Dessouki), "The Future of Parties in Egypt," *Rose al-Youssef*, December 5, 1983, pp. 32–33, 44–45, makes this point and suggests a framework for understanding Egyptian party politics which is similar but not identical to the one used in this chapter. Another useful discussion of this general issue is Mohamed Sid Ahmed, *The Future of the Party System in Egypt* (Cairo: Dar al-Mustaqbal al-Arabi, 1984). Both of the above are in Arabic.
4. Ali al-Din Hillal Dessouki, "Waiting for Mubarak," the *New York Times*, May 16, 1982.
5. Saad Eddin Ibrahim, "Spring of Fury," *Al-Ahram al-Iqtisadi*, May 2, 1984, pp. 39–41. (In Arabic)
6. For example, the program of the National Committee for the Defense of

Democracy, formed in 1983 by representatives of virtually all of Egypt's political opposition trends, was strikingly liberal in its overall tone. See: "Eight Solutions Presented by the Opposition for the Continuation of the Democratic Process," *Al-Shaab*,
October 18, 1983, pp. 1, 3. (In Arabic)

      7. R. Hrair Dekmejian, *Egypt Under Nasir: A Study In Political Dynamics* (Al-
bany: State University of New York Press, 1971) p. 282.

      8. Mark N. Cooper, *The Transformation of Egypt*, (London and Canberra:
Croom Helm; Baltimore: Johns Hopkins University Press), pp. 204–34, contains a
good discussion of the 1976 elections.

      9. An explanation of the Parties' Law can be found in Enid Hill, "Parties,
Elections and the Law," *Cairo Today* (April 1984), pp. 24–27.

      10. "Parties' Committee Objects to the Establishment of the Nasserite Party
by Kamal Ahmed," *Al-Gomhouria*, December 23, 1983, p. 1. (In Arabic)

      11. "Women's Votes: The Government's Trick to Forge Elections," *Al-Ahali*,
June 20, 1984, p. 6; "Fouad Serag al-Din Talks About the Overt Forging of Elections," *Al-Wafd*, May 31, 1984, p. 1.

      12. Abdel Latif al-Menaur, "Why Refrain from Participating in the Political
Game?" *Al-Ahram al-Iqtisadi*, December 5, 1983, pp. 18–22.

      13. *Al-Ahram*, May 30, 1984, p. 1.

      14. Raymond A. Hinnebusch, "The Reemergence of the Wafd Party: Glimpses
of the Liberal Opposition in Egypt," *International Journal of Middle Eastern Studies* 16,
(March 1984), pp. 99–121.

      15. *Al-Ahali*, October 19, 1983.

      16. Emad al-Din Adeeb, "The Alliance Between the Brotherhood and the
Pasha is the Last Bullet in the Body of the Sadatists," *Al-Majalla*, February 25, 1984,
p. 30.

      17. Ibid., pp. 30–36.

      18. Enid Hill, "What the Parties Stand For," *Cairo Today*, April 1984, pp. 28–
29, 62–65, explains briefly the main issues raised by each party.

      19. It was not possible to avoid subjective evaluation in selecting women to
be considered as among the political elite. Four women were selected because they
held leadership positions in major opposition parties or movements prior to the start
of the 1984 election campaign. Three others were identified by a "jury" of qualified
political observers as being the most important independent women in the political
opposition. The remaining nine individuals were selected because the press coverage
received during the 1984 campaign indicated that they were recognized as leaders
by their political peers. Egyptian press coverage was used for some of the data for
this chapter, but six women were interviewed at length by this writer or one of his
research assistants between September 1983 and June 1984. Those selected to constitute this representative sample of women in Egypt's political opposition were: Olfat
Kamel, Zeinab al-Ghazali, Afaf Mahfouz, Nawal al-Saadawi, Rizqah al-Belashi,
Hekmat Abu Zeid, Latifa Zayat, Shahenda Mogled (Muqalid), Amina Shafiq, Awatif
Abdel-Rahman, Farida al-Naqash, Mona Makram Obeid, Awatif Wali, Niemat
Hassan, Ragaa Rashad, and Laila Takla.

      20. Farkhounda Hassan, "My House First, Then Political Activity," *Rose El
Youssef*, February 27, 1984, pp. 18–19. (In Arabic)

21. See the section of the Tagamua program, especially its sections on women, in *Al-Ahali*, April 18, 1984, p. 11. (In Arabic)

22. Iqbal al-Sibei, "Nominating Women: Is It Forbidden or Permitted Religiously?" *Rose al-Youssef*, May 14, 1984, pp. 18–21. (In Arabic)

23. "The Strangest Request for Obedience Before the Personal Status Court. A Janitor Asks His Wife to Enter Into Obedience . . . In a Public Toilet," *Al-Ahram*, February 4, 1984, p. 14.

24. "Shahenda Mogled," *Al-Ahali*, September 28, 1983, p. 8. There is a brief discussion of this incident in Leonard Binder, *In A Moment of Enthusiasm* (Chicago: University of Chicago Press, 1978), pp. 341–42.

25. Raymond Baker, *Egypt's Uncertain Revolution Under Nasser and Sadat*, (Cambridge, Mass. and London: Harvard University Press), pp. 112, 205–209.

26. Shahenda Mogled, "I Shall Nominate Myself for the Third Time," *Rose al-Youssef*, March 12, 1984, p. 26.

27. Nawal al-Saadawi, *The Hidden Face of Eve: Women in the Muslim World*, trans. Sherif Hetata (Boston: Beacon Press, 1980), p. 103–104. This point was also made in an interview in April 1984, with one of my research assistants, Taroub Abdel Hadi. Another of Ms. Saadawi's books available in English is her novel, *Woman At Point Zero*, translated by Sherif Hetata (London: Zed Press, 1983).

28. Al-Saadawi, *Hidden Face of Eve*, p. 41.

29. Mustafa Amin, in his regular column "An Idea," *Al-Akhbar*, October 23, 1983, criticized the government for refusing to permit the group led by Nawal al-Saadawi to organize, indicating right wing as well as left wing support for her efforts.

30. Zeinab al-Ghazali, *Days From My Life* (Cairo: Dar al-Shuruq, 1982), p. 71. (In Arabic)

31. Interview, Zeinab al-Ghazali, October 1983.

32. Zeinab al-Ghazali, *Days From My Life*, p. 35.

33. A summary of the case, from her point of view, is found in her book, *Days From My Life*. A brief and objective account is in Karen Aboul Kheir, "The Muslim Brothers: Quest For An Islamic Alternative" (M.A. thesis, American University in Cairo, 1983), pp. 120–26.

34. Interview, Zeinab al-Ghazali, October 1983.

35. Al-Ghazali, *Days From My Life*, pp. 100–101.

36. *Al-Shaab*, May 15, 1984, p. 10.

37. *Al-Shaab*, May 29, 1984, p. 1.

38. In addition to Niemat Hassan's death, there were two other serious incidents reported in the May 1984 elections. Bothayna Shoukri, wife of Wafd candidate Ahmed Abdel Aziz Barakat, was shot by Shafiq Khafaza, cousin of an NDP candidate who was allegedly trying to frighten female Wafdists away from the polls. Mrs. Shoukri was injured seriously but not killed. Hussein Murad, a pollwatcher for the Wafd, was apparently beaten by the police and died soon after in Zagazig Hospital. See "Delegate of a Wafdist Nominee Killed in Ambiguous Circumstances," *Al-Wafd*, May 31, 1984; and "Cousin of an NDP Candidate Opens Fire to Frighten and Attacks the Wife of a Wafdist Candidate," *Al-Wafd*, May 31, 1984, p. 7. (In Arabic)

39. Interview, Afaf Mahfouz, January 1984.

40. Interview, Mona Makram Obeid, June 1984.

41. *Al-Ahram*, November 16, 1981.

42. Robert Bianchi, "Changing Patterns of Interest Representation in Modern Egypt" (American University in Cairo, 1984, unpublished paper).

43. Mervat Fahmy, "Women In the Elections: 'I Am the Egyptian Thatcher,' says Olfat Kamel," *Rose al-Youssef*, February 20, 1984, pp. 16-17. (In Arabic)

44. A recent example of this kind of writing is an essay by Awatif Abdel Rahman, "A Letter From a Forgotten Village," *Al-Ahali*, March 25, 1984, p. 12. (In Arabic)

45. The editorial in *Akhbar al-Yom* of June 23, 1984, by Musa Sabry, is a thinly veiled discussion of the possibly inappropriate background of Rifaat Mahgoub to serve as speaker of the People's Assembly in an era of increased political liberation.

CHAPTER 5—WOMEN IN BUSINESS

1. Joseph A. Schumpeter, *The Theory of Economic Development* (Cambridge: Harvard University Press, 1934), p. 93.

2. John Waterbury, *The Egypt of Nasser and Sadat: The Political Economy of Two Regimes* (Princeton, Princeton University Press, 1983), esp. pp. 57-204.

3. Those who wish to read more about this general topic should consult Robert Mabro, *The Egyptian Economy: 1952-1972* (Oxford: Clarendon Press, 1974); Donald Mead, *Growth and Structural Change in the Egyptian Economy* (Homewood, Illinois: Richard D. Irwin, 1967); Ikram, *Egypt: Economic Management in a Period of Transition* (Baltimore and London; Johns Hopkins University Press for the World Bank, 1980); and Waterbury, *The Egypt of Nasser and Sadat.*

4. Mead, *Growth and Structural Change*, pp. 272-73; Ikram, *Egypt*, pp. 19-20.

5. These figures are derived from Ikram, *Egypt*, pp. 20-21.

6. Ikram, *Egypt*, p. 21.

7. Nermine Mokhtar, "The Upper Economic Class in Egypt" (M.A. thesis, American University in Cairo, 1980).

8. Mark Cooper, *The Transformation of Egypt* (Baltimore: Johns Hopkins University Press, 1982), p. 63.

9. Joseph Fitchett, "U.S. AID Goals: Record Program, Maximum Impact," *International Herald Tribune*, June 7, 1983, p. 12S.

10. Ikram, *Egypt*, p. 171. There was an obvious need for an improved drainage system, especially in the Delta, even before the High Dam was built. It could be argued that it was the absence of these facilities, not the peasants' irrigation habits, which caused problems associated with waterlogging and a rising water table.

11. Ibid., p. 5.

12. Ibid., p. 246.

13. Saad Eddin Ibrahim, *The New Arab Social Order: A Study of the Social Impact of Arab Oil Wealth* (Boulder: Westview Press, 1982). This book raises questions and issues about the impact of oil wealth on Arab countries, even countries such as Egypt, which are less dependent on oil, and less affluent because of it, than Saudi Arabia. The book concentrates on Saudi Arabia and Egypt but deals theoretically with the entire Arab world.

14. Alice Brinton, "Up to 3.5 Million Workers Abroad," *International Herald Tribune*, June 7, 1983, p. 9S.

15. On development assistance programs in Egypt, see Earl L. Sullivan, ed., *The Impact of Development Assistance on Egypt* (Cairo: Cairo Papers in Social Service, Vol. 7, No. 3, September 1984).

16. William Baumol, "Entrepreneurship in Economic Theory," *The American Economic Review* 58 (May 1968), p. 65.

17. J. Bill and H. Askari, "Entrepreneurship and Economic Change in the Middle East" (unpublished paper, 1980, Austin, Texas); Nathaniel Leff, "Entrepreneurship and Economic Development: The Problem Revisited," *Journal of Economic Literature* 17 (March 1979), pp. 46–64; Peter Kilbey, ed., *Entrepreneurship and Economic Development* (New York: Free Press, 1971); Schumpeter, *The Theory of Economic Development*; Harvey Leibstein, "Entrepreneurship and Development," *American Economic Review* 58 (May 1968), pp. 72–83; Youssef Sayigh, *Entrepreneurs of Lebanon* (Cambridge: Harvard University Press, 1967); Gustave Papanek, *Pakistan's Development, Social Goals and Private Incentives* (Cambridge: Harvard University Press, 1967), and Baumol, "Entrepreneurship in Economic Theory."

18. Unless otherwise noted, information about the women in Egypt's business elite is based on interviews conducted in 1982 and 1983, with over forty people, including eleven of the twelve women who came eventually to be chosen for the study group. One woman was out of the country and information about her was provided by her sister. Interviews were conducted by this writer or by one of his research assistants and ranged in length from forty-five minutes to three hours. Two women were interviewed a second time and the interviews were taped. The entrepreneurs about whom this chapter is written were: Soad al-Sowaf, Zeinab al-Naggar, Nabela al-Shourbagy, Ina Tadrous Maggar, Niemat Alexane, Laila al-Tawil, Josse Dorra Fiani, Hoda Halim Abou Seif, Naela Hassan Ali Alouba, Amina Zaghloul, Hoda Abdel Meneim, and Laila al-Bannan.

19. Earl L. Sullivan, "Women and Work in Egypt," in *Women and Work in the Arab World* by Earl L. Sullivan and Karima Korayem, Cairo Papers in Social Science 4 (Cairo: December 1981), pp. 1–43.

20. Interview with Soad al-Sowaf, May 21, 1983, Soad al-Sowaf is considered by many of her male and female colleagues to be the most important female entrepreneur in Egypt. In general, quotations in the chapter will not be identified by name unless there is an obvious reason to do so.

21. The figure of 30 million £E was given to me by a person who was in a position to have accurate information on the topic. This person, for an obvious reason, does not wish to be identified. The data regarding the woman who started with 500 £E was the woman herself and corroborated by a reliable and informed source in the Egyptian financial community who wishes to remain anonymous. The use of anonymous sources presents an obvious problem: readers cannot go to the original and check for accuracy or reliability. Anonymous sources were not used often, and only in those cases where I had an unusually high degree of confidence in them for accuracy and reliability.

22. Brinton, "Up to 315 Million Workers Abroad," p. 9S.

23. Soad al-Sowaf, interview, May 21, 1983.

CHAPTER 6—WOMEN IN EGYPT'S POLITICAL AND ECONOMIC ELITE

1. Michael Gilsenan, *Recognizing Islam: Religion and Society in the Modern Arab World* (New York: Random House, Pantheon Books, 1982), pp. 171–72.

2. Cynthia Nelson, "Public and Private Politics: Women in the Middle Eastern World," *American Ethnologist* 1 (August 1974), pp. 551–63.

3. Gilsenan, *Recognizing Islam*, pp. 172–73. Gilsenan, in another book, demonstrates an acute awareness of social change and attributes the intensity of the debate over social norms, such as those pertaining to women, to a growing if perhaps subconscious awareness of their ambiguity. He concludes that, in the case of women, "the gains which were made during the past fifty years or so, limited as they were, are being lost." See Michael Gilsenan, "Social Trends," in ed. Patrick Seale, *The Shaping of an Arab Statesman: Abd al-Halim Sharaf and the Modern Arab World* (London: Quartet Books, 1983), p. 236.

4. This book is not the place for a bibliographical review of sexism in the West, but two recent books raise many issues relevant to this study: Betty Friedan, *The Second Stage* (New York: Summit Books, 1982), and Jean Bethke Elshtain, *Public Man, Private Woman: Women in Social and Political Thought* (Princeton: Princeton University Press, 1981).

5. One notable but ancillary feature I became aware of in the course of doing research for this book was the degree to which many of the women I was studying were informed about issues pertaining to women in various parts of the non-Western world, including the Far East. For example, some women in all four groups studied believed the Japanese experience has relevance to Egypt.

6. Saad Eddin Ibrahim, *Egypt in a Quarter Century: (1952–1977)*, (Beirut: Arab Promotion Institution, 1981), pp. 43–44. (In Arabic)

7. Laila el-Hamamsy, "The Changing Role of the Egyptian Women," *Middle East Forum* 33 (1958), p. 24; Laila el-Hamamsy, "The Role of Women in the Development of Egypt" *Middle East Forum* 33 (1958), pp. 592–601; Aziza Hussein, "The Role of Women in Social Reform in Egypt," *The Middle East Journal* 7 (Autumn 1953), pp. 440–50; Afaf Lutfi al-Sayyid Marsot, "The Revolutionary Gentlewoman in Egypt," in *Women in the Muslim World*, ed. Lois Beck and Nikki Keddie (Cambridge and London: Harvard University Press, 1978), pp. 261–76; Thomas Philipp, "Feminism and National Politics in Egypt" in *Women in the Muslim World*, pp. 277–94; and Safia Mohsen, "The Egyptian Woman: Between Modernity and Tradition," in *Many Sisters*, ed. Carolyn J. Matthiasson (New York: The Free Press, 1974), pp. 37–58.

8. Sullivan, "Women and Work in Egypt," in *Women and Work in the Arab World* by Earl L. Sullivan and Karima Korayem, Cairo Papers in Social Science 4 (Cairo: December 1981).

9. Cynthia Nelson, "Changing Roles of Men and Women: Illustrations From Egypt," *Anthropological Quarterly* 41 (April 1968), pp. 57–77.

10. Nelson, "Public and Private Politics."

11. James Bill and Hamied Askari, "Entrepreneurship and Economic Change in the Middle East" (unpublished paper, 1980, Austin, Texas); ed. Peter Kilbey, *Entrepreneurship and Economic Development* (New York: Free Press, 1971); Joseph A. Schumpeter, *The Theory of Economic Development* (Cambridge: Harvard University Press, 1934).

12. Schumpeter, *Theory of Economic Development*, pp. 93–94.

13. El-Hamamsy, "The Role of Women in the Development of Egypt"; Philipp, "Feminism and National Politics in Egypt"; Mohsen, "The Egyptian Woman: Between Modernity and Tradition"; Doria Shafik, "Egyptian Feminism" *Middle Eastern Affairs* III (August–September, 1952); Bahega Arafa, *The Social Activities of the Egyptian Feminist Union* (Cairo: Elias Modern Press, 1954).

14. Although she does not mention Egypt specifically, Jane Jaquette has discussed the positive aspects, from a feminist perspective, of a separate and protected female sphere of activity. See Jane S. Jaquette, "Women and Modernization Theory: A Decade of Feminist Criticism," *World Politics* 34 (January 1982), pp. 267–84.

15. Andrea Rugh, *Family in Contemporary Egypt* (Syracuse: Syracuse University Press, 1984), pp. 268–71.

16. Rugh, *Family in Contemporary Egypt*, pp. 256–60.

17. A study of people in the 20–40 age group would also afford comparison with research done on young women in Japan. See Susan J. Pharr, *Political Women in Japan: The Search for a Place in Political Life* (Berkeley and Los Angeles: University of California Press, 1981).

18. A few works which could form the beginning for some comparative work are: Adaljiza Sosa Riddell, "Female Political Elites in Mexico: 1974" in ed. Lynne Iglitzen and Ruth Ross, *Women in the World* (Santa Barbara: Clio, 1976), pp. 257–67; Jane S. Jaquette, "Female Political Participation in Latin America," in *Women in the World*, pp. 55–74; Virginia Spiro, *The Political Integration of Women: Roles, Socialization, and Politics* (London and New York: Tavistock Press, 1981); C. F. Epstein and R. L. Coser, eds., *Access to Power* (London: George Allen and Unwin, 1981); Jeane J. Kirkpatrick, *Political Women* (New York: Basic Books, 1974). Unfortunately, studies of third-world women generally are not as detailed as this book is, and most of the works cited above are on women in the West. More empirical work is needed, in my opinion, before advanced theoretical and comparative studies can be done.

Bibliography

Abdel-Kader, Soha. *The Status of Egyptian Women, 1900–1973*. Cairo: The Social Research Center, American University in Cairo, 1973.

————. "Survey of Trends in Research on Women," In *Social Science Research and Women in the Arab World*, pp. 139–75. Paris, London and Dover, N.H.: Frances Pinter Publishers, for UNESCO, 1984.

Abdulla, Ragai. "Case #520 that Stopped the Application of the Personal Status Law." *Al-Mussawer* (March 9, 1983), pp. 20–25, 72. (In Arabic)

Adeeb, Emad al-Din. "The Alliance Between the Brotherhood and the Pasha is the Last Bullet in the Body of the Sadatists." *Al-Majalla*, February 25, 1984, pp. 30–36. (In Arabic)

Akhavi, Shahrough. "Egypt: Neo-Patrimonial Elite." in *Political Elites and Political Development in the Middle East*, edited by Frank Tachau, pp. 69–113. Cambridge, Mass.: Schenkman, 1975.

Amin, Qasim. *The Emancipation of Women*. Cairo: N.P., 1899 and 1900. (In Arabic)

————. *The New Woman*. Cairo: N.P., 1901. (In Arabic)

Ansari, Hamied. "Authoritarianism and Liberalism Under Sadat: The Parliamentary Election of 1979." American University in Cairo, 1983.

Arafa, B. *The Social Activities of the Egyptian Feminist Union*. Cairo: Elias Modern Press, 1954.

Atiya, Nayra. *Khul-Khaal: Five Egyptian Women Tell Their Stories*. Syracuse: Syracuse University Press, 1982.

Attia, Rawya. "Rawya Attia Talks." *Rose al-Youssef*, July 22, 1957.

Baker, Raymond William. *Egypt's Uncertain Revolution Under Nasser and Sadat*. Cambridge, Mass. and London: Harvard University Press, 1978.

Baumol, William J. "Entrepreneurship in Economic Theory." *American Economic Review* 58 (May 1968), pp. 64–71.

Beck, Lois G., and Nikki Keddie, eds. *Women in the Muslim World.* Cambridge: Harvard University Press, 1978.

Bianchi, Robert. "Changing Patterns of Interest Group Representation in Modern Egypt." American University in Cairo, 1984.

Bill, J. A., and Askari, H. "Entrepreneurship and Economic Change in the Middle East." University of Texas, Austin, 1980.

Binder, Leonard. *In a Moment of Enthusiasm: Political Power and the Second Stratum in Egypt.* Chicago: University of Chicago Press, 1978.

Bowles, Gloria, and Renate Duelli Klein, eds. *Theories of Women's Studies.* London and Boston: Routledge and Kegan Paul, 1983.

Brinton, Alice, "Up to 3.5 Million Workers Abroad." *International Herald Tribune*, June 7, 1983, p. 9S.

CAPMAS, Population and Research Studies Center, *The Egyptian Woman in Two Decades, 1952–1972.* Cairo: Center for Public Mobilization and Statistics, 1974.

Charlton, Sue Ellen M. *Women In Third World Development.* Boulder and London: Westview Press, 1984.

Cole, Juan Ricardo. "Feminism, Class and Islam in Turn-of-the-Century Egypt." *International Journal of Middle Eastern Studies* 13 (November 1981), pp. 387–405.

Cooper, Mark Neal. *The Transformation of Egypt.* London and Canberra: Croom Helm; Baltimore: The Johns Hopkins University Press, 1982.

Dekmejian, R. Hrair. *Egypt Under Nasir: A Study in Political Dynamics.* Albany: State University of New York Press, 1971.

Dessouki, Ali E. Hillal. "Waiting for Mubarak." *The New York Times*, May 16, 1982.

————. "The Future of Parties in Egypt." *Rose al-Youssef*, December 5, 1983, pp. 32–33, 44–45. (In Arabic)

Dodd, P. C. "Youth and Women's Emancipation in the United Arab Republic." *The Middle East Journal* 22 (Spring 1968), pp. 159–72.

Elshtain, Jean Bethke. *Public Man, Private Woman: Women In Social and Political Thought.* Princeton: Princeton University Press, 1981.

Epstein, C. F., and R. L. Coser, eds. *Access to Power.* London: George Allen and Unwin, 1981.

Esposito, John L. *Women in Muslim Family Law.* Syracuse: Syracuse University Press, 1982.

Fitchett, Joseph. "U.S. AID Goals: Record Program, Maximum Impact." *International Herald Tribune*, June 7, 1983, p. 9S.

Fluehr-Lobban, Carolyn. "The Political Mobilization of Women in the Arab World." In *Women in Contemporary Muslim Societies*, edited with an introduction by Jane I. Smith, 235–59. Lewisburg, Pa.: Bucknell University Press, 1980.

Friedan, Betty. *The Second Stage*. New York: Summit Books, 1982.

Furnea, Elizabeth W., and Basima Bezirgan. *Middle Eastern Muslim Women Speak*. Austin: University of Texas Press, 1977.

Gallagher, Nancy. "Helping Others: Epidemics, Medical Aid and the Struggle For Power in Egypt." Santa Barbara, Calif.: book manuscript in progress, 1985.

al-Ghazali, Zeinab. *Days From My Life*. Cairo: Dar al-Shuruq, 1982. (In Arabic)

Gilsenan, Michael. "Social Trends." In *The Shaping of an Arab Statesman: Abd al-Halim Sharaf and the Modern Arab World*, edited by Patrick Seale, pp. 225–37. London: Quartet Books, 1983.

———. *Recognizing Islam: Religion and Society in the Modern Arab World*. New York: Random House, Pantheon Books, 1982.

Gran, P. *Islamic Roots of Capitalism: Egypt 1760–1840*. Austin: University of Texas Press, 1979.

el-Guindi, Fadwa. "Veiling Infitah With Muslim Ethic: Egypt's Contemporary Islamic Movement." *Social Problems* 28 (April 1981), pp. 465–85.

———. "Veiled Activism: Egyptian Women in the Contemporary Islamic Movement." *Femmes de la Mediterranee Peuples Mediterraneens* 22-23 (January–June 1983), pp. 79–89.

Hale, Sylvia. "Women as Change Agents: A Neglected Research Area." In E. A. (Nora) Cebotarev and Frances M. Shaver, *Women and Agricultural Production*. Toronto: Resources For Feminist Research, Volume 2, No. 1 (March 1982), pp. 42–46.

el-Hamamsy, Laila S. "The Changing Role of the Egyptian Women." *The Middle East Forum*, Vol. 33, No. 6 (1958), p. 24.

———. "The Role of Women in the Development of Egypt." *The Middle East Forum* Vol. 33, No. 6 (1958), pp. 592–601.

Hassan, Farkhounda. "My House First, Then Political Activity." *Rose al-Youssef*, February 27, 1984, pp. 18–19. (In Arabic)

Heikal, Mohamed. *Autumn of Fury: The Assassination of Sadat*. London: Andre Deutsch, 1983.

Hendricks, Bertus. "The Legal Left in Egypt." *Arab Studies Quarterly* 5 (Summer 1983), pp. 260–75.

Hennig, Margaret, and Ann Jardim. *The Managerial Woman*. New York: Simon and Schuster, Pocket Books, 1976.

Hill, Enid. *Mahkama! Studies in the Egyptian Legal System*. London: Ithaca Press, 1979.

———. "Parties, Elections and the Law." *Cairo Today*, April 1984, pp. 24–27.

———. "What the Parties Stand For." *Cairo Today*, April 1984, pp. 28–29, 62–65.

Hinnebusch, Raymond A. "The Reemergence of the Wafd Party: Glimpses of the Liberal Opposition in Egypt." *International Journal of Middle Eastern Studies* 16 (March 1984), pp. 99–121.

―――――. "Political Participation and the Authoritarian-Modernizing State in the Middle East: Limited Institutionalization and Political Activism in Syria and Egypt." Paper presented at the 1983 Annual Meeting of the Middle East Studies Association, Chicago, November 1983.

Hirst, David, and Irene Beeson. *Sadat*. London: Faber and Faber, 1981.

Hopwood, Derek. *Egypt: Politics and Society, 1945–1981*. London: George Allen and Unwin, 1982.

Hourani, Albert. *Arabic Thought in the Liberal Age, 1798–1939*. Cambridge: Cambridge University Press, 1983.

Howard-Merriam, Kathleen. "Women, Education, and the Professions in Egypt." *Comparative Education Review* 23 (June 1979), pp. 256–70.

―――――. "Egypt's Other Political Elite." *The Western Political Quarterly* 34 (March 1981), pp. 174–87.

Hussein, Aziza. "The Role of Women in Social Reform in Egypt." *The Middle East Journal*, Vol. 7, No. 4 (1954), pp. 440–50.

―――――. "Status of Women and Family Planning in a Developing Country: Egypt." In *Egypt: Population Problems and Prospects*, edited by Abdel R. Omran. Chapel Hill: Carolina Population Center, 1973.

Ibrahim, Barbara L. "Social Change and the Industrial Experience: Women As Production Workers in Urban Egypt." Ph.D. dissertation, Department of Sociology, Indiana University, 1980.

―――――. "Urban Labor Force Imbalances and Industrial Employment Policy —A Sociologist's View." In proceedings of Conference on Local Government Management in Egypt, Cairo, 1981.

Ibrahim, Saad Eddin. *Egypt in a Quarter of a Century (1952–1977)*. Beirut: Arab Promotion Institution, 1981. (In Arabic)

―――――. *The New Arab Social Order: A Study of the Social Impact of Oil Wealth*. Boulder, Colorado: Westview Press; London: Croom Helm, 1982.

―――――. "Spring of Fury." *Al-Ahram al-Iqtisadi*, May 2, 1983, pp. 39–41. (In Arabic)

Ikram, Khaled. *Egypt: Economic Management in a Period of Transition*. Baltimore and London: Johns Hopkins University Press, for the World Bank, 1980.

Issa, M. *The Egyptian Women's Participation in Labor Force: Secular Trends, Age Pattern and Determinates, 1907–1976*. Cairo: Center For Public Mobilization and Statistics, 1979.

Jaquette, Jane S. "Female Political Participation in Latin America." In *Women in the World: A Comparative Study*, edited by Lynne B. Iglitzen and Ruth Ross. Santa Barbara, Calif.: ABC-Clio Press, 1976.

————. "Women and Modernization Theory: A Decade of Feminist Criticism." *World Politics* 34 (January 1982), pp. 267–84.

Karawan, Ibrahim. "Sadat On The Road To Jerusalem." Paper presented at the Annual Meeting of the Middle East Studies Association, Seattle, November, 1981.

Kassem, Layla A. "The Opposition in Egypt: A Case Study of the Socialist Labor Party." M. A. Thesis, American University in Cairo, 1983.

Keddie, Nikki R. "Problems in the Study of Middle Eastern Women." *International Journal of Middle East Studies* 10 (April 1979), pp. 225–40.

Kilby, Peter, ed. *Entrepreneurship and Economic Development.* New York: Free Press, 1971.

Kirkpatrick, Jeane J. *Political Woman.* New York: Basic Books, 1974.

Lacouture, J. *Nasser.* Translated by D. Hofstadter. London: Secker and Warburg, 1973.

Lawhorne, Clifton O. "The Egyptian Press: An Official Fourth Estate." Paper presented at the annual convention of the Association for Education in Journalism, Athens, Ohio, July 1982.

Leff, Nathaniel. "Entrepreneurship and Economic Development: The Problem Revisited." *Journal of Economic Literature* 17 (March 1979), pp. 46–64.

Le Gassick, Trevor J. *Major Themes in Modern Arabic Thought: An Anthology.* Ann Arbor: University of Michigan Press, 1979.

Leibenstein, Harvey, "Entrepreneurship and Development." *American Economic Review* 58 (May 1968), pp. 72–83.

Mabro, Robert. *The Egyptian Economy: 1952–1972.* Oxford: Clarendon Press, 1974.

Mansfield, Peter. *Nasser's Egypt.* Harmondsworth: Penguin, 1969.

Mead, Donald C. *Growth and Structural Change in the Egyptian Economy.* Homewood, Illinois: Richard D. Irwin, 1967.

al-Menaur, Abdel Latif. "Why Refrain from Participating in the Political Game?" *Al-Ahram al-Iqtisadi*, December 5, 1983, pp. 18–22.

Mernissi, Fatima. *Beyond the Veil.* Cambridge: Schenkman, 1975.

Mikhail, Mona. *Images of Arab Women.* Washington, D.C.: Three Continents Press, 1981.

Mitchell, Richard P. *The Society of Muslim Brothers.* London: Oxford University Press, 1969.

Mogled, Shahenda. "I Shall Nominate Myself for the Third Time." *Rose El Youssef*, March 12, 1984, p. 26. (In Arabic)

Mohsen, S. K. "The Egyptian Woman: Between Modernity and Tradition." In *Many Sisters*, edited by Carolyn J. Matthiasson, pp. 37–58. New York: The Free Press, 1974.

Mokhtar, Nermine. "The Upper Economic Class in Egypt." M.A. Thesis, American University in Cairo, 1980.

Moore, Clement Henry. *Images of Development: Egyptian Engineers in Search of Industry.* Cambridge: M.I.T. Press, 1980.

NCER (National Center for Educational Research). *Women and Education in Egypt.* Cairo: Arab Republic of Egypt, 1980.

Nelson, Cynthia. "Changing Roles of Men and Women: Illustrations from Egypt." *Anthropological Quarterly* 41 (April 1968), pp. 57–77.

————. "Public and Private Politics: Women in the Middle Eastern World." *American Ethnologist* 1 (August 1974), pp. 551–63.

Newland, Kathleen. *Women in Politics: A Global Review.* Washington, D.C.: Worldwatch Institute, 1975.

Nowaihi, Mohammed. "Changing the Law on Personal Status within a Liberal Interpretation of the Sharia." In *Law and Social Change in Contemporary Egypt*, edited by Cynthia Nelson and Klause F. Koch, pp. 97–115. Cairo Papers in Social Science, Volume 2, No. 4, pp. 97–115. Cairo: American University in Cairo, 1979.

Othman, Amal. "The Legal Status of Women in Egypt." Ministry of Social Affairs, Cairo, unpublished paper, no date.

Papanek, G. F. *Pakistan's Development, Social Goals and Private Incentives.* Cambridge: Harvard University Press, 1967.

Pharr, Susan J. *Political Women in Japan: The Search for a Place in Political Life.* Berkeley and Los Angeles: University of California Press, 1981.

Philipp, T. "Feminism and Nationalist Politics in Egypt." In *Women in the Muslim World*, edited by Lois Beck and Nikki Keddie, pp. 277–94. Cambridge and London: Harvard University Press, 1978.

al-Qazzaz, A. *Women in the Middle East and North Africa: An Annotated Bibliography.* Middle East Monographs No. 2. Center for Middle Eastern Studies, University of Texas at Austin, 1977.

Raouf, Jihan Safwat. *Shelley in Arabic Literature in Egypt.* Cairo: Dar El Maaref, 1982. (In Arabic)

Rasheed, Baheega Sidky, et al. *The Egyptian Feminist Union.* Cairo: Dar El Maamoon Bookshop, 1973. (In Arabic and English)

Rassam, Amal. "Toward a Theoretical Framework for the Study of Women in the Arab World." In UNESCO, *Social Science Research and Women in the Arab World*, pp. 122–38. Paris, London and Dover, N.H.: Frances Pinter, publishers for UNESCO, 1984.

————. "Introduction: Arab Women: The Status of Research in the Social Sciences and the Status of Women." In UNESCO, *Social Science Research in the Arab World*, pp. 1–13. Paris, London and Dover, N.H.: Frances Pinter, publishers for UNESCO, 1984.

Riddell, Adaljiza Sosa. "Female Political Elites in Mexico: 1974." In *Women in the World: A Comparative Study*, edited by Lynne B. Iglitzen and Ruth Ross, pp. 257–67. Santa Barbara, Calif.: ABC-Clio Press, 1976.

Rugh, Andrea. *Family in Contemporary Egypt.* Syracuse: Syracuse University Press, 1984.

al-Saadawi, Nawal. *The Hidden Face of Eve: Women in the Muslim World.* Translated by Sherif Hetata. Boston: Beacon Press, 1980.

————. *Woman At Point Zero.* Translated by Sherif Hetata. London: Zed Press, 1983.

Sabet, Suzanne Saleh. "Social Action Research in Urban Egypt: A Case Study of Primary School Upgrading in Bulaq." M.A. Thesis, American University in Cairo, 1982.

Sadat, Anwar. *In Search of Identity.* London: William Collins/Fontana, 1978.

Safran, Nadav. *Egypt in Search of Political Community.* Cambridge: Harvard University Press, 1961.

Said, Amina. "The Arab Woman and the Challenge of Society." In *Middle Eastern Muslim Women Speak*, edited by Elizabeth W. Fernea and Basima Q. Bezirgan, pp. 374-390. Austin: University of Texas, 1977.

Said, Mustafa Kamel. "The Executive Branch in Egypt: Power in One Hand and Veto in the Other Hand." *Al-Ahram al-Iqtisadi*, August 8, 1983, pp. 36–39.

Sayigh, Youssef A. *Entrepreneurs of Lebanon.* Cambridge: Harvard University Press, 1967.

al-Sayyid-Marsot, Afaf Lutfi. *Egypt's Liberal Experiment: 1922–1936.* Berkeley and Los Angeles: University of California Press, 1977.

————. "The Revolutionary Gentlewoman in Egypt." In *Women in the Muslim World*, edited by Lois Beck and Nikki Keddie, pp. 261–76. Cambridge and London: Harvard University Press, 1978.

Schilling, Nancy Adams. "The Social and Political Roles of Arab Women: A Study in Conflict." In *Women in Contemporary Muslim Societies*, edited by Jane I. Smith. Lewisburg, Pa.: Bucknell University Press, 1980.

Schumpeter, Joseph. *The Theory of Economic Development: An Inquiry Into Profits, Capital, Credit, Interest and the Business Cycle.* Cambridge: Harvard University Press, 1934.

Shafik, Doria. "Egyptian Feminism." *Middle Eastern Affairs* III (August–September, 1952), pp. 233–38.

Shaltout, Mahmoud. "Women are Eligible to be Judges." *Rose al-Youssef*, December 17, 1962. (In Arabic)

al-Sibaei, Iqbal. "Nominating Women: Is It Forbidden or Permitted Religiously?" *Rose al-Youssef*, May 14, 1984, pp. 18–21. (In Arabic)

Sid-Ahmed, Mohammed. *The Future of the Party System in Egypt.* Cairo: Dar al-Mustaqbal al-Arabi, 1984. (In Arabic)

Smith, Jane I., ed. *Women in Contemporary Muslim Society.* Lewisburg, Pa.: Bucknell University Press, 1980.

Smock, Audrey Chapman, and Nadia Haggag Youssef. "Egypt: From Seclusion to Limited Participation." In *Women: Roles and Status in Eight Countries*, edited by Janet Zollinger Giele and Audrey Chapman Smock, pp. 35–79. New York: John Wiley and Sons, 1977.

Spiro, Virginia. *The Political Integration of Women: Roles, Socialization and Politics.* Urbana: University of Illinois Press, 1983.

Stacey, Margaret, and Marion Price. *Women, Power and Politics.* London and New York: Tavistock Press, 1981.

Stephens, R. *Nasser: A Political Biography.* London: Penguin, 1971.

Sullivan, Earl L. *The Impact of Development Assistance on Egypt.* Cairo: Cairo Papers in Social Science, Vol. 7, No. 3 (September 1984).

———. "Women in Egypt's Parliament." Paper delivered at the Annual Meeting of the Middle East Studies Association. Chicago, November 1983.

———. "Health, Development, and Women." In *Women, Health and Development*, edited by Cynthia Nelson. Cairo Papers in Social Science, Vol. 1, No. 1. Cairo: American University in Cairo, 1977.

———. "Women and Work in Egypt." In *Women and Work in the Arab World*, by Earl L. Sullivan and Karima Korayem. Cairo Papers in Social Science, Vol. 4, No. 4, December 1981.

Tessler, Mark A., and Jean F. O'Barr. "Gender and Participant Citizenship in Tunisia." *Journal of Arab Affairs*, Volume 2, Number 1 (1982), pp. 47–84.

Tomiche, Nada. "The Situation of Egyptian Women in the First Half of the 19th Century." In *Beginnings of Modernization in the Middle East*, edited by William Polk, et al., pp. 171–84. Chicago: University of Chicago Press, 1968.

Tucker, Judith. "Egyptian Women in the Work Force: A Historical Survey." *MERIP Reports* Number 50 (1976), pp. 3–9, 26.

———. "Decline of the Family Economy in Mid-Nineteenth Century Egypt." *Arab Studies Quarterly* 1 (Summer 1979), pp. 245–71.

UNESCO. *Social Science Research and Women in the Arab World.* Paris, London, and Dover, N.H.: Frances Pinter, Publishers for UNESCO, 1984.

Vatikiotis, P. J. *Nasser and His Generation.* New York: St. Martins Press, 1978.

———. *The History of Egypt*, 2nd edition. Baltimore: Johns Hopkins University Press, 1980.

Waterbury, John. *The Egypt of Nasser and Sadat: The Political Economy of Two Regimes.* Princeton: Princeton University Press, 1983.

Wellesley Editorial Committee. *Women and National Development: The Complexities of Change.* Chicago and London: University of Chicago Press, 1977.

Williams, John A. "Veiling in Egypt as a Political and Social Phenomenon."

In *Islam and Development*, edited by John Esposito. Syracuse: Syracuse University Press, 1980.

Women's Middle East Collective. *Women in the Middle East.* Cambridge: Women's Middle East Collective, 1973.

Woodsmall, Ruth Frances. *The Role of Women: A Study of the Role of Women, Their Activities and Organizations, in Lebanon, Egypt, Iraq, Jordan and Syria.* London and New York: The International Federation of Business and Professional Women, 1956.

Youssef, Nadia H. *Women and Work in Developing Societies.* Westport, Connecticut: The Greenwood Press, 1976.

———. "Women in Development: Urban Life and Labor." In *Women and World Development*, edited by Irene Tinker, pp. 70–77. New York: Overseas Development Council, 1976.

Index

WOMEN IN EGYPTIAN PUBLIC LIFE

was composed in 11-point Digital Compugraphic Baskerville and leaded 2 points
by Metricomp;
with initial capitals in Ryter Lighter by Rochester Mono/Headliners;
printed sheet-fed offset on 55-pound, acid-free Booktext, Natural HiBulk,
and smyth sewn and bound over 88-point binder's boards in Joanna Arrestox B
by BookCrafters;
with dust jackets printed in 2 colors by Philips Offset Company, Inc.;
and published by

SYRACUSE UNIVERSITY PRESS
SYRACUSE, NEW YORK 13244-5160